THE AI
MARKETING
PLAYBOOK

Second Edition

THE AI MARKETING PLAYBOOK

Concepts · Methods · Applications

Second Edition

Mark Lamplugh

MERCURY LEARNING AND INFORMATION
Boston, Massachusetts

Publisher: David Pallai
MERCURY LEARNING AND INFORMATION
121 High Street, 3rd Floor
Boston, MA 02110
info@merclearning.com
www.merclearning.com
800-232-0223

M. Lamplugh. *The AI Marketing Playbook: Concepts, Methods, Applications*.
ISBN: 978-1-50152-289-5

Library of Congress Control Number: 2024940125
242526321   This book is printed on acid-free paper in the United States of America.

Our titles are available for adoption, license, or bulk purchase by institutions, corporations, etc. For additional information, please contact the Customer Service Dept. at 800-232-0223(toll free).

To my son,
Alexei Mark Lamplugh

Contents

Preface   *xvii*

**Chapter 1:   Introduction to Artificial Intelligence
                    Marketing**   **1**

AI Marketing and Its Benefits   2

How AI Marketing Can Enhance Traditional Marketing
   Techniques   4

   Personalization and Targeting: A New Frontier   5

   Harnessing the Power of AI in Marketing   5

   Innovative Optimization and Efficiency   5

The History of AI in Marketing   6

   The Dawn of AI in Marketing   6

   The Rise of Big Data   6

   Personalization and Automation: A New Era in
     Marketing   7

   The Evolution of AI in Marketing: A Promising
     Outlook   8

The Impact of AI on the Marketing Industry   9

   Enhancing Personalization and Customer Experience
     with AI   9

   Revolutionizing Marketing Analytics and Optimization
     Through AI   9

   Predictive Analytics and Forecasting   10

   The Expanding Role of AI in Marketing's Future   10

Future Trends in AI Marketing   11

   Scaling Personalization with AI   11

From Chatbots to Advanced Conversational AI 11
Voice Search Optimization: Tuning into the Future 11
Predictive Analytics: A Crystal Ball for Marketers 11
Automated Content Creation: Turning the Page on
Tradition 12
Image and Video Recognition: A Smarter Vision 12
VR and AR 12
AI Marketing: Transforming the Marketing Industry 12
The Advantages of AI Marketing 13
Improving Conventional Marketing Methods 13
AI in Marketing: A Brief History 13
The Influence of AI on the Marketing Industry 13
Upcoming AI Marketing Trends 13

Chapter 2: **Understanding Artificial Intelligence and**
Machine Learning **15**
The Basics of AI and ML 16
What Exactly is AI? 16
What Exactly is Machine Learning (ML)? 16
AI and ML Examples 17
How AI is Used in Marketing 19
Data Examination 19
Marketing that is Tailored to the Individual 19
Making Content 19
Chatbots and Consumer Support 20
Algorithms for Supervised Learning 20
Algorithms for Unsupervised Learning 21
Applications of ML Algorithms 22
The Importance of Training Data for ML 23
The Role of Data Science in AI Marketing 25

Chapter 3: **Preparing Your Data for Artificial Intelligence** **29**
Importance of Data Hygiene and Quality 29
Structuring Data for ML Algorithms 29
Optimizing Data Collection and Storage for
AI Applications 30
Essential Data Preprocessing Methods 30
Revolutionizing AI Marketing with Tools and Platforms 30

Data Hygiene and Quality		30
Structure Data for Machine Learning Algorithms		33
Strategies for Collecting and Storing Data		36
Determine Essential Data		36
Select Suitable Data Sources		36
Utilize Data Management Platforms		37
Tap into Third-Party Data Providers		37
Prioritize Data Quality		37
Establish Data Governance Policies		37
Embrace Cloud-Based Storage Solutions		37
Prioritize Data Security Measures		37
Common Data Preprocessing Techniques		39
Tools and Platforms for Managing Data for AI Marketing		42
Chapter 4:	**Using Artificial Intelligence to Analyze Customer Behavior**	**47**
	How AI Can Be Used to Analyze Customer Behavior	48
	Predictive Analytics	48
	Sentiment Analysis	50
	Customer Segmentation	52
	Image Recognition	53
	How Businesses Have Successfully Used AI to Understand Their Customers	54
	Amazon	54
	Netflix	54
	Starbucks	54
	Techniques for Creating Customer Personas Using AI	55
	The Role of Clustering and Segmentation in Customer Analysis	57
	Definition of Clustering and Segmentation	57
	Benefits of Clustering and Segmentation	58
	Effective Use of Clustering and Segmentation in Marketing	58
	The Importance of Feedback Loops in Customer Analysis	58
	What Is a Feedback Loop?	59
	What Is the Significance of Feedback Loops in Customer Analysis?	59

Chapter 5:	**Personalization with Artificial Intelligence**	**63**
	Successful Personalization Strategies	70
	Personalization at Scale: Automating Individualized Experiences	71
	What Is AI Personalization at Scale?	71
	Why is AI Personalization Important?	72
	How to Automate Individualized Experiences with AI Personalization	72
	Examples of AI Personalization	72
	Ethical Considerations When Using AI for Personalization	73
	Measuring the ROI of Personalization with AI	75
Chapter 6:	**Chatbots and Artificial Intelligence-Powered Customer Service**	**79**
	Benefits of Using Chatbots and AI-Powered Customer Service	80
	Increased Efficiency	80
	Improved Customer Experiences	80
	Better Knowledge of the Data	80
	Profitable	81
	Scalable	81
	How Businesses Have Implemented Chatbots Successfully	81
	E-Commerce and Retail	81
	Banking and Finance	82
	Benefits of Using Chatbots and AI-Powered Customer Service	82
	Travel and Hospitality	83
	Health	83
	Designing Conversational Interfaces for Chatbots	85
	Why Is Conversational Interface Design Important for Chatbots?	85
	Best Practices for Designing Conversational Interfaces for Chatbots	85
	Best Practices for Training Chatbots with NLP	88
	The Future of AI-Powered Customer Service: Virtual Assistants and Voice-Activated Interfaces	91
	Virtual Assistants	91
	Voice-Enabled Interfaces	91
	The Future of AI-Powered Customer Service	93

Chapter 7: **Image and Video Recognition with Artificial Intelligence**   **95**

How AI Can Be Used for Image and Video Recognition   96

Successful Image and Video Detection Strategies   98

     Object Detection   98

     Face Recognition   98

     Emotion Detection   99

Applications of Computer Vision in Marketing   101

Techniques for Training Image Recognition Models   102

     Convolutional Neural Networks (CNNs)   103

     Learning Transfer   103

     Data Increase   103

     Learning Together   104

Ethical Considerations When Using AI for Image and Video Recognition   104

Summary   106

Chapter 8: **Using Artificial Intelligence (AI) for Social Media Marketing**   **109**

How AI Can Be Used for Social Media Marketing   110

     The History of AI in Social Media Marketing   110

     Using AI for Social Media Marketing   110

     Challenges When Using AI for Social Media Marketing   115

Successful Social Media Marketing Strategies   116

     Personalization   116

     Chatbots   116

     Analysis of Feelings with Sentiment Analysis   117

The Role of Sentiment Analysis in Social Media Marketing   119

     Understand the Audience   119

     Brand Reputation Monitoring   120

     Identification of Trends and Opportunities   120

     Measurement of Marketing Effectiveness   120

Predictive Analytics and Social Media Marketing   121

The Impact of AI on Social Media Advertising   124

Chapter 9: **Predictive Analytics with Artificial Intelligence (AI)**   **127**

How AI Can Be Used for Predictive Analytics   129

Types of Predictive Analytics 129

Successful Predictive Analytics Strategies 131

 Audience Segmentation 132

 Predicting Customer Abandonment 132

 Personalization of Content 132

 Predictive Scoring of Leads 133

The Basics of Predictive Modeling with Machine
Learning Algorithms 134

 Time Series Analysis and Predictive Analytics 137

 History of Time Series Analysis 137

 Time Series Analysis in Marketing 138

 Predictive Analytics in Marketing 139

 Methods of Time Series Analysis and Predictive
Analytics 139

 Natural Language Processing 142

 Recommendation Systems 143

Chapter 10:   **Email Marketing with Artificial
Intelligence (AI)**   **145**

How AI Can Be Used for Email Marketing 147

Examples of Successful Email Marketing
Strategies that Use AI 149

 Personalization 149

 Predictive Analytics 150

 Automated Emails 151

 Dynamic Content 152

 Benefits of AI in Email Marketing 154

Techniques for Optimizing Email Subject Lines with AI 154

 NLP 154

 Predictive Analytics 155

 Examples 155

Personalizing Email Content with AI 157

 Why Personalize Email Content? 157

 Benefits of Personalization 157

 How AI Can Personalize Email Content 158

 Examples of AI-Powered Email Personalization 158

Measuring the Effectiveness of Email Marketing with AI 160

 History of Email Marketing 160

	Measuring the Effectiveness of Email Marketing with AI	160
Chapter 11:	**Search Engine Optimization (SEO) with Artificial Intelligence (AI)**	**165**
	How AI Can Be Used for SEO	165
	Examples of Successful SEO Strategies that Use AI	166
	Techniques for Keyword Research with AI	166
	Optimizing Content for Search Engines with AI	166
	The Future of SEO with AI: Voice Search and NLP	167
	How AI Can Be Used for SEO	167
	Successful SEO Strategies that Use AI	170
	Content Optimization Using AI	170
	AI-Powered Keyword Research	170
	Voice Search Optimization Using AI	170
	Predictive Analytics Using AI	171
	AI-Powered Link Building	171
	Image Optimization Using AI	173
	Techniques for Keyword Research with AI	173
	Optimizing Content for Search Engines with AI	175
	Understanding AI and Search Engines	175
	Using AI to Optimize Content for Search Engines	175
	Content Creation	178
	Step-by-Step Instructions for Using AI for Content Creation	178
	Content Optimization	179
	Image and Video Optimization	180
	The Future of SEO with AI: Voice Search and NLP	182
	Voice Search	182
	NLP	183
Chapter 12:	**Using Artificial Intelligence for Content Marketing**	**187**
	How AI Can Be Used for Content Marketing	188
	Content Creation	188
	Content Optimization	189
	Personalization	190
	Content	190

Content Analysis   191

Successful Content Marketing Strategies that Use AI   192

The Role of AI in Content Ideation and Creation   194

Content Ideation   195

Content Creation   195

Personalizing Content for Different Audience
Segments with AI   198

What is Personalizing Content for Different Audience
Segments with AI?   198

Why is Personalizing Content with AI Important?   198

How to Personalize Content for Different Audience
Segments with AI   199

Measuring the Effectiveness of Content Marketing
with AI   201

Understanding Content Marketing   202

Measuring the Effectiveness of Content Marketing   202

How AI Can Help Measure the Effectiveness of
Content Marketing   202

Challenges of Using AI for Measuring the
Effectiveness of Content Marketing   203

**Chapter 13:   Marketing Automation with Artificial
Intelligence (AI)   207**

Successful Marketing Automation Strategies that Use AI   210

Here are Some Examples of Successful Marketing
Automation Strategies that Utilize AI   211

Techniques for Automating Lead Scoring and
Nurturing with AI   212

Step 1: Define the Ideal Customer Profile (ICP)   212

Step 2: Identify Key Buying Signals   212

Step 3: Use AI-Powered Lead Scoring Models   213

Step 4: Use AI-Powered Lead Nurturing Tools   213

Step 5: Integrate AI-Powered Tools into the CRM   213

Step 6: Monitor and Optimize AI-Powered Lead
Scoring and Nurturing   213

The Role of AI in Automated Email Campaigns and
Drip Marketing   214

Automated Email Campaigns   214

Drip Marketing   215

Using AI in Automated Email Campaigns and Drip
Marketing ... 216

Tips for Using AI in Automated Email Campaigns
and Drip Marketing ... 216

Challenges and Limitations of Using AI for Marketing
Automation ... 218

**Chapter 14: Using Artificial Intelligence (AI) for Sales
Enablement ... 223**

How AI Can Be Used for Sales Enablement ... 226

Benefits of Using AI for Sales Enablement ... 226

Challenges of Using AI to Help Sales ... 226

Best Practices for Using AI to Empower Sales ... 227

Successful Sales Enablement Strategies that Use AI ... 228

The Role of AI in Lead Generation and Qualification ... 230

What Are Lead Generation and Qualification? ... 231

The Role of AI in Lead Generation and Qualification ... 231

Advantages of Using AI to Generate and
Qualify Leads ... 232

Sales Forecasting with AI ... 234

The Impact of AI on Sales Productivity and Efficiency ... 236

Automated Lead Generation ... 237

Automated Sales Forecasting ... 238

AI-Powered Customer Service ... 239

Automated Sales Processes ... 239

**Chapter 15: Ethical Considerations and the Future of
Artificial Intelligence (AI) in Marketing ... 243**

Ethical Considerations When Using AI in Marketing ... 243

Potential Ethical Concerns with AI in Marketing ... 244

The Importance of Transparency and Privacy
When Using AI in Marketing ... 244

The Future of AI in Marketing: Emerging Technologies
and Trends ... 244

The Role of Human Expertise and Creativity in
AI-Powered Marketing ... 244

Ethical Considerations When Using AI in Marketing ... 245

Potential Ethical Concerns with AI in Marketing ... 246

Targeted Advertising ... 246

Personalization ... 247

Privacy 247

Bias 248

The Importance of Transparency and Privacy
When Using AI in Marketing 250

The Future of AI in Marketing: Emerging Technologies
and Trends 251

Emerging Technologies and Trends 252

Ethical Models and Standards 252

The Role of Human Expertise and Creativity in
AI-Powered Marketing 253

The Importance of Human Expertise in AI-Powered
Marketing 254

The Role of Creativity in AI-Powered Marketing 254

The Importance of Human Expertise in AI-Powered
Marketing 255

Ethical Considerations in AI Marketing 257

Potential Ethical Concerns with AI in Marketing 257

Transparency and Privacy in AI Marketing 257

Future of AI in Marketing 257

Role of Human Expertise and Creativity in
AI-Powered Marketing 257

Index 261

PREFACE

Welcome to the fascinating world of AI marketing, where technology and creativity converge to revolutionize how businesses engage with customers. This book will take you through the step-by-step process of how to integrate Artificial Intelligence (AI) into your existing marketing strategy to optimize your business, identify the best business practices to consider, and the power of personalizing content to customer preferences. Welcome to the future of marketing—powered by artificial intelligence.

In this first chapter, we'll explore the transformative power of AI and the effect it has on the marketing landscape. As technology continues to advance, the future holds even greater opportunities for innovation, personalization, and growth. By embracing AI and integrating it into your traditional marketing techniques and strategies, you'll position yourself at the forefront of the marketing industry, ready to harness this tool's full potential to achieve your business goals.

This chapter will focus on how AI can drive creative thinking and strategic planning by automating mundane tasks. You'll learn about the efficiency gains AI brings, which can reduce costs and increase the speed and accuracy of your marketing efforts. When used correctly, AI enables unparalleled personalization, crafting tailored messages that resonate with your audience, thereby fostering stronger customer relationships and deeper brand loyalty.

Finally, you'll uncover the history of AI in marketing, from its humble early days of data mining to the sophisticated machine learning and natural language processing technologies of today. You'll come to understand how AI has evolved to become an indispensable tool for modern marketers, offering real-time insights and driving significant improvements in return on investment (ROI).

Now that we've set the stage of how AI can be an additional tool to use, we can consider the intriguing realms of Artificial Intelligence (AI) and Machine Learning (ML). Chapter 2 is designed to provide you with a comprehensive understanding of each of these powerful technologies and their potential impact in the marketing sector.

In this chapter, you'll learn the foundational concepts of AI and ML, and how they differ from each other. While AI encompasses the development of computer systems that perform tasks requiring human intelligence, ML, a subset of AI, uses algorithms to learn from existing data and improve performance over time without explicit programming. You'll see how AI-powered chatbots can enhance customer service by managing routine inquiries, discover how predictive analytics helps businesses anticipate customer behavior and identify trends, and learn how personalization can help tailor marketing efforts to individual consumer preferences. This chapter also explores the different types of ML algorithms and the unique approach each takes to analyzing data and making predictions, be it through labeled datasets, finding patterns in unlabeled data, combining both, or learning through trial and error.

By the end of this chapter, you will have a solid grasp of the basics of AI and ML and be equipped with the right knowledge to start extracting valuable insights to enhance your marketing efforts and stay ahead in the competitive landscape.

Proper data preparation is the backbone of any successful AI initiative, and understanding the key steps involved will set you on the path to harnessing the full power of AI for your business. In Chapter 3, we will focus on preparing your data for AI applications, a crucial step to ensure that your models generate accurate and actionable insights. You'll learn the importance of data hygiene and quality. This is a critical stage of preparing your data for AI, where the groundwork is laid for powerful, data-driven marketing success. We will discuss best practices on how maintaining clean, accurate, and relevant data can prevent misleading or inconsistent results.

We'll also explore strategies for structuring, optimizing, and storing data collection for AI applications, as well as pre-processing techniques, which are essential for refining your data before it is used to train AI models. By focusing on these areas—data hygiene and quality, structuring data for machine learning algorithms, optimizing data collection and storage, employing common data pre-processing techniques, and leveraging the right tools and platforms—you can ensure that your AI models are built on a solid foundation. This preparation will enable your business to make informed decisions, enhance customer experiences, and drive growth through intelligent marketing strategies.

Now that the foundations of building an AI model have been covered, we can look into customer behavior. In our data-driven era, the sheer volume of information generated by customer interactions is staggering. Chapter 4 will guide you on how to harness AI to transform this data into actionable insights, leading to more personalized and effective marketing campaigns.

Throughout this chapter, you will explore various AI-powered tools that can help businesses gain a deeper understanding of their customers' needs, preferences, and behaviors. You'll see how predictive analytics can forecast future customer actions, sentiment analysis can gauge customer emotions, and segmentation can create targeted marketing strategies. Moreover, this chapter emphasizes the importance of feedback loops in customer analysis. By continuously gathering and analyzing feedback, businesses can refine their strategies to better meet customer needs.

In today's fast-paced and competitive market, providing personalized experiences has become essential for businesses aiming to enhance customer engagement and loyalty. AI has emerged as a game-changer in this regard, enabling companies to analyze vast amounts of customer data and create highly tailored experiences that resonate with individual preferences and behaviors.

Chapter 5 will explore how AI can be leveraged to offer personalized product recommendations, create dynamic email campaigns, suggest relevant content, and even tailor pricing strategies to individual customers. You'll discover how leading companies like Netflix, Amazon, and Spotify have successfully implemented AI-powered personalization to boost customer satisfaction and drive business growth. We will also address the ethical considerations associated with AI-driven personalization and emphasize the importance of transparency, fairness, and data privacy.

To ensure the effectiveness of your personalization strategies, we will discuss how to measure the return on investment (ROI) of AI-powered initiatives. By tracking key metrics such as conversion rates, customer engagement, and retention, you can make data-driven decisions to optimize your personalization efforts.

Next, Chapter 6 will provide a comprehensive overview of the landscape of chatbots and AI-powered customer service, exploring their profound impact on enhancing customer interactions, streamlining operations, and ultimately driving business growth. From providing 24/7 availability and faster response times to reducing operational costs and delivering personalized experiences, these technologies can significantly improve customer satisfaction and engagement.

The chapter will also cover the crucial aspects of designing effective conversational interfaces for chatbots and delve into best practices for training chatbots with natural language processing (NLP). You will learn about defining the chatbot's personality, creating seamless user experiences, and providing clear navigation options to ensure that interactions are intuitive and engaging.

As we look to the future of AI-powered customer service, this chapter will also explore the potential of virtual assistants and voice-activated interfaces. These emerging technologies promise to revolutionize customer interactions by offering more natural and intuitive ways to engage with businesses. We will discuss the benefits and challenges of these advancements and provide insights on how to prepare for their integration.

Chapter 7 provides a thorough exploration of image and video recognition with AI, and how it can transform the way businesses understand and engage with visual content, providing a comprehensive overview of its applications, benefits, and best practices. You'll learn how AI algorithms can swiftly and accurately identify and classify images and videos, enabling businesses to leverage this technology for a variety of marketing strategies. The benefits of

AI-driven image and video recognition are immense, ranging from enhanced personalization and improved customer experiences to increased efficiency in marketing campaigns.

The chapter will also cover various applications of computer vision in marketing and how AI can be used to analyze advertisements, providing insights that help businesses fine-tune their campaigns for maximum impact. Ethical considerations are crucial when using AI for image and video recognition, and this chapter will address these important issues. We'll explore potential biases, privacy concerns, and the steps businesses can take to ensure their AI implementations are fair, transparent, and respectful of user privacy.

Next, we will discuss techniques for training image recognition models. You'll learn about machine learning algorithms, including convolutional neural networks (CNNs) and object detection models, and how they can be trained on large datasets to accurately recognize objects, faces, and scenes in images and videos. This section will provide practical guidance on building and refining these models to achieve high accuracy.

Next, Chapter 8 provides a comprehensive overview of the multifaceted ways AI can be utilized in social media marketing. From automating content creation and scheduling to conducting sophisticated sentiment analysis and predictive modeling, AI offers numerous advantages that can elevate your social media presence. Through practical examples and actionable insights, this chapter aims to equip you with the knowledge and tools to harness AI for your social media marketing strategies effectively, providing you with a competitive edge in today's digital landscape. AI-powered tools can help businesses identify specific target audiences and optimize their ad campaigns for maximum impact. By leveraging AI, you can ensure your ads reach the right people at the right time, enhancing your ROI and overall campaign effectiveness.

By automating tasks, personalizing content, and improving customer engagement, AI enables businesses to analyze vast amounts of social media data quickly and efficiently. Machine learning (ML) algorithms and natural language processing (NLP) can uncover trends, patterns, and insights that inform and optimize marketing strategies. By assessing the tone and sentiment of social media posts, businesses can gain a deeper understanding of customer feedback and tailor their marketing strategies accordingly.

By understanding both the capabilities and limitations of AI-powered predictive analytics, businesses can make more informed decisions and use these technologies to enhance their marketing efforts. Chapter 9 provides a thorough exploration of how AI can be used for predictive analytics, providing a comprehensive overview of its applications, techniques, and limitations. By leveraging AI, companies can analyze vast datasets more rapidly and accurately, uncovering patterns and making predictions that human analysts might miss. This section covers various AI techniques such as regression, decision trees, neural networks, and clustering, highlighting how they contribute to creating robust predictive models to forecast future outcomes based on historical data.

Next, the fundamentals of predictive modeling with ML algorithms are explained. This involves the process of collecting and preprocessing data, selecting the appropriate ML algorithm, and dividing data into training and testing sets. This chapter also explores time series analysis, a critical technique for analyzing sequential data points over time. Predictive analytics can be applied to time series data to forecast future values, such as stock prices, product demand, or website traffic. Despite its benefits, predictive analytics with AI has its limitations and requires continuous monitoring and updating of predictive models to maintain accuracy and ensure best ethical practices are considered.

As AI technology continues to evolve, the future of email marketing promises even more innovative and impactful strategies. Email marketing remains a cornerstone of digital marketing, allowing businesses to communicate directly with their audience and customers. In Chapter 10, we explore how AI can be utilized to enhance various aspects of email marketing, from segmentation and personalization to optimization and testing. With the integration of AI, businesses can elevate their email marketing strategies to drive more engagement, conversions, and revenue. AI significantly enhances email marketing by optimizing segmentation, personalization, optimization, and testing.

By leveraging AI-powered tools, businesses can create more targeted, engaging, and effective email campaigns that drive better results and increase customer retention and sales. AI algorithms can analyze vast amounts of customer data, segment audiences based on demographics, behavior, interests, and past interactions, and tailor emails to specific groups. This leads to increased open rates, click-through rates, and conversions by delivering more relevant content to the recipients.

AI can analyze performance data from past emails to predict the best-performing subject lines for future campaigns. It can also generate personalized subject lines based on customer data, which significantly increases open and engagement rates and predict the expected results of future email campaigns, helping businesses optimize their strategies for better performance.

As AI continues to evolve, the future of SEO will become even more exciting, with new opportunities for personalization, voice search, and natural language processing. Embracing these technologies will position your business for success in the ever-changing digital landscape. Chapter 11 focuses on how, by using AI-powered tools and techniques, marketers can identify the most effective SEO strategies, conduct keyword research, optimize content for search engines, and stay ahead of the latest SEO trends.

Search engines use complex algorithms to determine the relevance and value of a website and rank it in search results. These algorithms are constantly evolving, making it difficult for marketers to keep up with the latest SEO techniques. This is where AI can help. AI-powered tools and techniques can analyze large volumes of data and help marketers identify the most effective SEO strategies. AI can enhance SEO through content optimization, link building, keyword research, and user behavior analysis. By leveraging these capabilities, you can ensure your website remains competitive and visible in search engine results.

The future of SEO is closely tied to the development of AI, particularly in the areas of voice search and natural language processing (NLP). Voice search is expected to become a major player in SEO, with AI tools helping to identify common voice search queries and optimize content accordingly. As AI becomes more advanced, NLP will become more sophisticated, allowing search engines to better understand the meaning of words and phrases and identify the most relevant content for search queries.

By harnessing the power of AI, you can enhance every aspect of your content marketing strategy, from ideation and creation to personalization and performance measurement. As AI technologies continue to evolve, their impact on content marketing will only grow, making it essential for marketers to stay abreast of these advancements and leverage them to stay competitive in the digital landscape. In Chapter 12, you will discover how AI can revolutionize various aspects of content marketing, from ideation and creation to personalization and measurement. AI can significantly enhance content marketing by automating content creation, generating innovative ideas, and personalizing content for different audience segments. By leveraging AI, marketers can streamline the content creation process, ensuring high-quality output at scale.

AI also plays a crucial role in measuring content marketing effectiveness. AI-powered tools can automate the generation of various content formats, including articles, blogs, social media posts, and videos, optimizing content by analyzing its readability, keyword density, and structure, ensuring it is both search engine-friendly and appealing to the target audience. Then, AI-powered analytics tools provide real-time insights into content performance, tracking metrics such as engagement rates, conversion rates, and customer lifetime value. By identifying patterns and trends, these tools help marketers make data-driven decisions to refine their content strategies as well as identify the best channels and optimal times for distributing content, maximizing its reach and impact.

By now, the topics of personalization and optimization will be familiar. Next up is marketing automation: the process of using technology to automate repetitive marketing tasks. In Chapter 13, we'll explore how, by integrating marketing automation, businesses can streamline their efforts, personalize campaigns, and make data-driven decisions that lead to better outcomes in a more efficient and effective manner.

One of the key benefits of using AI in marketing automation is its ability to analyze large volumes of data to uncover patterns and preferences. AI algorithms can process customer behavior and demographic data to create highly targeted marketing messages using techniques like predictive modeling and machine learning algorithms to identify and prioritize promising leads. This automation ensures that marketing efforts are directed toward leads with the highest conversion potential, thereby increasing engagement and conversions.

Automated email campaigns and drip marketing also benefit from AI. By analyzing customer behavior and preferences, AI can personalize email content, subject lines, and send times, making the campaigns more effective. This automation saves time and resources while delivering targeted and impactful messages. AI's ability to automate repetitive tasks is another crucial aspect of sales enablement. Tasks such as data entry and lead qualification can be automated using AI, freeing up sales teams to focus on building relationships and closing deals. AI tools can analyze a prospect's behavior and demographics to determine their likelihood of becoming a customer, helping sales teams prioritize their efforts on the most promising leads.

Chapter 14 covers how AI can enhance various aspects of sales, providing comprehensive insights into its application for lead generation, qualification, sales forecasting, and improving overall sales productivity and efficiency.

Sales enablement involves equipping sales teams with the right tools, resources, and information to engage prospects effectively, nurture relationships, and close deals. For instance, AI-powered tools can suggest products or services based on a customer's browsing and purchasing history, allowing sales teams to make personalized recommendations that are more likely to result in a sale.

Lead generation and qualification, as well as sales forecasting, are pivotal areas where AI makes a substantial impact. AI can analyze data from various sources, such as browsing history and social media activity, to identify and qualify potential customers. It can then analyze customer behavior, market trends, and other factors to produce accurate sales forecasts. These forecasts enable sales teams to plan their activities and resources more effectively, enhancing overall performance and profitability.

AI's impact on sales productivity and efficiency is profound. By automating routine tasks and providing insights into customer behavior, AI allows sales teams to tailor their approaches and make more relevant recommendations.

AI is a profound tool with incredible transformative potential for marketing and sales. However, the core of marketing can never be forgotten. Chapter 15, the last chapter in this book, will explore how AI can enhance CRM systems, making them more intelligent, intuitive, and responsive to the needs of businesses and customers alike. We will examine how AI can provide deeper insights into customer behavior, predict future customer actions, and automate personalized communication, thereby fostering stronger and more meaningful relationships with customers.

The integration of AI into CRM systems represents a paradigm shift, transforming traditional CRM from a static repository of customer information into a dynamic, intelligent platform that actively drives customer engagement and loyalty. We'll discuss the importance of data quality and integration, the selection of appropriate AI tools, and the training and support needed for teams to effectively utilize these systems. By following these guidelines, businesses can ensure a smooth and successful integration of AI into their CRM processes.

This book provides the fundamentals you'll need to integrate strategies in your marketing campaigns and create processes that save time and money, while also giving you ideas on creating content to reach your target audience. After reading this book you'll have a great understanding of how you can use AI to grow your marketing experience.

Mark Lamplugh
August 2024

CHAPTER 1

INTRODUCTION TO ARTIFICIAL INTELLIGENCE MARKETING

A rtificial intelligence (AI) has been transforming the world of marketing, offering new ways to approach and understand consumers, optimize marketing strategies, and drive business growth. AI marketing involves using machine learning (ML) algorithms and predictive analytics to automate marketing processes, gain insights from data, and personalize customer experiences. AI marketing offers several benefits, including increased efficiency, cost-effectiveness, accuracy, and speed, allowing businesses to reach the right audience with the right message at the right time.

Defining AI Marketing and Its Remarkable Benefits:

AI marketing is the application of AI technologies to streamline, enhance, and customize various marketing activities throughout the customer journey, from lead generation to retention. Embrace these outstanding benefits of AI marketing:

- *Exceptional efficiency:* Automating mundane tasks such as data analysis, reporting, and segmentation with AI allows marketing professionals to devote time to more strategic initiatives.
- *Budget-friendly innovation:* By automating tasks and minimizing human intervention, AI significantly reduces marketing-related expenses, including hiring and training personnel.
- *Delivering personal touch:* Using consumer behavior data analysis, preferences, and interests, AI crafts tailored marketing messages and offers to boost customer engagement and foster loyalty.
- *Pinpoint accuracy:* The ability of AI to rapidly analyze vast data sets ensures that marketers make well-informed, data-driven decisions derived from valuable insights.

- *Lightning-fast processing:* Real-time data processing in AI empowers marketers to promptly adapt to evolving consumer needs and market trends.

Elevating Traditional Marketing Techniques with AI Marketing:

AI marketing can amplify conventional marketing approaches in numerous ways, including:

- *Precise audience targeting:* Leveraging consumer data analysis, AI identifies target audiences and distributes customized messages through a range of channels like email, social media, or mobile apps.
- *Creative content generation:* Based on consumer data and preferences, AI can skillfully produce bespoke content that resonates deeply with the intended audience.
- *Effortless A/B testing:* Automating the A/B testing procedure with AI permits marketers to assess multiple variations of a campaign swiftly and accurately, optimizing overall effectiveness.
- *Powerful predictive analytics:* Gleaning insights from data analysis, AI projects future trends, behaviors, and results which enable marketers to make strategic adjustments accordingly.

AI marketing is transforming the marketing industry, providing businesses with new ways to reach and engage with their customers, optimize their strategies, and drive growth. As AI technology continues to advance, the future of AI marketing looks promising, with new opportunities for personalization, automation, and innovation.

AI MARKETING AND ITS BENEFITS

At its core, AI marketing –harnesses sophisticated technologies like ML, natural language processing (NLP), and predictive analytics to fine-tune and individualize marketing strategies and initiatives. As a popular choice for businesses of all sizes, AI marketing offers an array of impressive benefits:

1. *Personalization:* By examining vast quantities of customer data, AI marketing allows businesses to tailor their marketing efforts with personalized recommendations and suggestions based on their audience's unique interests and habits. This leads to enhanced customer engagement and higher conversion rates.

2. *Efficiency:* Thanks to AI marketing tools that automate various processes, marketers can dedicate more time to strategizing and generating creative content. The result? Marketing campaigns achieve greater levels of productivity and efficiency.

3. *Predictive Analytics:* Leveraging AI marketing is key in identifying trends and patterns in customer behavior—empowering businesses to forecast future inclinations and adjust their marketing approaches accordingly. This ensures companies remain competitive by anticipating shifts in consumer demand.

4. *Improved ROI:* With AI marketing's ability to pinpoint the most effective channels and tactics for engaging target audiences, businesses can optimize their marketing budgets—an essential step toward increasing return on investment (ROI) and overall profitability.

5. *Real-time insights:* Offering a real-time look at customer behavior and campaign performance, AI marketing tools grant marketers the flexibility to make prompt adjustments, ensuring campaigns are continually optimized. The outcome? A higher level of agility and responsiveness in all endeavors.

By encompassing personalized outreach, heightened efficiency, predictive analytics, improved ROI, and real-time insights, AI marketing delivers an abundance of advantages for organizations keen on polishing their promotional pursuits. As technological advancements lay the groundwork for the future, the role of AI in shaping the marketing landscape will only continue to grow in significance.

Step-by-Step Guide to Integrating AI Into Marketing Strategies

1. **Assess Current Marketing Processes**

   - Evaluate existing marketing strategies and tools.
   - Identify areas where AI can enhance efficiency, such as data analysis, customer segmentation, and personalization.

2. **Define Objectives and Goals**

   - Determine what the desired achievements are with AI integration (e.g., increased customer engagement, improved ROI, enhanced personalization).
   - Set clear, measurable goals for AI implementation in the marketing strategy.

3. **Select the Right AI Technologies**

   - Research AI tools and solutions relevant to marketing needs (e.g., AI-driven analytics platforms, chatbots, personalized recommendation systems).

- Consider factors like compatibility with existing tools, budget, and ease of integration.

4. **Plan the Integration Process:**

- Develop a roadmap for integrating AI into all marketing processes, including timelines and milestones.
- Ensure cross-departmental collaboration to align marketing objectives with AI capabilities.

5. **Implement AI Solutions:**

- Start with pilot projects to test the effectiveness of AI in specific marketing areas.
- Gradually expand the use of AI tools across different marketing channels and campaigns.

6. **Monitor and Optimize:**

- Regularly assess the performance of AI implementations against existing goals.
- Use insights gained from AI analytics to continuously optimize and refine marketing strategies.

7. **Training the Team:**

- Educate the marketing team on AI capabilities and best practices.
- Encourage ongoing learning and adaptation to new AI technologies and trends.

8. **Stay Updated on AI Advancements:**

- Keep abreast of the latest developments in AI technology and marketing applications.
- Regularly evaluate new AI tools and techniques that could enhance marketing efforts.

HOW AI MARKETING CAN ENHANCE TRADITIONAL MARKETING TECHNIQUES

AI has been revolutionizing the realm of marketing for quite some time. By tapping into the capabilities of ML algorithms, predictive analytics, and other AI-driven tools, businesses can amass and scrutinize enormous volumes of data, tailor customer experiences, and fine-tune their marketing tactics. This chapter delves deep into the ways AI marketing can amplify traditional marketing methods, concentrating on real-life examples and implementations.

Personalization and Targeting: A New Frontier

A key advantage of AI marketing lies in its capacity to individualize and direct marketing messages to specific customers. AI algorithms evaluate customer data to unveil distinctive patterns, preferences, and habits that can be utilized to craft bespoke marketing campaigns. Take Netflix as an example—the streaming giant employs AI algorithms to examine user viewing trends and tastes, subsequently propelling personalized content recommendations. This strategy has proven immensely successful, with customized suggestions accounting for up to 80% of Netflix's views.

E-commerce platforms like Amazon offer yet another illustration of AI-fueled personalization in action. Amazon harnesses ML algorithms to study customer behavior and anticipate future purchases. Armed with this information, Amazon can suggest products tailored to individual customers' interests. This technique has played a significant role in cementing Amazon's status as one of the most triumphant e-commerce platforms worldwide.

Harnessing the Power of AI in Marketing

AI serves as a catalyst for revitalizing traditional marketing approaches through the employment of predictive analytics. This technique utilizes historical data to ascertain patterns and trends, which assists in forecasting future outcomes. Predictive analytics can determine customer churn probabilities, product popularity potentials, and marketing campaigns' successes.

A prime example of predictive analytics in action can be observed at the retail giant, Target. Incorporating ML algorithms, Target assesses customer data to identify those with a higher likelihood of becoming pregnant. Consequently, the company then tailors marketing campaigns that promote baby products to the identified customers. Target's pregnancy prediction model has garnered significant success by accurately identifying 25% of pregnant customers within a mere two weeks.

Innovative Optimization and Efficiency

AI can streamline and enhance traditional marketing strategies by introducing optimal efficiency and effectiveness. Through the analysis of vast data sets, AI algorithms outline patterns and trends which aid in optimizing marketing campaigns. AI enables the discovery of optimal times for sending marketing emails, identification of effective social media channels, and selection of impactful marketing messages.

The online advertising industry showcases a spectacular example of AI-driven optimization. Here, advertisers employ ML algorithms to study user behavior and predict which ads resonate the most with specific audiences. Advertisements are then tailored accordingly for maximum efficacy. AI-powered advertising campaigns have consistently outperformed conventional approaches.

AI marketing possesses immense potential to redefine traditional marketing methods radically. By utilizing advanced ML algorithms, predictive analytics, and other AI-powered tools, businesses can curate personalized customer experiences, optimize their marketing tactics, and improve overall efficiency and effectiveness.

Although AI marketing remains in its infancy stage, it is evident that it will play an increasingly crucial part in the future of marketing. As AI technology continues to evolve, people can anticipate even more inventive and efficient techniques emerging, further enriching customer experiences and propelling business success.

THE HISTORY OF AI IN MARKETING

AI has become a game changer in the marketing industry in recent years. From personalization to automation, AI has revolutionized the way businesses reach their customers and make sales. This chapter will explore the history of AI in marketing and its impact on the industry.

The Dawn of AI in Marketing

Tracing the roots of AI in marketing leads back to the 1990s when businesses began employing data mining methods to examine customer behavior and inclinations. This technique relied substantively on statistical models while working with data sets that were often restricted in terms of size and scope.

As the new millennium unfolded, ML algorithms and NLP emerged, revolutionizing the landscape of AI technology. Armed with these advanced tools, companies delved into larger and more intricate data sets, attaining precise insights into customer actions.

One of the pioneering instances of AI in marketing was the creation of recommendation engines. In 1998, Amazon unveiled its groundbreaking recommendation system that tapped into collaborative filtering to propose products to customers rooted in their browsing and purchasing history. This innovation proved pivotal, driving Amazon's sales skyward and enhancing customer experiences.

Around this time, chatbots also entered the marketing realm. Fueled by NLP and ML, these virtual aides could address consumer inquiries, put forth suggestions, and even facilitate transactions effortlessly.

The Rise of Big Data

A major turning point for AI in marketing arose with the advent of big data. As an ever-growing number of companies collected immense customer data, the demand for cutting-edge data analysis tools surged.

AI presented an answer to this burgeoning need. Utilizing ML algorithms and NLP, businesses could now scrutinize customer data at scale and unearth insights that would have been otherwise elusive with manual analysis.

One prominent example during this era was the inception of predictive analytics in marketing. Industry giants like IBM and SAS developed software solutions capable of forecasting customer behavior, empowering businesses to fine-tune their marketing strategies for optimal returns on investment.

Personalization and Automation: A New Era in Marketing

The emergence of big data and AI has revolutionized personalization and automation in the marketing landscape. By deciphering customer data, companies can now craft tailored marketing messages to individual consumers, offering a more customized experience.

A prime example of this innovation is Netflix's recommendation algorithm. By evaluating a user's viewing history and preferences, Netflix can suggest relevant TV shows and movies that will captivate their interest, enhancing the user experience and boosting engagement.

AI has also empowered companies to automate various marketing processes, ranging from lead generation to customer service. Chatbots serve as a fitting illustration; they manage customer inquiries and issues, allowing human agents to concentrate on more intricate tasks.

Step-by-Step Instructions for Leveraging the History of AI in Marketing

1. **Research AI's Evolution in Marketing:**

   - Investigate the progression of AI in marketing to understand how it has evolved and impacted the field.
   - Look into different eras of marketing to see how AI technologies have been integrated over time.

2. **Highlight Key Developments:**

   - Identify and examine major milestones and technological breakthroughs in the history of AI in marketing.
   - Understand how these developments have shaped current marketing practices and AI applications.

3. **Analyze Success Stories:**

   - Study cases of successful AI implementation in marketing across various industries.
   - Gain insights into effective AI strategies and the results they produce.

4. **Incorporate Lessons into Current Strategies:**

   - Use the historical insights gained to inform and enhance current AI marketing strategies.

- Ensure that the approach is influenced by proven methods and learnings from past successes.

5. **Anticipate Future AI Trends:**

- Stay updated on the latest advancements in AI technology and predictive trends in the marketing sector.
- Prepare for future shifts in the industry by understanding potential developments and their implications for AI in marketing.

The Evolution of AI in Marketing: A Promising Outlook

The application of AI in marketing endeavors is set to expand exponentially in upcoming years. As an increasing number of companies adopt digital transformation strategies, the demand for advanced data analysis tools will be more evident than ever before.

Voice search is one domain where AI is poised to make substantial contributions. With the emergence of voice-activated assistants like Siri and Alexa, businesses are compelled to optimize their content for this channel, calling for NLP and ML algorithms.

Furthermore, AI is predicted to significantly influence the creation of augmented reality (AR) and virtual reality (VR) experiences. By utilizing AI-driven chatbots and recommendation systems, companies will be capable of crafting more immersive and captivating AR/VR experiences for their clientele.

From its humble beginnings involving data mining to its present capabilities in predictive analytics, AI has revolutionized the way businesses approach customer behavior, fostering personalized and immersive interactions. As technological advancements continue unabated, the role of AI within the marketing industry will become increasingly indispensable. With applications spanning voice search to AR/VR experiences, AI is set to empower businesses by cultivating innovative connections with customers.

Nevertheless, it is crucial to recognize that incorporating AI into marketing practices presents its own set of challenges. As companies become more reliant on AI solutions, there arises a potential for diminishing human interactions, potentially resulting in decreased trust and engagement from customers.

To navigate these obstacles successfully, marketers must find the perfect equilibrium between AI implementation and human engagement—all while maintaining exceptional customer experiences. By striking this balance, businesses can fully leverage AI's potential to spur growth and remain at the forefront of their industries.

The story of the integration of AI within marketing has been a captivating one—from data mining origins to predictive analytics advents and customization capabilities. The technology is predicted to play a pivotal part in shaping voice search techniques along with AR/VR experiences' development.

Undoubtedly, it is an exhilarating period for the marketing industry, and AI-embracing businesses can.

THE IMPACT OF AI ON THE MARKETING INDUSTRY

AI is revolutionizing the marketing industry. With the advent of advanced ML algorithms and deep neural networks, businesses can now leverage the power of AI to make data-driven decisions and provide personalized experiences to their customers. This chapter will explore the impact of AI on the marketing industry, discuss some examples of how AI is being used in marketing today, and explore the potential for AI in the future.

Enhancing Personalization and Customer Experience with AI

AI has revolutionized the marketing landscape by enabling businesses to offer their customers highly personalized experiences. Through AI, organizations can gather and scrutinize extensive customer data that reveals preferences, behaviors, and demographics. This invaluable information empowers businesses to develop tailored marketing strategies and product recommendations specific to everyone.

Amazon's recommendation engine exemplifies the power of AI-driven personalization. The engine studies a customer's purchase history and browsing habits to suggest products that pique their interests, increasing the probability of sales. McKinsey reports that companies utilizing AI for personalization can witness sales gains between 6-10%.

Another avenue where AI enhances the customer experience is through AI-driven chatbots. These chatbots can address a wide variety of customer inquiries while providing instantaneous responses, elevating customer satisfaction, and diminishing response times. This proves particularly beneficial for businesses inundated with customer inquiries, like e-commerce Web sites or customer service departments.

Revolutionizing Marketing Analytics and Optimization Through AI

AI also transforms how businesses analyze and refine their marketing ventures. Utilizing ML algorithms to examine massive quantities of data allows organizations to derive insights into customer behavior and preferences while identifying patterns and trends that would be challenging to detect manually.

One instance of this integration is in Google's Smart Bidding feature, which harnesses ML algorithms to optimize real-time ad bids according to parameters such as device, location, and time. This results in more prudent advertising expenditure and an amplified ROI.

Additionally, AI technology can optimize Web site and app design by analyzing user behavior and engagement metrics. Identifying areas requiring improvement enables businesses to test alternate design variations that perform optimally. Although manual A/B testing can be time-intensive and expensive, implementing AI for this purpose increases efficiency while reducing costs.

Predictive Analytics and Forecasting

AI can also be used for predictive analytics, which involves using historical data to make predictions about future events. In the marketing industry, this can be used to forecast sales, predict customer churn, and identify emerging trends.

One example of this is Netflix's recommendation engine, which uses ML algorithms to predict which movies and TV shows customers are likely to enjoy based on their viewing history. This not only improves the customer experience but also helps Netflix make more informed decisions about which content to produce and license.

Predictive lead scoring, which involves using AI to identify the most promising leads for sales teams to pursue. By analyzing factors such as demographic data, past behavior, and engagement metrics, businesses can identify leads that are most likely to convert and prioritize them accordingly.

The Expanding Role of AI in Marketing's Future

The swift advancement of AI technology opens a world of boundless possibilities for the marketing sector. Experts foresee a future where significant aspects of the marketing lifecycle are automated, such as ad copy creation, design, customer behavior analysis, and product recommendations.

One notable domain where AI is making considerable progress is NLP. NLP trains machines to comprehend and interpret human language, profoundly influencing marketing strategies. Businesses can harness NLP-driven chatbots to deliver enhanced, personalized customer service or employ NLP algorithms to scrutinize customer feedback and sentiments, leading to improvements in products and services.

The potential of AI also extends to AR and VR. With AI-powered analyses of customer behaviors and preferences, businesses can develop immersive and customized AR and VR experiences that captivate customers and fuel sales.

However, as is the case with any nascent technology, adopting AI in marketing brings its share of potential hurdles and risks. One key issue is the propensity for AI to reinforce bias and discrimination in areas like hiring and lending. Furthermore, there is a growing concern about AI undermining privacy and security as businesses accumulate and examine vast amounts of personal data on their customers.

To address these challenges, it is crucial for businesses, policymakers, and AI developers to collaboratively establish ethical guidelines, best practices for AI implementation in marketing, and promote transparency and accountability in algorithms and models.

The influence of AI on the marketing industry is substantial, with further growth anticipated. Utilizing this powerful technology enables businesses to provide tailored experiences to customers while optimizing their marketing strategies and making informed decisions about products and services. Nevertheless, it is essential to tread cautiously when approaching the use of AI in marketing – prioritizing ethical considerations and best practices.

FUTURE TRENDS IN AI MARKETING

AI is making waves in the world of marketing. The use of AI in marketing has been growing rapidly in recent years, and this trend is expected to continue well into the future. AI has the potential to transform the way marketers approach their work, from understanding customers and their behavior, to targeting them with more personalized and relevant content, to automating various marketing tasks.

Here are some of the future trends in AI marketing that are expected to emerge in the coming years.

Scaling Personalization with AI

A core advantage of incorporating AI in marketing lies in its capacity to customize content and communication on a grand scale. By employing AI, marketers can scrutinize extensive customer data, paving the way for more individualized experiences. Consequently, customers are met with precisely targeted content, catering to their unique requirements and interests instead of generic messages that hold little relevance.

The prowess of AI enables an in-depth analysis of a client's purchase history, browsing habits, and social media engagement to craft a highly accurate portrait of their interests and preferences. This valuable data is then employed to deliver customized product suggestions and promotional offers.

From Chatbots to Advanced Conversational AI

Chatbots serve as an embodiment of conversational AI that streamline customer service processes through automation. Numerous businesses currently utilize chatbots for responding to customer queries, delivering product recommendations, and even overseeing order processing.

Looking ahead, chatbots are poised to become increasingly sophisticated and adept. Thanks to advancements in NLP and ML, chatbots will be equipped to comprehend and address more intricate inquiries while engaging customers in more fluid and captivating conversations.

Voice Search Optimization: Tuning into the Future

As smart speakers and virtual assistants like Amazon Alexa and Google Home surge in popularity, voice search has become a force to be reckoned with. To stay ahead of the curve, marketers must adapt and optimize their content for voice search queries. By harnessing the power of AI algorithms to analyze user patterns and preferences, marketers can craft content tailored to voice search, boosting their visibility in this emerging platform.

Predictive Analytics: A Crystal Ball for Marketers

AI is revolutionizing marketing through the magic of predictive analytics. By employing ML algorithms to dissect customer data, marketers can anticipate future behaviors and make strategic decisions on which products to display, which demographics to engage, and how to fine-tune pricing for maximum impact.

Automated Content Creation: Turning the Page on Tradition

Creating content can be a laborious process, but AI is ready to streamline it. With AI-powered automation, marketers can generate headlines, draft product descriptions, and even compose entire articles effortlessly. Although this technology is still budding, expect to see groundbreaking AI-powered content creation tools that enable marketers to produce high-quality content efficiently while freeing up resources for other marketing endeavors.

Image and Video Recognition: A Smarter Vision

AI's ability to scrutinize images and videos for objects, people, and additional elements opens new avenues for marketing. Potential applications include spotting products within multimedia for eCommerce sites, pinpointing logos in social media posts, or discerning emotions in customer photos. As this technology advances further, expect to see marketers incorporating image and video recognition into personalized and relevant content-creation strategies.

VR and AR

Users can encounter a virtual environment or digital overlays in the real-world using AR and VR technology. Many marketing strategies may be implemented with these technologies, including developing immersive brand experiences, presenting things in 3D, and even enabling buyers to try products before they buy.

Readers can anticipate seeing increasingly more inventive and compelling experiences developed for customers as AI becomes more integrated with AR and VR.

AI is expected to play a significant role in marketing in the future. AI can change how marketers approach their business, from mass personalization to automated content generation and predictive analytics. It is likely people will see even more fascinating and cutting-edge uses of AI in marketing as technology continues to progress and improve. Businesses may remain ahead of the curve and improve client engagement in the years to come by embracing these trends and integrating AI into their marketing efforts.

AI Marketing: Transforming the Marketing Industry

AI is changing how organizations work, and the marketing sector is no exception. AI is rapidly transforming the marketing environment, giving marketers a strong tool to better understand their consumers, boost productivity, and drive sales. AI marketing is the use of AI technology to automate and optimize marketing processes, as well as to give insights that allow marketers to make better decisions.

The Advantages of AI Marketing

AI marketing delivers a variety of advantages, including improved customer experiences, personalized marketing messaging, increased efficiency, and campaign optimization. Customer data may be analyzed by AI to uncover trends that allow for improved targeting, customization, and engagement. AI may also be used to automate tedious processes, allowing marketers to focus on more strategic projects.

Improving Conventional Marketing Methods

AI marketing may supplement traditional marketing methods by offering a more tailored approach. AI can scan massive volumes of data to discover client preferences and habits, enabling more focused and personalized marketing communications. AI may also be used to optimize marketing strategies, lowering costs while boosting efficiency. Furthermore, AI can deliver real-time analytics and insights to marketers, allowing them to make smarter decisions and swiftly change campaigns based on performance data.

AI in Marketing: A Brief History

AI has been used in marketing for decades, but recent advances in AI technology have enabled marketers to utilize it in new and more successful ways. Companies began employing data mining techniques to examine client data and uncover trends in the 1990s. Companies began utilizing ML in the early 2000s to evaluate client behavior and optimize marketing strategies. Marketers have been able to leverage AI in new and inventive ways in recent years, thanks to the availability of enormous amounts of data and the development of more powerful AI algorithms.

The Influence of AI on the Marketing Industry

AI has had an enormous influence on the marketing business. AI has helped marketers to analyze customer data more efficiently, resulting in more focused and personalized marketing communications. AI has also simplified the automation of monotonous operations, allowing marketers to focus on more strategic projects. Furthermore, AI has helped marketers to improve marketing strategies in real-time, lowering costs and enhancing efficiency. As a result, AI has become an indispensable tool for marketers, and businesses that do not use AI in their marketing activities risk falling behind their competitors.

Upcoming AI Marketing Trends

In the future, AI is predicted to continue to disrupt the marketing business in novel ways. The growing use of NLP and chatbots to create more personalized and engaging consumer experiences is one trend. Another rising trend is the use of AI with other new technologies such as VR and AR to create more immersive marketing experiences. Furthermore, AI is predicted to play an increasingly significant role in influencer marketing, allowing marketers to discover and collaborate with influencers who are most likely to resonate with their target audience.

AI marketing is changing the way companies promote their products and services. Marketers may better understand their clients, tailor marketing messages, boost efficiency, and optimize marketing campaigns by utilizing AI technology. Although AI has a long history in marketing, current breakthroughs in AI technology have enabled marketers to leverage AI in new and more successful ways. AI has had a huge influence on the marketing sector, and future developments in AI marketing are predicted to continue to revolutionize the industry in new and unique ways. Companies that adopt AI marketing will, in the end, be better positioned to satisfy their consumers' requirements and remain ahead of their competition.

CHAPTER 2

UNDERSTANDING ARTIFICIAL INTELLIGENCE AND MACHINE LEARNING

Artificial Intelligence (AI) and machine learning (ML) have become buzzwords in a variety of disciplines, including marketing. Businesses are looking for methods to use AI and ML to improve their marketing efforts as technology progresses. But, before delving into the intricacies of AI in marketing, it is critical to first grasp what AI and ML are.

The development of computer systems that can do activities that would normally require human intellect, such as visual perception, speech recognition, decision-making, and language translation, is referred to as *artificial intelligence* (AI). *Machine learning* (ML) is a subset of AI that employs algorithms to allow computers to learn from data and improve their performance without being explicitly programmed.

AI is applied in marketing in a variety of ways, from chatbots and virtual assistants to predictive analytics and personalization. AI-powered chatbots may provide customer service and answer frequently asked queries, freeing up human workers for more difficult activities. Personalization helps firms to personalize their marketing efforts to consumers' tastes, whilst predictive analytics may assist organizations to foresee customer behavior and spot trends.

ML algorithms are classified into four types: supervised learning, unsupervised learning, semisupervised learning, and reinforcement learning. *Supervised learning* is the process of using labeled data to train a computer system to predict outcomes based on fresh, unlabeled data. *Unsupervised learning* is the process of examining unstructured data to uncover patterns and correlations without any prior knowledge.

To increase accuracy, *semisupervised learning* blends labeled and unlabeled data, whereas *reinforcement learning* uses rewards and punishments to educate a computer system to make judgments.

When it comes to ML, the value of training data cannot be emphasized. The accuracy of the ML model is determined by the quality and amount of training data. As a result, it is critical to ensure that the training data is representative of the target population, devoid of biases, and large enough to avoid overfitting.

Data science is important in AI marketing because it uses huge data to extract valuable insights and inform decision-making. Data scientists uncover patterns, trends, and correlations in massive volumes of data using techniques such as data mining, ML, and predictive analytics. Businesses may use this information to better their marketing tactics, improve customer experiences, and eventually boost revenue.

AI and ML have enormous promise in marketing, and their applications are expanding. Understanding the fundamentals of AI and ML, as well as the various types of ML algorithms, the significance of training data, and the role of data science in AI marketing, is critical for businesses looking to leverage these technologies to improve their marketing efforts.

THE BASICS OF AI AND ML

AI is a rapidly evolving technology that is changing the way people live and work. It has been in development for decades, but it is only in the last few years that AI has become a mainstream topic of discussion. One of the most significant branches of AI is ML, which is a subset of AI that enables computers to learn from data and improve their performance over time without being explicitly programmed. This chapter explains the basics of AI and ML, and their differences, and provide examples of how they are being used in various industries.

What Exactly is AI?

AI is a subfield of computer science that focuses on the development of intelligent machines that can think, reason, and learn in the same way that people can. AI may be used to automate processes, forecast outcomes, and solve issues that would otherwise need human intellect. It is classified into two types: narrow or weak AI and general or strong AI.

Narrow AI is intended to do specialized tasks such as facial recognition, chess play, and automobile driving. It is trained to accomplish a specific job and cannot learn beyond that task's scope. General AI, on the other hand, is intended to accomplish any intellectual work that a person can complete. It is capable of reasoning, understanding natural language, and learning from experience.

What Exactly is Machine Learning (ML)?

Machine learning (ML) is a kind of AI that allows computers to learn from data and improve their performance over time without being explicitly programmed. ML algorithms examine enormous volumes of data, discover patterns, and generate predictions based on that data using statistical methods.

ML is classified into three types: supervised learning, unsupervised learning, and reinforcement learning.

The most prevalent kind of ML is supervised learning. It entails training a model with labeled input and knowing the proper output. The system learns to identify patterns in data and then makes predictions based on those patterns. A supervised learning system may be trained to recognize photographs of cats and dogs.

Unsupervised learning is the process of training a model with unlabeled input in which the right output is uncertain. The algorithm learns to recognize patterns in the data and group data points that are similar together. An unsupervised learning algorithm can be used to categorize clients based on their shopping history.

Reinforcement learning is the process of teaching a model to make decisions based on input from its surroundings. The model learns via trial and error and adapts its behavior based on input. A reinforcement learning method may be used to train a robot in how to navigate a maze.

AI and ML Examples

AI and ML are being utilized to increase productivity, accuracy, and decision-making in a variety of sectors. Here are a couple such examples:

- *Healthcare:* AI and ML are being used to analyze medical pictures, diagnose ailments, and create individualized treatment regimens. IBM Watson Health uses ML to evaluate medical information and make individualized treatment suggestions.
- *Finance:* AI and ML are being used to detect fraud, forecast market trends, and automate financial research. JPMorgan Bank uses ML to evaluate vast volumes of financial data and generate investment suggestions.
- *Retail:* AI and ML are being utilized to improve consumer experience, customize suggestions, and optimize inventory management. Amazon utilizes ML to propose things to customers based on their previous purchases.
- *Transportation:* AI and ML are being utilized to improve transportation safety, efficiency, and sustainability. Tesla's Autopilot technology employs ML to navigate roadways and avoid crashes.
- *Education:* AI and ML are being used to tailor learning, provide students feedback, and construct adaptive learning systems. Carnegie Learning is utilizing ML to tailor math teaching for kids.

AI and ML are quickly revolutionizing industries such as healthcare, banking, retail, transportation, and education.

They allow computers to learn from data and improve over time without being explicitly programmed. AI and ML have the potential to automate jobs, make predictions, and solve issues that would normally need human intellect due to their capacity to analyze massive volumes of data and find patterns. As technology advances, expect to see even more inventive applications of AI and ML in the coming years.

Step-by-Step Instructions: Getting Started with AI and ML

1. **Understand the Definitions**

   - AI: Learn that AI involves creating computer systems that can perform tasks typically requiring human intelligence, such as recognizing speech, making decisions, and translating languages.
   - ML: Understand that ML is a subset of AI where machines learn from data to make decisions and improve over time without being explicitly programmed.

2. **Recognize the Significance of AI and ML in Various Sectors**

   - Identify how AI and ML are being used across different industries like healthcare, finance, marketing, and education.
   - Explore specific examples, such as AI in customer service (chatbots) and ML in predictive analytics for marketing strategies.

3. **Distinguish Between Different Types of AI**

   - Learn about narrow AI, which is designed for specific tasks (like facial recognition or Internet searches), and general AI, which simulates human intelligence more broadly and can perform a variety of tasks.

4. **Explore the Fundamentals of ML**

   - Dive into the three main types of ML: supervised learning (where the model learns from labelled data), unsupervised learning (where it identifies patterns in data without explicit labels), and reinforcement learning (where it learns through trial and error using feedback from its actions).

5. **Practical Engagement with AI and ML Concepts**

   - Use online resources or platforms that offer AI and ML simulations to see these concepts in action. Experiment with simple ML models using datasets available online to understand how ML algorithms learn and make predictions.

6. **Reflect on the Ethical Implications:**

   - Consider the ethical aspects of AI and ML, such as privacy concerns, bias in data, and the impact of automation on employment. Reflect on how these technologies should be applied responsibly in society and business.

HOW AI IS USED IN MARKETING

In recent years, AI has transformed the way organization's function, particularly in the field of marketing. Marketers are using AI to analyze massive volumes of data, develop tailored experiences, and improve marketing strategies. This chapter investigates the numerous applications of AI in marketing, with a particular emphasis on the book sector. We will examine how AI may assist publishers and writers in gaining insights into reader preferences and habits, developing effective marketing campaigns, and providing tailored reading experiences.

Data Examination

AI-powered systems may sift through massive volumes of data to give insights into reader preferences and behavior. Publishers and authors may utilize this information to better understand their readers' traits, reading habits, and preferences. Companies may also examine sales statistics, social media activity, and other indicators to see how effective their marketing strategies are. AI-powered technologies can measure how many people saw an author's book advertisement, how many clicked on the advertisement, and how many purchased the book.

Furthermore, AI may assist authors and publishers in identifying reader behavior trends, such as which genres or authors are popular, what themes are popular, and how long readers spend on a book. This information can help them to create more targeted marketing campaigns that speak directly to readers' interests.

Marketing that is Tailored to the Individual

Customization is a marketing term for good reason. Customers are more likely to interact with marketing information that is targeted to their specific interests and preferences. AI-powered solutions can assist publishers and writers in providing readers with customized marketing experiences. Publishers might recommend books to readers based on their prior purchases and reading history. AI may also be used to develop tailored adverts based on the reader's interests and preferences.

Customization might also include the book's format. AI-powered systems may evaluate reader data to identify whether formats, such as audio, ebook, or print, are ideal for the book. If a reader has a history of purchasing audiobooks, the publisher can make an audio version of the book, boosting the reader's chance of purchasing.

Making Content

AI may assist with content production in a variety of ways, including the generation of book summaries and descriptions, the creation of interesting book names, and even the design of book covers. Natural language processing (NLP) is used in this technology to evaluate text and generate new content.

AI-powered content creation systems can evaluate a book's content, determine the key themes and subjects, and provide an accurate summary of the book's content.

Similarly, AI may use reader reviews to produce book titles that are more likely to catch the interest of readers. It may also evaluate visual components such as color, font, and photos to generate more appealing book covers.

Chatbots and Consumer Support

Chatbots powered by AI may provide 24/7 customer service, addressing commonly asked queries and directing readers to the appropriate resources. Chatbots may also assist publishers and authors in learning about reader preferences, such as which books are popular and what problems readers are experiencing. They can also give a personalized reading experience by recommending books based on prior purchases and the reading history of the reader.

Moreover, chatbots may be utilized to give readers real-time feedback, such as updates on new releases, promotions, and other essential information. This contributes to a more interesting and dynamic reading experience for readers.

AI is changing the way publishers and authors advertise their books. AI-powered systems can analyze massive volumes of data, generate tailored experiences, and optimize marketing strategies. Publishers and writers may use AI to gather insights into consumer preferences and habits, build targeted marketing efforts, and give tailored reading experiences. AI is unquestionably the future of book marketing.

As AI evolves and improves, expect to see even more creative applications of this technology in book marketing and other sectors. Yet, while AI can help to automate many marketing jobs, it cannot replace human creativity and insight. Marketers must continue to strike a balance between the benefits of AI and the human touch that comes through personalization interaction and creative thinking. To summarize, AI is altering the way publishers and writers sell their books, providing them with important data and tools to develop more effective campaigns and individualized reading experiences. As AI technology advances, it will surely become increasingly relevant in the realm of book marketing and beyond.

To summarize, AI is altering the way publishers and writers sell their books, providing them with important data and tools to develop more effective campaigns and individualized reading experiences. As AI technology advances, it will surely become increasingly relevant in the realm of book marketing and beyond.

Algorithms for Supervised Learning

Supervised learning is a sort of ML in which the model learns from labeled data, which means that the input data has already been labeled with the desired output. The goal of supervised learning is to develop a mapping function that, using labeled data, translates the input to the output. There are several types of supervised learning algorithms, including:

- *Regression:* Regression algorithms are used to forecast continuous variables such as housing prices, stock prices, or weather conditions. The goal of regression is to train a function that translates the properties of the input to a continuous output.
- *Classification:* Classification algorithms are used to predict discrete values such as whether an email is spam or not, whether a client will buy a product or not, and whether a patient has an illness. The goal of classification is to learn a function that transfers the attributes of the input to a discrete output.
- *Decision tree algorithms:* Decision tree algorithms are utilized for classification as well as regression problems. With the training data, they construct a decision tree that may be used to generate predictions.
- *Support vector machines (SVM):* SVM is a classification technique that finds a hyperplane that divides data into as many classes as possible. SVM is often used in binary classification problems.
- *Neural networks:* A form of deep learning method, neural networks can learn complicated nonlinear mappings from input to output. Neural networks may be used for classification as well as regression.

Algorithms for Unsupervised Learning

Unsupervised learning is a sort of ML in which the model learns from unlabeled data, that is, input data that has not been labeled with the appropriate output. Unsupervised learning seeks to discover the underlying structure of data, such as patterns, correlations, and clusters. Unsupervised learning algorithms come in a variety of types, including:

- *Q-learning:* Q-learning is a reinforcement learning algorithm that learns the best action-value function by updating the Q-value of each state-action combination repeatedly based on the reward received and the projected future reward.
- *Deep reinforcement learning:* Deep reinforcement learning is a sort of reinforcement learning in which the policy is learned using deep neural networks. Deep reinforcement learning has been successfully used to Atari games, Go, and other games.
- *Policy gradient:* Policy gradient is a reinforcement learning algorithm that directly learns policy by maximizing the parameters of a policy function using gradient descent.

Applications of ML Algorithms

ML algorithms have numerous applications in various fields. Following are some examples:

- *Image recognition:* Convolutional neural networks (CNNs) and other ML methods are used for image identification tasks such as recognizing objects in photos, recognizing faces, and so on.
- *NLP:* For NLP tasks such as language translation, sentiment analysis, and others, ML methods such as recurrent neural networks (RNNs) and transformer models are utilized.
- *Recommendation systems:* ML methods such as collaborative filtering and content-based filtering are used in recommendation systems to propose items to consumers, movies to viewers, and other services.
- *Fraud detection:* ML methods such as anomaly detection and decision trees are used to detect fraud, such as credit card fraud and insurance fraud.
- *Autonomous vehicles:* Reinforcement learning, and other ML techniques are employed in autonomous vehicles such as self-driving automobiles and drones.

ML algorithms have transformed the science of AI and have a wide range of applications. Many types of ML algorithms have been examined, such as supervised learning, unsupervised learning, and reinforcement learning, as well as their applications, in this post. Understanding these techniques is critical for creating successful ML models capable of solving real-world issues.

Step-by-Step Instructions: Implementing Different ML Algorithms

1. **Understand and Categorize Problems:**

   - Review the problem you need to solve and determine if it is a classification, regression, clustering, or decision-making task.
   - Categorize the problem as supervised learning if you have labelled data (e.g., email spam classification), unsupervised learning if you have unlabeled data (e.g., customer segmentation), or reinforcement learning if the problem involves decision-making through trial and error (e.g., a game or a robot's navigation).

2. **Select Appropriate Algorithms for Each Type of Learning:**

   - For supervised learning tasks, consider algorithms like Linear Regression for regression problems or SVMs for classification tasks.
   - For unsupervised learning tasks, explore algorithms like K-Means for clustering or Principal Component Analysis for dimensionality reduction.

- For reinforcement learning tasks, investigate algorithms like Q-Learning or Deep Q-Networks (DQN).

3. **Train a Simple Model Using a Chosen Algorithm:**

   - Start with a dataset that is suitable for your ML problem. Ensure the data is clean and preprocessed appropriately.
   - Use a ML library like scikit-learn in Python to train a model with your chosen algorithm. Use the fit method in scikit-learn to train your model on your training data.
   - Monitor the training process to ensure that the model is learning effectively.

4. **Evaluate the Model's Performance:**

   - After training, evaluate your model's performance using appropriate metrics, such as accuracy and precision for classification problems or mean squared error for regression problems.
   - Use a validation or test set to assess the model's ability to generalize to unseen data.
   - If the performance is unsatisfactory, consider tuning the model's parameters, trying a different algorithm, or revisiting your data preprocessing steps.

5. **Iterate and Improve:**

   - ML is an iterative process. Based on the model evaluation, you may need to revise your approach, adjust hyperparameters, or even collect more data.
   - Continue refining your model to improve its performance on the task at hand.
   - By following these steps, you can systematically implement and evaluate different ML algorithms, enhancing your understanding and ability to leverage AI for various applications.

THE IMPORTANCE OF TRAINING DATA FOR ML

ML has improved quickly in recent years and is now considered an essential component of AI. ML has advanced due to the availability of vast volumes of data, which allows machines to learn and increase their accuracy over time. This is when practice data comes in handy. The backbone of ML is training data, which is used to train algorithms to execute specific tasks. This chapter will go through the significance of training data in ML.

What exactly is training data? It is a subset of data utilized by ML algorithms to study patterns and generate predictions and is known as training data. It is the data that is utilized to train the ML model to identify various patterns and correlations in data. This training data is labeled with correct answers and utilized to assist the ML model in learning and improving.

Building a decent ML model requires a lot of training data. It aids the model's learning and accuracy over time. Some of the reasons why training data is crucial for ML are as follows:

- *Prediction accuracy:* The quality and quantity of training data have a significant impact on the accuracy of ML models. If the training data is correct, the ML model can generate accurate predictions. If the training data is incorrect, the ML model will produce incorrect predictions. This is why having high-quality training data is critical.
- *Generalization ML:* This seeks to create models that can generalize to new data. This means that the ML model should be able to forecast accurate data that it has never seen before. The training data is critical to obtaining generalization. The ML model learns to find patterns and correlations that are applicable to new data by training it on a broad set of data.
- *Extraction of characteristics:* The process of choosing and transforming raw data into a set of features that may be utilized for ML is known as feature extraction. The quality of the input data used to train the ML model is determined by feature extraction, which is a vital stage in the ML process. High-quality training data aids in feature extraction and allows the ML model to learn important data characteristics.
- *Choosing an algorithm:* There are several ML algorithms, each with its own set of advantages and disadvantages. The method chosen is determined by the job and the data required to train the model. High-quality training data can aid in the selection of the best ML algorithm for the job.
- *Model efficiency:* The quality of the training data has a direct impact on the performance of a ML model. The ML model will function effectively if the training data is of good quality. The ML model, on the other hand, will perform badly if the training data is of poor quality.
- *Fairness and bias:* If the training data is skewed, ML models might be prejudiced and unjust. This might result in incorrect predictions and prejudice. To guarantee that the ML model is fair and impartial, it is critical to have varied and unbiased training data.
- *Price and time training:* Data collection and labeling is costly and time-consuming. Nonetheless, it is required for developing accurate and dependable ML models. ML models may be erroneous and fail to function as predicted in the absence of high-quality training data, resulting in additional expenses and effort required for retraining and improving the model.

Training data is an essential part of ML. It is the backbone of ML algorithms and plays a critical role in building accurate and reliable models. High-quality training data is essential for accurate predictions, generalization, feature extraction, algorithm selection, model performance, fairness, and reducing costs and time. As the field of ML continues to advance, the importance of high-quality training data will continue to grow. With the increasing availability of data, it is important to ensure that the training data is diverse, accurate, and unbiased to develop fair and reliable ML models. It is also vital to remember that collecting training data is not a one-time task. The training data must be updated and improved as new data becomes available to guarantee that the ML model continues to progress and remain accurate. This necessitates continual efforts to acquire and categorize data, as well as monitoring and pupating ML model's performance as needed.

ML relies heavily on training data. The accuracy, generalization, feature extraction, algorithm selection, model performance, fairness, and cost and time efficiency of the ML model are all directly affected by the quality and quantity of training data. As the area of ML expands, it is critical to prioritize the acquisition and curation of high-quality training data to construct accurate and dependable ML models.

Step-by-Step Instructions: Preparing and Utilizing Training Data for ML

1. **Collect and Organize Your Data Sources:**

    • Identify the data needed for your ML project.
    • Gather data from various sources like databases, online repositories, or through data collection tools.

2. **Cleanse and Preprocess the Data for ML Purposes:**

    • Remove irrelevant or redundant data to streamline the dataset.
    • Handle missing data through methods like imputation or removal.
    • Normalize or standardize the data to ensure consistency in scale and format.

3. **Understand How to Split Data into Training and Testing Sets:**

    • Divide your data into a training set (typically 70%–80% of the dataset) to train the model, and a testing set (20%–30%) to evaluate its performance.
    • Ensure the split provides a representative sample of the overall data, maintaining the distribution of key variables.
    • These instructions guide the process of preparing and utilizing training data, which is crucial for developing effective ML models.

THE ROLE OF DATA SCIENCE IN AI MARKETING

Data science is critical in AI marketing. ML algorithms and other AI techniques are used in AI marketing to analyze and understand enormous amounts of data from diverse sources to acquire insights into customer behavior and preferences. The core of this process is data science, which allows organizations to collect, process, and analyze enormous amounts of information to obtain a better knowledge of their consumers and make educated decisions regarding marketing tactics.

Following are some ways data science is used in AI marketing:

Data collection: Data collection is one of the most important tasks of data science in AI marketing. Data scientists acquire information from a variety of sources, including social media, search engines, and customer databases, using techniques such as web scraping, data mining, and data extraction.

Data cleaning and preparation: After collecting the data, data scientists clean and preprocess it to eliminate any inconsistencies, mistakes, or missing numbers. They also convert the data into an analysis-ready format.

Data analysis and modeling: Data scientists examine data and construct models that forecast consumer behavior and preferences using different analytical approaches like statistical analysis, ML algorithms, and predictive modeling. These models assist organizations in making educated marketing strategies and campaign selections.

Personalization and targeting: Data science is used in AI marketing to build individualized and targeted marketing efforts. Businesses may understand their customer's preferences, habits, and interests by analyzing their data and creating marketing strategies that are personalized to their individual requirements.

Customer segmentation: Data science aids in the identification of various client categories based on their behavior, tastes, and demographics. This data may be utilized to develop tailored marketing initiatives that are more likely to appeal to each customer demographic.

Optimization: Data science also aids in the optimization of marketing initiatives by revealing what works and what doesn't. Businesses may utilize data from previous campaigns to discover what elements led to the campaign's success or failure and use that information to optimize future efforts by evaluating data from previous campaigns.

Step-by-Step Instructions: Leveraging Data Science for AI-Driven Marketing

1. **Data Collection and Integration:**

   - Gather customer data from various sources like social media, Web site analytics, and customer relationship management (CRM) systems.
   - Integrate and consolidate data into a central repository for analysis.

2. **Data Cleaning and Preparation:**

   - Clean the data by removing inconsistencies, duplicates, and irrelevant information.

- Prepare the data for analysis by categorizing, coding, and normalizing it as needed.

3. **Data Analysis and Insight Generation:**

   - Analyze the cleaned data using statistical methods and ML algorithms to uncover patterns, trends, and insights.
   - Translate these insights into actionable marketing strategies and decisions.

4. **Implementation of Data-Driven Strategies:**

   - Develop marketing campaigns and initiatives based on the insights gained from data analysis.
   - Personalize customer experiences and communications based on their behaviors and preferences.

5. **Continuous Monitoring and Refinement:**

   - Use analytics tools to monitor the performance of marketing campaigns and initiatives.
   - Continuously refine and optimize marketing strategies based on data-driven insights and market feedback.

By following these steps, businesses can harness the power of AI and ML in their industry-specific applications and leverage data science to enhance AI-driven marketing strategies, ensuring a more targeted and effective approach to customer engagement and business growth.

Data science is an important part of AI marketing. It allows companies to collect, analyze, and analyze massive volumes of consumer data to acquire insights into customer behavior and preferences. This data may be utilized to develop personalized and targeted marketing campaigns, optimize marketing tactics, and make smart marketing budget and resource decisions.

Numerous crucial issues on understanding AI and ML have been addressed in this chapter. The chapter began by outlining the fundamentals of AI and ML, including the distinctions between supervised and unsupervised learning, as well as the significance of algorithms and data in these processes.

PREPARING YOUR DATA FOR ARTIFICIAL INTELLIGENCE

E mbarking on the journey to harness the power of artificial intelligence (AI) for your business is an exciting endeavor, and a crucial aspect of this process is preparing your data. High-quality, well-structured data is the backbone of effective AI models and is essential to the success of your organization. This chapter delves into the key steps for data preparation in AI, encompassing data hygiene and quality, structuring data for machine learning (ML) algorithms, strategies for collecting and storing data, popular data preprocessing techniques, and tools and platforms for streamlining data management in AI marketing.

Importance of Data Hygiene and Quality

The foundation of successful AI implementation lies in maintaining excellent data hygiene and quality. Data hygiene focuses on eliminating errors, discrepancies, and imprecisions in your data by removing duplicates, rectifying spelling mistakes, and ensuring that data values adhere to expected parameters. Data quality pertains to the accuracy, comprehensiveness, and relevance of your data. Ensuring high-quality data guarantees accurate forecasts and insights while preventing your AI models from generating false or biased outcomes.

Structuring Data for ML Algorithms

Preparing your data for ML algorithms entails formatting it in a way that can be easily processed and analyzed by AI models. This includes choosing suitable data types, organizing your information into labeled datasets, and developing feature engineering pipelines that convert raw data into a usable format for your AI models. Adequately structured data enhances the accuracy and efficiency of your AI models.

Optimizing Data Collection and Storage for AI Applications

To harness the true potential of AI, it is crucial to gather and store data in a readily accessible and usable manner. This entails outlining precise data collection procedures, ensuring consistent data capture, and choosing suitable storage options that promote effective data retrieval and analysis. Cutting-edge storage solutions for AI consist of cloud-based platforms, distributed file systems, and data warehouses.

Essential Data Preprocessing Methods

Prior to training your AI models, it's imperative to refine your data through preprocessing techniques, enhancing its quality, and preparing it for thorough analysis. Widely adopted preprocessing methods involve data cleansing, normalization, feature scaling, and feature extraction. By employing these tactics, you can eliminate noise from your data, minimize the influence of outliers, and generate new features vital to your AI models.

Revolutionizing AI Marketing with Tools and Platforms

An array of tools and platforms are at your disposal to effectively manage data for AI marketing initiatives. These encompass data integration platforms, quality software solutions, governance tools, as well as state-of-the-art AI platforms offering prebuilt models and workflows. Choosing the fitting tools and platforms is paramount in guaranteeing proper data management while generating precise and actionable insights through AI modeling.

Preparing your data for AI is a crucial step in harnessing AI to deliver commercial value. You can ensure that your AI models generate accurate and relevant insights that drive your business forward by focusing on data hygiene and quality, structuring data for ML algorithms, selecting appropriate strategies for collecting and storing data, employing common data pre-processing techniques, and leveraging tools and platforms for managing data.

DATA HYGIENE AND QUALITY

Data hygiene and quality are critical parts of every data-driven project because they directly influence the dependability and utility of the data insights. This portion of Chapter 3 covers the significance of data hygiene and quality, as well as some best practices for maintaining clean and correct data.

Data hygiene refers to the meticulous process of cleaning and preparing data for analysis. This crucial procedure identifies and corrects errors, inconsistencies, and inaccuracies within the data set, ensuring the reliability and accuracy of subsequent analyses.

It is impossible to overestimate the significance of data hygiene and quality. Incorrect conclusions, faulty analysis, and lost resources can all result from poor data hygiene and quality. Incorrect data can also have a detrimental influence on decision-making and company outcomes. High-quality data, on the other hand, may give significant insights, stimulate innovation, and assist companies in making educated decisions.

It is critical to follow basic best practices to guarantee that data cleanliness and quality are maintained throughout a project. Among these practices are:

Best Practices for Data Hygiene:

- *Data Validation:* This involves verifying the correctness and completeness of data by cross-checking against other sources or comparing it to past data to identify discrepancies.
- *Data Governance:* Refers to the management and regulation of data throughout its lifecycle. This includes developing rules and processes for data collection, storage, and use, as well as delegating data management responsibilities.
- *Ongoing Monitoring and Maintenance:* Data hygiene and quality require continuous effort. Regular activities should include audits, updating data standards, and re-profiling and cleansing data as necessary.
- *Data Security:* A critical aspect of data hygiene, involving protection against unauthorized access, data encryption, and implementing backup and recovery processes.

Common Challenges in Maintaining Data Hygiene:

- *Data Silos:* Occur when information is compartmentalized within various systems or departments, hindering integration and analysis, often leading to inconsistencies and inaccuracies.
- *Incomplete or Inconsistent Data:* Gaps or discrepancies in data entry can result in incomplete or inconsistent information, complicating the extraction of valuable insights.
- *Resource Constraints:* Proper data hygiene and quality maintenance require significant resources, such as skilled staff and technology, which may be scarce in some organizations.
- *Data Volume:* The increasing amount of data can make maintaining its hygiene and quality more complex, demanding extensive resources for profiling, cleaning, and validating large datasets.
- *Data Integration:* Integrating data from various sources, especially when stored in different formats or systems, poses challenges that can introduce further inconsistencies and inaccuracies.

Data hygiene and quality are essential components of any data-driven project. They ensure that the data is accurate, complete, consistent, and reliable, allowing organizations to make informed decisions based on trustworthy insights. To maintain data hygiene and quality, organizations should follow best practices such as data profiling and cleaning, standardization, data validation, data governance, regular monitoring and maintenance, and data security. Despite the challenges of maintaining data hygiene and quality, it is crucial for organizations to invest in these practices to ensure the accuracy and reliability of their data. By doing so, they can drive innovation, optimize business outcomes, and gain a competitive edge in the marketplace.

Data Hygiene and Quality: Step-by-Step Guide for Marketers

Objective: *To cleanse and ensure the quality of marketing data before its utilization in AI applications.*

Step 1: Data Audit

- Conduct a thorough audit of your existing data to identify inaccuracies, inconsistencies, and gaps.
- Tools: Use data profiling tools to assess the quality and structure of your data.

Step 2: Cleaning Data

- Remove duplicates to avoid redundancy and potential biases in AI analysis.
- Correct errors such as misspellings, incorrect entries, and inconsistencies in naming conventions.
- Tools: Implement data cleaning software that can automate the detection and rectification of common data issues.

Step 3: Data Validation

- Establish validation rules to ensure that incoming data meets predefined quality standards.
- Validate data for accuracy, completeness, and consistency using automated validation tools.
- Tools: Utilize data validation tools to automate checks for data integrity and accuracy.

Step 4: Standardization and Normalization

- Standardize data formats across all datasets to ensure uniformity (e.g., date formats, currency, etc.).
- Normalize data to bring different scales into alignment, facilitating comparative analysis and machine learning.
- Tools: Use data transformation tools to automate standardization and normalization processes.

Step 5: Data Governance

- Develop a data governance framework that defines policies, procedures, and standards for data management.
- Assign roles and responsibilities for data quality management to ensure ongoing oversight.
- Tools: Implement data governance software to monitor compliance with data policies and standards.

Step 6: Regular Monitoring and Maintenance

- Schedule regular data quality reviews to continually assess and improve the data hygiene processes.
- Update and refine data cleaning, validation, and standardization practices as needed based on monitoring feedback.
- Tools: Use data monitoring tools to track data quality over time and highlight areas for improvement.

Step 7: Data Security

- Implement robust data security measures to protect data integrity and privacy.
- Ensure that data cleaning and processing activities comply with data protection regulations like GDPR or CCPA. The GDPR is a comprehensive data protection law that came into effect in the European Union (EU) on May 25, 2018. The CCPA, which took effect on January 1, 2020, is a state statute intended to enhance privacy rights and consumer protection for residents of California, USA.
- Tools: Use security and compliance tools to safeguard data and ensure regulatory adherence.

By following these steps, marketers can significantly enhance the hygiene and quality of their data, ensuring that their AI applications are powered by reliable and accurate information, leading to better marketing decisions and strategies.

STRUCTURE DATA FOR MACHINE LEARNING ALGORITHMS

ML algorithms have gained significant traction in the marketing landscape, enabling businesses to enhance their decision-making and predictions regarding customers, products, and marketing tactics. To maximize the potential of these algorithms, it is crucial to properly structure the data tailored to the specific algorithm being utilized.

The initial step in this data structuring process is pinpointing the variables pertinent to the problem at hand. If predicting customer churn is the objective, relevant variables may encompass factors such as age, gender, purchase history, and engagement with marketing initiatives.

Following variable identification, assembling data from various sources like databases or APIs becomes essential. Ensuring data accuracy, completeness, and representation of the target population is a top priority. Moreover, addressing data privacy and ethical considerations when acquiring and utilizing data is vital.

After data collection comes preprocessing which consists of cleaning the data, attending to missing values, and encoding categorical variables. Data cleaning entails rectifying errors or inconsistencies while missing values can be addressed by techniques such as imputation or employing regression or decision trees. Categorical variables like gender or product classifications require encoding into numeric values for compatibility with ML algorithms.

Post-preprocessing, the data must be divided into training and testing sets. The former sets the algorithm while the latter evaluates its efficiency. Ensuring representativeness and independence between these sets is crucial. A wide post-preprocessing-accepted proportion is 70% for training and 30% for testing purposes.

After dividing the data, one must choose a suitable ML algorithm among numerous types such as linear regression, logistic regression, decision trees, random forests, or neural networks. The chosen algorithm depends on factors including problem nature, data type, and desired output.

Lastly, it's time to train the selected algorithm using the obtained training set. This allows the algorithm to learn from available data while fine-tuning its parameters to minimize error discrepancies between forecasted outputs and actual results.

As businesses embrace the power of ML, structuring data becomes a critical step toward more accurate predictions and smarter decisions. This involves identifying relevant variables, collecting, and pre-processing data, splitting it into training and testing sets, selecting the right algorithm, training it, and evaluating its performance.

But the journey does not end here. Once the algorithm is trained, it's time to evaluate its performance using the testing set. This crucial step involves comparing the predicted output with the actual output and calculating key metrics like accuracy, precision, recall, and F1 score. These metrics provide a clear picture of how well the algorithm is performing and help fine-tune it if necessary.

But that's not all. Interpreting the results is just as important. By understanding the relationships between input and output variables and identifying patterns or trends, businesses can gain valuable insights into their data. Feature importance analysis or visualizations are some techniques that can help in this regard.

Structuring data for ML and following these essential steps can empower businesses to make more informed decisions about their marketing strategies.

With accurate predictions and insights, they can stay ahead of the competition and drive growth for their business.

Structuring Data for ML Algorithms
Objective: *To prepare and organize data effectively for use in ML models.*
Step-by-Step Instructions

1. **Identify Relevant Variables:**

   - Analyze the objectives of your ML project to determine which variables are necessary.
   - Select variables that significantly impact the outcome you are trying to predict or analyze.

2. **Collect and Assemble Data:**

   - Gather data from various sources, such as internal databases, customer relationship management (CRM) systems, social media platforms, or third-party data providers.
   - Consolidate this data into a centralized repository to facilitate easy access and analysis.

3. **Clean the Data:**

   - Remove any irrelevant or redundant information that does not contribute to the learning process.
   - Correct errors, such as misspellings or incorrect values, to improve data accuracy.

4. **Label the Data (for supervised learning):**

   - Ensure each data point in your dataset has a corresponding label or outcome for training purposes.
   - in a customer churn model, label each customer record as "churned" or "retained."

5. **Format and Structure the Data:**

   - Organize data into a structured format, such as tables, where each row represents a data point, and each column represents a feature.
   - Ensure that the data format is compatible with the ML tools or platforms you will be using.

6. **Perform Feature Engineering:**

   - Transform raw data into features that better represent the underlying problem to the predictive models.

- This can include creating new variables from existing data, like extracting day of the week from date stamps, or combining multiple variables into a single feature.

7. **Split the Data into Training and Testing Sets:**

- Divide your data into two sets: one for training the ML model and the other for testing its performance.
- A common split ratio is 70% for training and 30% for testing, but this can vary based on the size and specifics of your data.

8. **Normalize or Scale the Features:**

- Standardize the range of independent variables or features of data.
- Scaling can be crucial for algorithms that are sensitive to the scale of input data, like distance-based algorithms or neural networks.

9. **Finalize the Dataset:**

- Ensure the final structured dataset is saved in a format that is accessible and usable for the ML algorithms you plan to use.
- Verify that the dataset includes all necessary features and labels and is split correctly into training and testing sets.

By following these steps, marketers can effectively structure their data to optimize the performance of ML algorithms, leading to more accurate and actionable insights from their AI-driven marketing strategies.

STRATEGIES FOR COLLECTING AND STORING DATA

Collecting and storing data is a critical aspect of AI marketing. The data collected is used to train ML models that power personalized marketing campaigns, product recommendations, and other data-driven initiatives. However, collecting and storing data comes with its own set of challenges. This section explores some strategies for collecting and storing data for AI marketing.

Determine Essential Data

Prior to gathering data, it is crucial to pinpoint the specific types of data required. This enables the identification of appropriate data sources and methods of collection. When accumulating data for a recommendation engine, consider user behavior patterns, purchase records, and characteristics of products.

Select Suitable Data Sources

Align your chosen data sources with your data needs. A vast array of sources can be utilized, such as customer transactions, social media interactions, client feedback, Web analysis, and survey results. Focus on sources that contribute the most relevant information to enhance marketing efforts.

Utilize Data Management Platforms

Employing data management platforms (DMPs) can assist in collecting and storing data. DMPs offer the ability to consolidate data from diverse sources and establish a comprehensive view of your clientele. Furthermore, utilizing a DMP enables you to segment your data and craft tailored audiences for specialized marketing strategies.

Tap into Third-Party Data Providers

Collaborating with third-party data providers can supplement your existing data with valuable insights. These providers can offer demographic, psychographic, and behavioural information that may be beyond your reach. However, it is imperative to ensure the data obtained from third-party providers is both precise and current.

Prioritize Data Quality

High-quality data is fundamental for successful AI marketing endeavors. Inaccurate or subpar data quality can yield unreliable insights and defective models. To guarantee top-notch data quality, implement robust standards, perform regular audits, and routinely clean your data.

Establish Data Governance Policies

Implementing sound data governance policies aids in maintaining accurate, secure, and regulatory-compliant data. These policies should address the procedures for collecting, storing, processing, and utilizing data. Moreover, they should delineate roles and responsibilities concerning data management while outlining guidelines for access and sharing of information.

Embrace Cloud-Based Storage Solutions

The rising popularity of cloud-based storage solutions is paving the way for efficient data storage. Offering scalability, flexibility, and cost-effectiveness, these storage options surpass traditional methods of data preservation. Equipped with advanced security measures like encryption and multifactor authentication, cloud storage ensures your data stays protected.

Prioritize Data Security Measures

Safeguarding your customers' information and your business' reputation is paramount. Implementing strong security protocols such as access controls, encryption, and firewalls is essential to shield your data from unauthorized access, theft, and cyber threats. Having a well-structured data breach response plan in place is also crucial to address any security incidents.

Gather and save data skillfully to fuel AI-driven marketing efforts. This will empower businesses to comprehend their customers' behavior and preferences better, leading to tailor-made marketing campaigns that captivate their target audience. By adopting the strategies delineated in this section, businesses can collect pristine data, and ensure top-notch security and compliance.

Optimizing Data Collection and Storage for AI Applications
Step-by-Step Instructions

1. **Define Data Requirements:**

    - Identify the specific types of data needed for your AI applications, such as customer behavior, transactional data, or social media interactions.
    - Determine the volume, variety, velocity, and veracity of the data required to meet the objectives of your AI initiatives.

2. **Establish Data Collection Methods:**

    - Select the appropriate data collection methods, which could include Web scraping, API integrations, surveys, or using IoT devices.
    - Ensure that the data collection methods comply with legal and ethical standards, particularly concerning user consent and data privacy.

3. **Design a Scalable Data Storage Solution:**

    - Choose a storage solution that can scale with your data needs, considering factors like data growth, accessibility, and security.
    - Evaluate options like cloud storage, on-premises databases, or hybrid models, focusing on flexibility, cost, and integration capabilities.

4. **Implement Data Standardization Processes:**

    - Standardize data formats, naming conventions, and storage practices to ensure consistency across various sources and systems.
    - Develop a data dictionary or schema that defines each data element, its format, and its relationship to other data elements.

5. **Ensure Data Quality and Integrity:**

    - Implement processes for continuous data quality checks, including validation, de-duplication, and cleansing, to maintain the integrity of your data.
    - Use automated tools where possible to streamline the data quality assurance process.

6. **Develop a Comprehensive Data Backup and Recovery Plan:**

   • Establish regular backup schedules to protect data against loss or corruption.
   • Create a disaster recovery plan that outlines procedures for restoring data in case of a system failure or data breach.

7. **Adopt Advanced Data Security Measures:**

   • Implement robust security protocols such as encryption, access controls, and network security to protect data from unauthorized access and cyber threats.
   • Regularly update security measures to counter evolving cyber risks and comply with data protection regulations.

8. **Monitor and Evaluate Data Storage Performance:**

   • Use monitoring tools to track the performance of your data storage and retrieval systems, identifying any bottlenecks or inefficiencies.
   • Regularly review and optimize your data storage infrastructure to ensure it meets the demands of your AI applications effectively.

By following these steps, organizations can optimize their data collection and storage practices, ensuring that the data is not only accessible and usable for AI applications but also secure, reliable, and scalable to meet future needs.

COMMON DATA PREPROCESSING TECHNIQUES

Each ML project, including AI marketing, requires data pre-processing. The data generated for AI marketing campaigns are frequently unstructured, incomplete, or noisy, which might have an impact on the model's effectiveness. Data pre-processing approaches strive to clean, convert, and prepare data for analysis and modeling. This section will go through some of the most prevalent data pre-processing techniques used in AI marketing, along with some examples.

Data cleaning: The process of discovering and repairing or deleting mistakes, inconsistencies, and missing data from a dataset is known as data cleaning. This phase is critical since it has the potential to impact the model's accuracy. There are various methods for cleaning data, including:

   • *Missing data handling*: Missing data can be treated in a variety of methods, including imputation, deletion, and interpolation. If a customer's age is missing, replace it with the dataset's average age or remove the entire record.
   • *Remove duplicates*: Duplicate data might induce bias in the model and must be removed. If the same customer's data is entered twice in the dataset, one of them must be removed.

- *Error correction*: Data mistakes can potentially impair model accuracy. If a customer's email address is misspelled, fix it to prevent promotional emails from being sent to the incorrect address.
- *Data transformation:* Data transformation is the process of changing data from one form to another, normalization, or scaling. The following are some examples of common data transformation techniques:

    a. *Normalization:* The process of adjusting the values of the variables to a standard range is known as normalization. If there is a dataset with client ages ranging from 18 to 65, it's acceptable to normalize the numbers to a range of 0 to 1.

    b. *Scaling:* Scaling is the process of altering variables so that their range of values is similar. If there is a dataset comprising variables like age, salary, and buying hi\story, feel free to scale them to have a comparable range of values.

- *Feature Selection:* In feature selection, the most relevant variables in the dataset are chosen for modeling. This step is critical since it can lower the dataset's dimensionality and increase the model's performance. The following are some examples of frequent feature selection techniques:

    a. *Correlation analysis:* The process of discovering variables that are highly associated with the target variable is known as correlation analysis. When anticipating a customer's purchasing behavior, determine the factors that have the strongest connection with the customer's buying history.

    b. *Principal Component Analysis (PCA):* PCA is a technique for reducing dataset dimensionality by finding the most significant variables. If there is a dataset with several variables, PCA can discover the variables that account for most of the variation in the data.

- *Data Integration:* Data integration is the process of merging data from several sources to form a cohesive dataset. This stage is critical in AI marketing since it provides users with a comprehensive picture of the customer's activity. The following are some examples of frequent data integration techniques:

    a. *Sampling:* Sampling is the process of reducing the amount of a dataset by picking a subset of it. If there is a huge data set with millions of customer records, minimize its size by selecting a random sample of the data.

    b. *Dimensionality reduction:* This is the process of lowering the number of variables in a dataset while retaining its critical information. If there is a dataset with several variables, one may reduce the dimensionality of the dataset using techniques such as PCA.

Data preprocessing is an important stage in artificial intelligence marketing since it prepares the data for analysis and modeling. Data cleaning, data transformation, feature selection, data integration, and data reduction are all popular data preprocessing procedures. Each approach has advantages and limits, and the right technique is determined by the nature of the data and the modeling aims. AI marketers that use these strategies effectively may enhance the accuracy and efficiency of their models, resulting in improved consumer insights and more effective marketing campaigns.

Step-by-Step Instructions for Data Pre-processing in ML

1. **Data Cleaning**

   - Identify and remove duplicate records to prevent skewed analysis.
   - Fix or remove erroneous data entries, such as incorrect dates or misspelled words.
   - Handle missing values by either deleting the rows, imputing the missing values with statistical measures (mean, median, mode), or using prediction models.

2. **Data Normalization**

   - Scale the data to a small, specified range like 0 to 1 or -1 to 1. This can be done using methods like Min-Max scaling.
   - Apply normalization to ensure that the model is not biased toward variables with larger scales.

3. **Feature Scaling**

   - Use standardization to center the data around the mean with a unit standard deviation. This means subtracting the meaning of each feature and then dividing it by the standard deviation.
   - Standardize features when your algorithm is sensitive to the scale of the input data, like in the case of support vector machines (SVMs) or k-nearest neighbors.

4. **Feature Extraction**

   - Transform raw data into features that better represent the underlying structure of the data. This can be done using techniques like Principal Component Analysis (PCA) or Autoencoders in deep learning.
   - Identify and select the most important variables that have a strong relationship with the output variable.

5. **Data Transformation**

- Convert categorical data into numerical values using one-hot encoding or label encoding.
- Transform nonlinear data into a more suitable form for linear models by applying log or exponential transformations.

6. **Data Integration**

- Combine data from various sources to create a comprehensive view. This might involve merging different datasets, aligning columns, and resolving conflicts in data values.

7. **Data Reduction**

- Reduce the number of data input variables by selecting only the relevant features. This can help improve model performance and reduce computational complexity.

8. **Validation of Preprocessing Steps**

- After preprocessing, validate the changes by visualizing the data and checking the summary statistics to ensure that the data is now clean, normalized, and ready for modeling.
- Perform exploratory data analysis (EDA) to understand the distributions, relationships, and correlations of the preprocessed features.

By following these steps, you can effectively preprocess your data, enhancing the quality and performance of your ML models. This process is essential in ensuring that your AI applications can derive meaningful and accurate insights from the data.

TOOLS AND PLATFORMS FOR MANAGING DATA FOR AI MARKETING

Data is an important part of AI marketing. AI marketing tactics would be unable to forecast customer behavior, tailor marketing efforts, or uncover patterns and trends in consumer preferences in the absence of data. As a result, efficient data management is critical for any firm that wishes to properly employ AI marketing.

There are a variety of tools and systems available to assist firms in managing data for AI marketing. This section will look at some of the most prominent tools and systems for handling data for AI marketing, as well as their applications.

Platforms for Customer Relationship Management (CRM): CRM systems are used to manage and analyze customer data. These systems enable firms to consolidate consumer data and track customer interactions across numerous media. Businesses may get insights into customer behavior, preferences, and purchase history by analyzing this data and using this knowledge to tailor marketing activities. Salesforce, HubSpot, and Zoho are among the major CRM solutions.

Data Management Platforms (DMPs): DMPs collect, analyze, and manage massive amounts of data from a variety of sources, including Web site analytics, social media platforms, and advertising campaigns. Businesses may use DMPs to develop extensive customer profiles, segment their audiences, and tailor marketing efforts based on consumer behavior and interests. Adobe Audience Manager, Oracle BlueKai, and Lotame are among prominent DMPs.

BI Platforms: BI platforms are used to analyze vast amounts of data and produce reports, dashboards, and visualizations. By finding patterns, trends, and insights in consumer behavior and preferences, these platforms empower organizations to make data-driven decisions. Tableau, Power BI, and QlikView are some prominent BI solutions.

ML Platforms: AI models that can evaluate data and make predictions are built and deployed using ML platforms. Businesses may use these platforms to automate marketing activities, customize consumer experiences, and improve marketing campaigns. Google Cloud AI Platform, Amazon SageMaker, and Microsoft Azure Machine Learning are other major ML platforms.

Marketing Automation Platforms: These systems are used to automate repetitive marketing processes including email campaigns, social media posting, and lead nurturing. Businesses may use these platforms to tailor marketing efforts based on client behavior and interests, as well as track the performance of marketing initiatives. Marketo, Pardot, and HubSpot are three major marketing automation solutions.

Step-by-Step Instructions: Selecting and Utilizing Tools and Platforms for AI Marketing

By following these steps, marketers can effectively select and utilize the right tools and platforms for their AI Marketing needs.

Step 1: Identify Your Needs

- Evaluate your current marketing strategies and identify areas where AI can add value.
- Determine the specific tasks you need to automate or enhance with AI, such as customer segmentation, predictive analytics, or personalized content creation.

Step 2: Research Available Tools and Platforms

- Explore various AI marketing tools and platforms that cater to your identified needs. Consider factors such as functionality, scalability, integration capabilities, user-friendliness, and cost.
- Look for tools that offer features like data integration, analytics, ML models, and automation workflows.

Step 3: Assess Compatibility with Existing Systems

- Ensure the selected tools or platforms can seamlessly integrate with your existing marketing stack, including CRM systems, DMPs, and analytics tools.
- Check for compatibility with your data formats and workflows to avoid potential integration issues.

Step 4: Evaluate Security and Compliance

- Verify that the tools and platforms comply with relevant data protection regulations, such as GDPR or CCPA, to safeguard customer data.
- Assess the security measures implemented by the vendor, including data encryption, access controls, and audit trails.

Step 5: Conduct Trials and Demos

- Before committing to a purchase, take advantage of free trials or demos offered by the vendors to test the tool's functionality and assess its fit with your marketing needs.
- Use this period to evaluate the ease of use, effectiveness, and potential impact on your marketing outcomes.

Step 6: Implement and Train Your Team

- Once a tool or platform is selected, implement it into your marketing operations.
- Provide training for your marketing team to ensure they understand how to use the innovative technology effectively. This may include training sessions, workshops, or online courses provided by the vendor.

Step 7: Monitor and Optimize

- Continuously monitor the performance of the tools and platforms to ensure they are delivering the desired results.
- Be prepared to adjust or optimize based on performance data, user feedback, and evolving marketing goals.

Step 8: Stay Updated

- Keep abreast of the latest developments and updates in AI marketing technology to ensure your tools and platforms remain current and competitive.
- Regularly review new features, updates, and best practices to enhance your AI marketing strategies.

Data management for AI marketing necessitates a mix of technologies and platforms that allow firms to successfully gather, analyze, and utilize consumer data. CRM platforms, DMPs, BI platforms, ML platforms, and marketing automation platforms are some of the most popular data management tools and platforms for AI marketing. Businesses may obtain insights into customer behavior and preferences, tailor marketing efforts, and optimize marketing campaigns for better outcomes by employing these tools and platforms.

In Chapter 3 of the *AI Marketing Playbook*, the focus is on preparing data for AI, which is essential for ML algorithms to be effective in marketing. The chapter discusses the importance of data hygiene and quality, structuring data, strategies for collecting and storing data, common data preprocessing techniques, and tools and platforms for managing data for AI marketing.

The chapter emphasized the need for clean and high-quality data to ensure accurate predictions and effective decision-making. Data hygiene involves removing errors, duplicates, and inconsistencies from data. Quality data is free from biases and is relevant to the business problem at hand. The chapter explains that data quality can be maintained by regularly auditing and monitoring data, creating data standards and policies, and involving experts in data management.

To structure data for ML algorithms, the chapter recommends using a data structure that is easy for the algorithm to process. Data should be in a format that the algorithm can recognize, such as a table or matrix. Data should also be labeled, meaning each data point has a corresponding label or target variable.

The chapter then discussed strategies for collecting and storing data, such as using customer relationship management (CRM) software, social media listening tools, and web analytics platforms. The chapter also advises businesses to use cloud-based storage solutions, which are scalable and cost-effective.

Common data preprocessing techniques are then covered in the chapter, including data normalization, outlier removal, feature scaling, and dimensionality reduction. These techniques are essential for improving the quality of data and reducing noise, which can affect the accuracy of predictions.

The chapter explored tools and platforms for managing data for AI marketing, such as Amazon Web Services (AWS), Google Cloud, and Microsoft Azure. These platforms provide businesses with the infrastructure, tools, and resources needed to store, process, and analyze substantial amounts of data efficiently. The chapter advises businesses to choose a platform that suits their needs and budget, as well as one that offers high-quality security features.

Chapter 3 of *AI Marketing Playbook* provided a comprehensive guide to preparing data for AI marketing. By focusing on data hygiene and quality, structuring data for ML algorithms, and using effective data preprocessing techniques and tools, businesses can maximize the potential of AI for marketing purposes.

USING ARTIFICIAL INTELLIGENCE TO ANALYZE CUSTOMER BEHAVIOR

Welcome to Chapter 4 of the *AI Marketing Playbook*, where readers will explore how artificial intelligence (AI) can be used to analyze customer behavior. With the ever-increasing amount of data generated by customers' interactions with businesses, it has become crucial for companies to leverage AI in analyzing this data to gain valuable insights into their customers' behavior. By doing so, businesses can create more personalized and effective marketing campaigns that lead to higher customer engagement, loyalty, and satisfaction.

In this chapter, readers will dive into the many ways in which AI can be used to analyze customer behavior. The chapter will examine how AI-powered tools can help businesses gain a better understanding of their customers, including their needs, preferences, and behaviors. Discussion also explores how businesses have successfully used AI to understand their customers, citing real-world examples of companies that have used AI to improve their marketing efforts.

Furthermore, the chapter will explore techniques for creating customer personas using AI, a powerful tool for segmenting customers and tailoring marketing messages to specific groups. There are discussions about how clustering and segmentation can be used to identify distinct groups of customers with similar characteristics and behaviors, helping businesses to tailor their marketing strategies to these groups.

The chapter explores the importance of feedback loops in customer analysis. By constantly gathering feedback from customers, businesses can gain valuable insights into their needs, preferences, and behaviors, allowing them to continually refine their marketing strategies to better meet their customers' needs. Additionally, the chapter will examine how AI-powered tools can be used to gather and analyze feedback, enabling businesses to make data-driven decisions and improve their marketing efforts.

Overall, this chapter will provide readers with a comprehensive understanding of how AI can be used to analyze customer behavior and how businesses can leverage this technology to improve their marketing strategies. Whether a marketer, a business owner, or simply interested in the potential of AI, this chapter will offer valuable insights and practical advice for using AI to better understand and engage with customers.

HOW AI CAN BE USED TO ANALYZE CUSTOMER BEHAVIOR

In today's digital age, customer behavior analysis has become more important than ever. With the help of AI, businesses can now analyze customer behavior at an unprecedented level of granularity. In this section, there is discussion about how AI can be used to analyze customer behavior, along with some examples.

Predictive Analytics

AI-powered predictive analytics can assist organizations in identifying trends in consumer behavior that might otherwise be missed through manual analysis. AI algorithms may anticipate future consumer behavior, such as purchasing patterns, product preferences, and even the possibility of churn, by evaluating prior customer data. This data may then be utilized to tailor marketing campaigns, improve customer experiences, and optimize product offers.

Netflix recommends material to its customers based on their watching history, reviews, and preferences. The company's technology predicts what the viewer will watch next, and the recommendations are tailored to everyone.

Implementing Predictive Analytics for Customer Behavior

Step-by-Step Instructions

1.   **Define Objectives and Goals**

     • Identify specific behaviors or trends you want to predict (e.g., purchase patterns, customer churn).
     • Set clear, measurable goals for the predictive model (e.g., reduce churn rate by 10% within six months).

2.   **Collect and Aggregate Data**

     • Gather historical customer data from various sources such as transaction records, Web site analytics, customer service interactions, and social media activity.

- Ensure the data is comprehensive, covering several aspects of customer behavior and interactions.

3. **Clean and Preprocess Data**

- Clean the data to remove inconsistencies, duplicates, and irrelevant information.
- Preprocess the data by normalizing values, encoding categorical variables, and handling missing data to prepare it for analysis.

4. **Select the Predictive Modeling Technique**

- Choose an appropriate predictive modeling technique based on the objective, such as regression analysis for continuous outcomes or classification for discrete actions.
- Consider techniques like decision trees, random forests, neural networks, or logistic regression based on the complexity of behavior patterns.

5. **Divide the Dataset**

- Split the data into training and testing sets, typically with a 70–30 or 80–20 ratio.
- Use the training set to build and train the model, and the testing set to evaluate its performance.

6. **Develop and Train the Predictive Model**

- Use the selected algorithm to create the predictive model.
- Train the model using the training dataset, adjusting parameters to optimize performance.

7. **Test and Validate the Model**

- Evaluate the model's performance using the testing set to ensure accuracy in predictions.
- Use metrics like accuracy, precision, recall, and the area under the ROC curve (AUC) for evaluation.

8. **Refine and Optimize the Model**

- Based on testing results, refine the model by adjusting parameters, adding, or removing features, or trying different algorithms if necessary.
- Continuously iterate to improve prediction accuracy and meet the predefined goals.

9. Deploy the Model

- Once the model performs satisfactorily, integrate it into your business processes for real-time predictions or periodic analysis.
- Ensure the deployment infrastructure can handle the load and provides timely insights.

10. Monitor and Update the Model

- Regularly monitor the model's performance in real-world conditions and collect feedback.
- Update the model periodically with new data and insights to maintain its relevance and accuracy over time.

By following these steps, businesses can implement predictive analytics to gain insights into customer behavior, enabling proactive decision-making and more personalized customer engagement strategies.

Sentiment Analysis

AI-powered sentiment analysis can help businesses to understand how customers feel about their products, services, and brand. By analyzing customer feedback from social media, customer reviews, and other sources, AI algorithms can determine whether the sentiment is positive, negative, or neutral. This information can be used to identify areas of improvement, resolve customer complaints, and even predict customer behavior.

Example: Airbnb uses sentiment analysis to monitor customer feedback and improve the guest experience. The company's AI algorithms analyze customer reviews to identify common themes and issues, which are then used to make improvements to the platform.

Conducting Sentiment Analysis to Gauge Customer Emotions Step-by-Step Instructions

1. Select AI Sentiment Analysis Tools:

- Research and choose AI-powered sentiment analysis tools that best fit your business needs. Popular options include IBM Watson, Google Cloud Natural Language, and Sentiment Analyzer.

2. Gather Customer Feedback Data:

- Collect data from various sources where customer feedback is available, such as social media platforms, customer reviews, survey responses, and support tickets.

3. Prepare the Data for Analysis:

- Cleanse the data by removing irrelevant content, correcting typos, and standardizing formats.
- Organize the data into a structured format that is compatible with the chosen sentiment analysis tool.

4. Perform Sentiment Analysis:

- Input the prepared data into the sentiment analysis tool.
- Run the analysis to categorize feedback into sentiments such as positive, negative, or neutral.

5. Analyze the Results:

- Evaluate the sentiment analysis output to identify trends, patterns, and areas of concern or opportunity.
- Pay special attention to recurring themes in negative feedback to pinpoint areas for improvement.

6. Integrate Findings into Business Strategy:

- Use the insights gained from sentiment analysis to inform marketing strategies, product development, and customer service approaches.
- Address negative sentiments by making necessary changes and enhancements to products or services.

7. Monitor and Update:

- Regularly update the sentiment analysis process with new data to keep insights current.
- Continually refine the sentiment analysis approach based on evolving business needs and feedback trends.

8. Report and Share Insights:

- Compile the findings into reports and share them with relevant stakeholders to drive informed decision-making.
- Use visualizations to present sentiment trends and impacts on customer behavior and business outcomes.

By systematically conducting sentiment analysis using AI tools, businesses can effectively gauge customer emotions and sentiments, leading to better-informed strategies and improved customer experiences.

Customer Segmentation

AI-powered consumer segmentation may assist firms in identifying groups of customers that have similar qualities, requirements, and habits. AI algorithms may segment clients based on demographics, purchasing behaviors, and other variables by evaluating customer data. This data may be utilized to tailor marketing campaigns, generate targeted campaigns, and enhance consumer experiences.

Customer segmentation is used by Amazon to customize product suggestions and incentives. The AI algorithms used by the firm analyze consumer data to identify groups with similar purchasing behaviors and then offer items and promotions based on those tendencies.

Step-by-Step Instructions

1. **Define Segmentation Goals:**

   • Clarify what you aim to achieve with customer segmentation. Objectives could include improving targeted marketing, enhancing product recommendations, or increasing customer retention.

2. **Collect and Prepare Data:**

   • Gather comprehensive customer data from various sources such as sales records, online behavior analytics, social media interactions, and customer feedback.
   • Cleanse and prepare the data by removing inconsistencies and irrelevant information to ensure accuracy in segmentation.

3. **Choose AI Segmentation Tools:**

   • Select AI tools and platforms that offer advanced segmentation capabilities. Consider tools that can handle large datasets and provide detailed analytical features.

4. **Segmentation Analysis:**

   • Use the AI tool to analyze the customer data and segment the customers into distinct groups based on common characteristics such as demographics, purchasing behavior's, preferences, and engagement levels.

5. **Review and Refine Segments:**

   • Evaluate the generated customer segments to ensure they are meaningful and align with your business objectives.
   • Refine the segmentation by adjusting parameters or criteria as needed to better define customer groups.

6. **Develop Targeted Strategies:**

    • Create tailored marketing strategies for each customer segment, focusing on their specific needs, preferences, and behaviors.
    • Develop personalized communication plans, product offerings, and promotional activities to enhance engagement and conversion within each segment.

7. **Implement and Monitor:**

    • Roll out targeted campaigns and strategies for each segment, closely monitoring the performance and customer response.
    • Use AI tools to continuously analyze the effectiveness of segmentation and the impact of targeted actions on customer behavior.

8. **Iterate and Optimize:**

    • Based on performance data and customer feedback, iterate, and refine segmentation models and strategies.
    • Continuously update customer data and segmentation parameters to adapt to changing customer behaviors and market trends.

9. **Report and Communicate Results:**

    • Compile detailed reports on segmentation outcomes, campaign performance, and ROI for each segment.
    • Share insights and successes across the organization to inform broader business strategies and decisions.

By following these steps and leveraging AI for customer segmentation, businesses can achieve more precise targeting in their marketing efforts, leading to increased efficiency, higher customer satisfaction, and improved overall business performance.

Image Recognition

AI-powered picture identification may assist organizations in better understanding how their customers engage with their products and brand. AI algorithms can uncover trends in how people use items and interact with brands by analyzing photos from social media, customer reviews, and other sources. This data may be utilized to enhance product design, develop more successful marketing strategies, and even detect counterfeit goods.

Coca-Cola employs picture recognition to monitor how their goods are used and exhibited in shops. The AI algorithms used by the corporation scan photographs from social media and other sources to discover trends in how its goods are eaten, and then utilize that knowledge to enhance marketing and product design.

Customer behavior analysis enabled by AI has the potential to transform how organizations perceive and interact with their consumers. Businesses may acquire insights into consumer behavior that would be hard to unearth through manual study by employing AI algorithms to examine customer data. This data may then be utilized to tailor marketing activities, improve customer experiences, and optimize product offers, resulting in more revenue and better customer engagement.

HOW BUSINESSES HAVE SUCCESSFULLY USED AI TO UNDERSTAND THEIR CUSTOMERS

AI has the potential to revolutionize the way businesses understand their customers. By analyzing large volumes of data, AI can provide businesses with insights into consumer behavior and preferences, allowing them to make informed decisions about product development, marketing strategies, and customer engagement. This chapter will discuss several examples of how businesses have successfully used AI to understand their customers.

Amazon

Amazon, one of the world's largest online retailers, has been employing AI to better understand its consumers for several years. Amazon analyzes consumer data such as purchase history, browsing behavior, and search queries using AI algorithms to deliver tailored suggestions to each customer. Amazon may use AI to give highly relevant and individualized suggestions to each consumer, boosting the possibility of a purchase.

Amazon also uses AI to improve the efficiency of its supply chain operations. Amazon can estimate demand for items by analyzing consumer data, allowing it to optimize inventory management and shorten the time it takes to deliver products to customers.

Netflix

Netflix is a popular video streaming service that uses AI to understand its customers' viewing habits. By analyzing viewing history, search queries, and user ratings, Netflix can provide personalized recommendations for movies and TV shows. Netflix's recommendation engine is powered by AI algorithms that can identify patterns in customer behavior, such as the types of movies or TV shows they watch and when they watch them.

Netflix also uses AI to optimize its content creation process. By analyzing customer data, Netflix can identify popular genres and themes, allowing it to produce content that is more likely to resonate with its audience.

Starbucks

Starbucks is a multinational coffeehouse business that employs AI to better understand its consumers' preferences and purchasing patterns. Starbucks analyzes user data, such as purchase history, mobile orders, and social media activity, using AI algorithms to deliver individualized suggestions to each customer. Based on previous purchases, Starbucks' AI-powered recommendation engine may also offer new goods that consumers are likely to be interested in.

Starbucks also used AI to enhance its supply chain operations. Starbucks can estimate demand for certain items by studying consumer data, allowing it to optimize inventory management and avoid waste.

AI has the potential to revolutionize the way businesses understand their customers. By analyzing large volumes of data, AI can provide businesses with insights into consumer behavior and preferences, allowing them to make informed decisions about product development, marketing strategies, and customer engagement. The examples discussed in this chapter demonstrate how businesses across industries are successfully using AI to understand their customers and provide personalized experiences that drive customer loyalty and growth.

TECHNIQUES FOR CREATING CUSTOMER PERSONAS USING AI

Chapter 4 of the *AI Marketing Playbook* is crucial reading for any marketer seeking to improve their understanding of customers and create accurate personas. In this chapter, you will learn about various techniques for creating customer personas using AI and how to use data to develop more accurate and nuanced representations for your audience.

The chapter started by explaining what customer personas are and why they are essential for marketing. A customer persona is a detailed representation of your target audience that helps you understand their needs, wants, and behaviors. By creating accurate customer personas, you can tailor your marketing efforts to meet your audience's unique needs and improve your marketing ROI.

The next section of the chapter covered the traditional approach to creating customer personas, which involves conducting market research, surveys, and focus groups. While this approach can yield valuable insights, it is time-consuming and expensive. The use of AI can help speed up this process and deliver more accurate and nuanced personas.

The next part introduced different AI techniques for creating customer personas, such as natural language processing (NLP) and machine learning (ML). NLP can help you analyze enormous amounts of unstructured data from social media, customer feedback, and customer support logs to identify patterns in customer behavior and preferences. ML can help you segment your audience based on various attributes, such as demographics, behavior, and interests.

Then Chapter 4 discussed the importance of data privacy and ethical considerations when using AI to create customer personas. It is essential to use customer data responsibly and transparently to build trust with your audience.

This chapter provides a step-by-step guide to creating customer personas using AI. The process involves collecting data, cleaning, and organizing the data, identifying patterns and insights, and developing personas based on those insights. The chapter also provides tips on how to validate your personas and ensure they are accurate and useful.

Chapter 4 provided valuable insights into using AI to create customer personas. By leveraging AI techniques, marketers can gain a deeper understanding of their audience and deliver more personalized and effective marketing campaigns. The chapter also emphasizes the importance of data privacy and ethical considerations when using AI, which is crucial for building trust with your customers.

Creating Customer Personas with AI
Step-by-Step Instructions

1. **Define Objectives:**

   - Identify the goals of creating customer personas, such as improving product development, tailoring marketing messages, or enhancing customer service.

2. **Collect and Aggregate Data:**

   - Gather comprehensive customer data from various sources like (customer relationship management) CRM systems, social media analytics, purchase histories, and customer surveys.

3. **Select AI Analysis Tools:**

   - Choose AI tools that specialize in data analysis and customer profiling, like IBM Watson, Salesforce Einstein, or custom ML models.

4. **Analyze and Segment Data:**

   - Use AI tools to analyze the collected data, identifying patterns and behaviors that distinguish different customer groups.
   - Segment the customer base into distinct personas based on shared characteristics, such as demographics, buying behaviors, interests, and needs.

5. **Develop Personas:**

   - Create detailed profiles for each customer segment, including name, age range, preferences, pain points, and motivations to make the personas relatable.

6. **Validate and Refine Personas:**

    • Test the accuracy of the customer personas through targeted marketing campaigns or focus groups and refine them based on feedback and performance.

7. **Integrate Personas into Marketing Strategy:**

    • Use the developed personas to tailor marketing campaigns, product development, and customer service strategies to meet the specific needs of each group.

8. **Review and Update Regularly:**

    • Periodically review and update the personas using the latest customer data and AI insights to ensure they remain accurate and relevant.

THE ROLE OF CLUSTERING AND SEGMENTATION IN CUSTOMER ANALYSIS

Clustering and segmentation are powerful tools in customer analysis that can help businesses better understand their customers and tailor their marketing efforts to meet their specific needs. The following sections explore the role of clustering and segmentation in customer analysis, including their definitions, benefits, and how they can be used effectively in marketing.

Definition of Clustering and Segmentation

Clustering and segmentation are two data analysis strategies for grouping comparable data points together. Clustering and segmentation are techniques used in consumer analysis to categorize customers based on shared features or behavior.

Clustering is the process of grouping consumers based on their similarities to one another without knowing what these commonalities are. This is accomplished via the use of algorithms that examine data points and decide which consumers have the most in common with one another. Clustering can assist firms in identifying previously unknown patterns and correlations within their consumer base.

The practice of breaking a customer base into groups based on shared factors such as demographics, habits, or wants is known as segmentation. Businesses may use segmentation to better understand their consumers' wants and preferences, allowing them to build customized marketing initiatives that are more likely to resonate with certain groups.

Benefits of Clustering and Segmentation

Clustering and segmentation have various advantages in consumer analysis. Businesses may acquire insights into their consumers' behavior and preferences by detecting patterns and similarities among them, allowing them to design targeted marketing efforts that are more successful at reaching certain groups of customers. This can result in higher levels of customer happiness, loyalty, and sales.

Clustering and segmentation can also assist companies in identifying new growth and innovation possibilities. Businesses may produce new products and services that are personalized to their customers' individual demands by studying their consumers' wants and preferences.

Moreover, clustering and segmentation may help businesses save time and money by focusing their marketing efforts on the most profitable consumer categories. Businesses may use their marketing efforts more efficiently and effectively if they identify the categories that create the most income.

Effective Use of Clustering and Segmentation in Marketing

Businesses must first determine the criteria that are most essential in distinguishing their clients to employ clustering and segmentation effectively in marketing. These factors can include demographic information like age, gender, and income, as well as behavioral information like purchase history, Web site interactions, and social media activity.

Businesses may use clustering and segmentation algorithms to categorize clients based on these criteria after they have been detected. These groups may then be studied to uncover trends and similarities among customers and to develop targeted marketing campaigns customized to each group's requirements and preferences.

It is vital to highlight that clustering and segmentation are continual processes that need constant monitoring and correction. Businesses must be able to adjust their marketing tactics to match changing client behavior and preferences.

Clustering and segmentation are important customer analytic methods that may help organizations acquire insights into their customers' behavior and preferences, as well as design focused marketing efforts that are more effective at reaching certain groups of consumers. Businesses that use clustering and segmentation successfully may boost customer happiness, loyalty, and revenue while also identifying new prospects for development and innovation.

THE IMPORTANCE OF FEEDBACK LOOPS IN CUSTOMER ANALYSIS

In the world of marketing, understanding your customers is essential. The better you know your customers, the more effective your marketing campaigns will be. One of the best ways to get to know your customers is through feedback loops. Feedback loops are essential tools that help you gather, analyze, and act on customer feedback. This section discusses the importance of feedback loops in customer analysis.

What Is a Feedback Loop?

A feedback loop is a process where you collect feedback from customers, analyze that feedback, and then act based on the results of that analysis. The feedback loop can be broken down into three stages:

Collect feedback: In this stage, you gather information from your customers. This can be done through surveys, customer reviews, social media, or other feedback mechanisms.

Analyze feedback: Once you have collected feedback, you need to analyze it to identify patterns, trends, and insights. This stage involves data analysis and interpretation.

Act: Based on the feedback analysis insights, you may optimize your marketing campaigns or other elements of your business. This might include alterations to your products, services, or marketing techniques.

What Is the Significance of Feedback Loops in Customer Analysis?

Customer satisfaction: Feedback loops are critical for determining consumer satisfaction. You may find areas where your clients are dissatisfied and then make efforts to improve those areas by gathering feedback.

Feedback loops are particularly important in product development. By studying client input, you may understand what features and functionalities your consumers desire and need, and then build products that match those demands.

Marketing improvements: Feedback loops are critical for enhancing marketing strategies. You may understand which marketing messages resonate with your clients and alter your marketing initiatives accordingly by evaluating customer feedback.

Customer retention: Feedback loops can aid in customer retention. You may demonstrate to your clients that you appreciate their opinions and are devoted to satisfying their requirements by responding to their complaints and adjusting based on their comments.

Competitive edge: Feedback loops might provide you with an advantage. You may produce goods, services, and marketing efforts that better satisfy the demands of your clients if you understand them better than your rivals.

Customer feedback loops are critical instruments for customer analysis. You may increase customer happiness, product development, marketing campaigns, customer retention, and gain a competitive edge by gathering feedback, evaluating it, and acting on the results. Integrating feedback loops into your marketing plan may help you gain a deeper understanding of your clients and, as a result, generate company success.

Utilizing Feedback Loops for Continuous Improvement
Step-by-Step Instructions

1. **Establish Feedback Channels:**

   • Set up various channels for collecting customer feedback, such as surveys, social media, customer support interactions, and online reviews.

2. **Integrate AI Analytics Tools:**

   • Use AI tools to analyze the collected feedback data continuously. Tools like sentiment analysis, text analytics, or customer behavior prediction models can provide deep insights.

3. **Process and Analyze Feedback:**

   • Regularly process the feedback through the AI analytics tools to identify trends, customer satisfaction levels, and areas needing improvement.

4. **Act on Insights:**

   • Use the insights gained from the feedback analysis to make informed decisions on product enhancements, service improvements, and marketing adjustments.

5. **Implement Changes:**

   • Apply the necessary changes based on the feedback analysis to improve customer satisfaction, product quality, and overall service delivery.

6. **Communicate Changes to Customers:**

   • Inform customers about the changes made in response to their feedback, showing them that their input is valued and acted upon.

7. **Monitor Outcomes:**

   • Continuously monitor how the changes impact customer satisfaction and business performance, using AI tools to track progress and outcomes.

8. **Iterate the Process:**

   • Establish a continuous cycle of feedback, analysis, implementation, and monitoring to ensure ongoing improvement and adaptation to customer needs.

By leveraging AI to create customer personas and utilizing feedback loops, businesses can gain a deeper understanding of their customers and continuously improve their products, services, and marketing strategies.

Chapter 4 looked at how AI may be used to evaluate consumer behavior in a variety of ways.

One of the key advantages of AI is that it may help businesses obtain a better knowledge of their clients, allowing them to make more educated decisions about how to sell their products and services. AI may be used to evaluate consumer data like purchase histories, search queries, and social media interactions to find patterns and trends that human analysts may not see right away.

There are several examples of businesses that have effectively used AI to better understand their customers. Amazon utilizes AI to tailor product suggestions for its consumers based on their browsing and purchasing histories. Similarly, Netflix utilizes AI to propose movies and TV series to its subscribers based on their watching habits. The idea in both situations is to give clients with a more personalized experience that caters to their specific requirements and preferences.

Using AI to create client personas is another effective way for studying customer behavior. Businesses may construct rich personas that capture the essence of distinct client categories by evaluating data about their demographics, hobbies, and behavior. These personas may then be utilized to inform marketing and sales tactics, as well as product development initiatives.

Customer analysis also benefits from clustering and segmentation. Clustering is the process of grouping consumers together based on behavioral similarities, whereas segmentation is the process of splitting customers into various groups based on demographics or other factors. Both strategies may be used to uncover trends in consumer behavior and create targeted marketing efforts that will appeal to certain client groups.

Lastly, feedback loops are critical for effective consumer analysis. Businesses may acquire useful insights into what works well and what needs to be improved by soliciting feedback from customers about their experiences with a product or service. This input may then be utilized to improve marketing and product initiatives, as well as to inspire future AI-powered consumer behavior assessments.

PERSONALIZATION WITH ARTIFICIAL INTELLIGENCE

In today's fast-paced and highly competitive market, businesses are constantly seeking ways to provide personalized experiences for their customers. Personalization has become a key driver of customer engagement and loyalty, and artificial intelligence (AI) has proven to be a significant change in this regard.

AI can be used to analyze vast amounts of customer data, including purchase history, browsing behavior, and demographic information, to create highly personalized experiences. AI-powered personalization can help businesses provide relevant recommendations, personalized content, and targeted offers to customers in real time.

There are numerous successful examples of personalization strategies powered by AI. Netflix uses AI algorithms to recommend movies and TV shows to users based on their viewing history and preferences. Amazon, however, uses AI to offer product recommendations and personalized emails to customers.

Personalization at scale is made possible by automating individualized experiences through AI. With AI, businesses can offer personalization to every customer at a scale, which was previously impossible to achieve manually.

While the benefits of AI-powered personalization are many, there are also ethical considerations that must be considered. The use of customer data and AI algorithms to create personalized experiences must be transparent, and customers must have control over their data.

Measuring the return on investment (ROI) of personalization with AI is critical to determining the success of personalization strategies. Metrics such as customer engagement, conversion rates, and customer satisfaction can be used to measure the impact of personalization on business outcomes.

Personalization with AI is a powerful tool for businesses seeking to provide personalized experiences to their customers at a scale. While there are ethical considerations that must be addressed, the benefits of AI-powered personalization are numerous, and measuring the ROI of personalization strategies is critical to their success.

AI has revolutionized the way marketers approach personalization. With the help of AI, businesses can analyze vast amounts of customer data and offer tailored experiences to their users. This section explores how AI can be used for personalization and provides examples of its implementation.

Personalized product recommendations: One of the most common ways AI is used for personalization is by recommending products to customers based on their past purchases and behavior. By analyzing customer data, AI algorithms can predict which products a customer is most likely to be interested in and suggest them to the customer. Amazon uses AI to recommend products to customers based on their browsing history, purchase history, and other data points.

Step-by-Step Instructions: Implementing Predictive Analytics for Personalized Product Recommendations

1. **Define Objectives**

   • Identify the goals of your personalized recommendation system, such as increasing sales, improving customer engagement, or enhancing user experience.

2. **Collect and Prepare Data**

   • Gather comprehensive customer data, including purchase history, browsing behavior, and demographic information.
   • Clean and preprocess the data to ensure accuracy and consistency.

3. **Select a Predictive Analytics Model**

   • Choose an appropriate machine learning (ML) model for predictive analytics, such as collaborative filtering, content-based filtering, or hybrid models.

4. **Train the Model**

   • Use historical data to train your selected model, ensuring it can accurately predict customer preferences and behaviors.

5. **Test and Validate the Model**

   • Evaluate the model's performance using a separate set of test data to ensure accuracy and effectiveness in making recommendations.

6. **Implement the Model**

   • Integrate the trained model into your product recommendation system to start generating personalized suggestions for customers.

7. **Monitor and Refine**

   • Continuously monitor the performance of your recommendation system and adjust the model as needed based on customer feedback and changing behaviors.

8. **Ensure Privacy and Transparency**

   • Inform customers about how their data is being used for personalized recommendations and adhere to data protection regulations to maintain trust and compliance.

By following these steps, businesses can implement predictive analytics to create personalized product recommendations that resonate with individual customer preferences, leading to improved customer satisfaction and increased business performance.

Personalized email campaigns: AI can also be used to personalize email campaigns to individual customers. By analyzing customer data such as past purchases, Web site activity, and demographics, AI algorithms can suggest personalized content and offers to include in an email campaign. If a customer has previously purchased running shoes from a retailer, AI can suggest sending them an email campaign featuring the latest running shoe releases.

Step-by-Step Instructions: Using AI for Personalized Email Campaigns

1. **Define Campaign Goals**

   • Clearly outline what you aim to achieve with personalized email campaigns, such as increasing engagement, driving sales, or improving customer retention.

2. **Collect and Segment Customer Data**

   • Gather comprehensive data from various sources like customer relationship management (CRM) systems, Web site analytics, and purchase histories.
   • Segment customers based on demographics, behavior patterns, and purchase history to tailor the email content.

3. **Choose an AI-Powered Email Marketing Platform**

   • Select a platform that offers AI capabilities for personalization, such as automated segmentation, content optimization, and behavior-based triggers.

4. **Develop Personalized Content**

   • Create dynamic content templates that can be automatically customized for each recipient based on their data and past interactions.

5. **Set Up Behavioral Triggers**

   • Implement AI-driven triggers for sending emails based on specific customer actions or milestones, like cart abandonment, product browsing, or subscription renewal dates.

6. **Test and Optimize Campaigns**

   • Use A/B testing to compare various aspects of your email campaigns, such as subject lines, content, and sending times, to determine what works best for different segments.

7. **Launch and Monitor**

   • Roll out personalized email campaigns and closely monitor key metrics such as open rates, click-through rates, and conversion rates to evaluate effectiveness.

8. **Gather Feedback and Refine**

   • Collect customer feedback through surveys or analyzing email interactions to continuously refine and improve the personalization strategy.

9. **Ensure Compliance and Privacy**

   • Ensure all personalized email campaigns comply with data protection regulations like GDPR and maintain transparency with customers about how their data is used.

By implementing these steps, businesses can effectively use AI to craft personalized email campaigns that resonate with individual customers, leading to higher engagement and better marketing outcomes.

Personalized content recommendations: AI can also be used to recommend personalized content to customers. By analyzing customer data such as past content consumption, interests, and behavior, AI algorithms can suggest content that is most relevant to each customer. Netflix uses AI to recommend movies and TV shows to users based on their viewing history and ratings.

Step-by-Step Instructions: Leveraging AI for Personalized Content Recommendations

1. **Define Objectives and Scope**

   • Identify the goals for personalized content recommendations, such as increasing user engagement, boosting time spent on a site, or enhancing content discoverability.

2. **Collect and Analyze Customer Data**

   • Gather data from various touchpoints like browsing history, interaction logs, purchase records, and social media activity to understand customer preferences and behaviors.

3. **Implement AI and ML Models**

   • Use AI algorithms, such as collaborative filtering, content-based filtering, or hybrid models, to analyze customer data and identify patterns and preferences.

4. **Develop a Recommendation Engine**

   • Build or integrate a recommendation engine that processes customer data in real time and generates personalized content suggestions.

5. **Integrate Recommendations Across Platforms**

   • Ensure the recommendation engine is seamlessly integrated across all customer-facing platforms, such as Web sites, apps, and social media, to provide consistent personalized experiences.

6. **Test and Optimize the Recommendation System**

   • Conduct A/B testing to compare different recommendation algorithms and configurations, optimizing for key performance indicators like engagement rate, click-through rate, and conversion rate.

7. **Monitor User Interaction and Feedback**

   • Regularly analyze how customers interact with recommended content and gather direct feedback to refine and improve the recommendation algorithms.

8. **Ensure Ethical Use of Data**

   • Maintain transparency with customers about how their data is used for personalized recommendations and adhere to data privacy regulations and ethical standards.

9. **Update and Evolve AI Models**

   - Continuously update the AI models with new data and insights and adapt to changing customer preferences and market trends to keep the recommendations relevant and effective.

By following these steps, businesses can effectively leverage AI to provide personalized content recommendations, enhancing customer experience and engagement through tailored content that resonates with individual preferences and behaviors.

Personalized pricing: AI can also be used to personalize pricing for individual customers. By analyzing customer data such as past purchases and demographics, AI algorithms can suggest pricing that is tailored to each customer. Airlines use AI to personalize pricing for customers based on factors such as their location, travel history, and purchasing behavior.

Step-by-Step Instructions: Applying AI for Personalized Pricing

1. **Define Pricing Strategy Objectives**

   - Establish clear goals for personalized pricing, such as increasing sales, improving customer loyalty, or maximizing profit margins.

2. **Collect and Analyze Customer Data**

   - Gather comprehensive data on customer behavior, including purchase history, browsing patterns, and engagement levels with the business.

3. **Develop a Segmentation Model**

   - Use AI algorithms to segment customers based on their price sensitivity, purchasing behavior, and engagement history.

4. **Implement Predictive Analytics**

   - Apply predictive analytics to forecast how different customer segments are likely to respond to various pricing strategies.

5. **Create a Dynamic Pricing Model**

   - Develop a dynamic pricing model that utilizes AI to adjust prices in real time based on customer data and predefined business rules.

6. **Integrate the Pricing Model with Sales Platforms**

   - Ensure the dynamic pricing model is fully integrated with online and offline sales platforms to allow for seamless price adjustments.

7. **Test and Optimize the Pricing Strategy**

   • Conduct controlled tests to evaluate the effectiveness of personalized pricing strategies and use the insights to optimize the model continuously.

8. **Monitor Customer Response and Market Trends**

   • Regularly assess customer reactions to price changes and stay updated with market trends to adjust the pricing strategy accordingly.

9. **Ensure Transparency and Fairness**

   • Maintain ethical standards by being transparent with customers about personalized pricing practices and ensuring prices are fair and nondiscriminatory.

10. **Review and Adjust the AI Model Regularly**

   • Periodically review the AI model for accuracy and relevance, making necessary adjustments to reflect changes in customer behavior and market conditions.

Implementing AI-driven personalized pricing allows businesses to optimize their pricing strategies dynamically, catering to individual customer preferences and market conditions, leading to enhanced customer satisfaction and improved business performance.

Personalized Web site experience: AI can also be used to personalize the Web site experience for individual customers. By analyzing customer data such as past Web site activity, behavior, and preferences, AI algorithms can suggest personalized content and offers to show to each customer. A clothing retailer could use AI to personalize the homepage of their Web site to show products that are most likely to interest each customer based on their past purchases and browsing history.

Step-by-Step Instructions: Personalized Website Experience

1. **Analyze User Behavior and Preferences**

   • Collect and analyze data on user interactions, browsing patterns, and engagement with the Web site to understand preferences and behavior.

2. **Segment Users Based on Behavior**

   • Use AI algorithms to segment users into distinct groups based on their behavior and preferences identified from the collected data.

3. **Design Personalized User Experiences**

   • Develop customized Web site layouts, content, and interaction paths for each user segment to enhance their browsing experience.

4. **Implement AI-Driven Content Recommendation**

   • Integrate AI tools to dynamically recommend content, products, or services tailored to individual user preferences and past behavior.

5. **Optimize Website Navigation and Search**

   • Use AI to personalize the navigation and search functionalities, making it easier for users to find relevant content and products.

6. **Test and Optimize Personalized Experiences**

   • Continuously test distinct aspects of personalized Web site experiences and use the insights to optimize user engagement and satisfaction.

7. **Monitor User Feedback and Behavior**

   • Regularly monitor user feedback and behavior changes to refine the personalization strategies and ensure they meet user needs.

AI can be a powerful tool for personalization, allowing businesses to tailor experiences to individual customers in a way that was not possible before. By analyzing vast amounts of customer data, AI algorithms can provide personalized product recommendations, email campaigns, content recommendations, pricing, and Web site experiences. Businesses that embrace AI-powered personalization can improve customer satisfaction and increase sales.

SUCCESSFUL PERSONALIZATION STRATEGIES

Personalization has been an increasingly vital component of marketing in recent years, as customers want firms to understand their unique requirements and preferences. AI is becoming increasingly crucial in providing personalized experiences since it can assist in automating the process of assessing consumer data and adapting marketing messaging. Following are some instances of effective AI-powered personalization strategies:

Amazon: Amazon has aggressively invested in AI to provide tailored experiences to its consumers. One way it accomplishes this is through its recommendation engine, which analyzes consumer activity and recommends things that they are likely to be interested in. This has been a key factor in Amazon's success, as it has helped to drive increased sales and customer loyalty.

Netflix: Netflix is another firm that has successfully employed AI. Its recommendation engine analyzes client watching habits to suggest series and movies that they are likely to appreciate. Customers are more inclined to spend time watching material that is relevant to their interests, which has contributed to greater engagement on the platform.

Spotify: Another firm that has employed AI to provide individualized experiences to its consumers is Spotify. Its recommendation engine analyzes consumer listening habits to suggest music and playlists that they are likely to appreciate. Customers are more inclined to spend time listening to music that is relevant to their interests, which has contributed to increasing engagement on the platform.

Sephora: Sephora is a beauty business that uses AI to provide individualized experiences to its consumers. Its Color IQ technology analyzes consumer skin tone and recommends items that are a suitable fit for their complexion using ML algorithms. Customers are more inclined to acquire items that are adapted to their specific demands, which has resulted in greater sales and client loyalty.

Starbucks: Starbucks has embraced AI to provide individualized experiences to its consumers via its mobile app. The software analyzes client purchase habits to suggest drinks and foods that they are likely to appreciate. Customers are more inclined to acquire things that are personalized to their specific interests, which has contributed to improved sales and client loyalty.

These are just a few instances of effective AI-powered personalization initiatives. Businesses may provide more relevant and engaging experiences to their consumers by harnessing the power of ML algorithms to evaluate customer data, which can help generate greater sales and customer loyalty.

PERSONALIZATION AT SCALE: AUTOMATING INDIVIDUALIZED EXPERIENCES

Personalization has been a buzzword in the world of marketing for a while now. With the increasing amount of data and the use of AI, businesses can now automate individualized experiences at a scale. This section of the *AI Marketing Playbook* explores how to use AI to automate individualized experiences for customers.

What Is AI Personalization at Scale?

The use of AI to customize consumer experiences on a big scale is known as AI personalization at scale. This implies that companies may give individualized experiences to millions of clients without requiring human participation. At scale, AI personalization entails analyzing massive quantities of data to understand customer behavior and preferences, and then leveraging that data to offer tailored experiences.

Why is AI Personalization Important?

AI personalization is critical because it helps organizations to give relevant experiences to their consumers. Consumers nowadays demand tailored experiences from the businesses with which they interact. Customization promotes better client interactions and increases consumer loyalty.

Businesses can give individualized experiences to millions of consumers with AI personalization, guaranteeing that each client feels noticed and understood. AI customization may also help organizations save time and money. Businesses may provide personalized experiences at a scale without hiring more people by automating the personalization process.

How to Automate Individualized Experiences with AI Personalization

Businesses must take the following actions to automate personalized experiences using AI personalization:

Gather information: The first step toward automating personalized experiences with AI personalization is data collection. Customer data such as purchase history, browsing habits, and demographic information are included. Companies may gather data via a variety of methods, including Web sites, social media, and mobile apps.

Analyze data: After gathering the data, the following step is to examine it. This entails identifying trends in client behavior and preferences using ML techniques. Companies may utilize this data to establish consumer groups based on their preferences, activity, and demographics.

Customize experiences: After the consumer segments are defined, organizations may utilize this information to tailor their interactions with them. Personalized product suggestions, targeted marketing, and tailored content are examples of this. AI-powered customization solutions can help businesses automate the personalization process.

Test and optimize: It is critical to continuously test and optimize the personalization process. A/B testing may be used by businesses to discover which personalization tactics are most effective. Furthermore, organizations may utilize ML algorithms to continuously refine the personalization process.

- *Track performance*: Lastly, organizations must track the effectiveness of their AI-powered personalization efforts. This includes monitoring client engagement, conversion rates, and satisfaction. Businesses may find areas for improvement and adjust their personalization strategy accordingly by monitoring results.

Examples of AI Personalization

There are several examples of AI personalization in action. Here are a few:

Amazon: An excellent example of AI personalization in action is Amazon. Customers are recommended items based on their purchase history and browsing activity by AI-powered recommendation engines.

Netflix: Netflix personalizes content suggestions for its viewers using AI-powered algorithms. To propose material that is likely to interest each user, the firm analyzes data such as viewing history, time of day, and device type.

Spotify: To customize music suggestions for its customers, Spotify employs AI-powered algorithms. To propose music that is likely to appeal to each user, the firm analyzes data such as listening history, playlists, and time of day.

AI personalization at scale is a strong technology that companies may employ to provide personalized experiences to their consumers. Businesses may develop consumer groups and customize experiences by gathering and analyzing customer data. Businesses can automate the personalization process using AI-powered personalization solutions, saving time and money while providing individualized experiences at scale.

Businesses must gather and analyze consumer data, personalize experiences, test, and refine the customization process, and continuously monitor performance to effectively adopt AI personalization at scale. Businesses may strengthen their ties with their consumers, boost customer loyalty, and promote business growth by doing so.

Amazon, Netflix, and Spotify are three instances of AI personalization in action. These businesses have used AI-powered algorithms to provide tailored experiences for their consumers, which has resulted in improved engagement, contentment, and loyalty.

AI personalization at scale is a game-changer for businesses looking to deliver individualized experiences to their customers. By leveraging the power of AI, businesses can automate the personalization process, save time and money, and build stronger relationships with their customers. As technology continues to evolve, AI personalization at scale is poised to become an increasingly important aspect of marketing and customer experience management.

ETHICAL CONSIDERATIONS WHEN USING AI FOR PERSONALIZATION

When it comes to using AI for personalization in marketing, it's important to consider ethical considerations to ensure that the use of AI doesn't violate people's privacy or lead to discrimination or bias. This section of the *AI Marketing Playbook* explores the ethical considerations that need to be considered when using AI for personalization.

Transparency and accountability: One of the key ethical considerations in using AI for personalization is transparency and accountability. It's important to be transparent about how AI is used to personalize marketing efforts and to be accountable for any outcomes or consequences that result from that use. That means making sure people understand how their data is being used and giving them control over their data.

Privacy: Privacy is an important ethical consideration when using AI for personalization. Organizations must ensure that data is collected and used in accordance with relevant data protection laws and regulations. They must also obtain user consent before collecting or using their data.

Bias and discrimination: Another key ethical consideration when using AI for personalization is avoiding bias and discrimination. AI algorithms can sometimes make biased or discriminatory decisions based on factors such as race, gender, or age. To avoid this, companies must ensure that their algorithms are unbiased and do not perpetuate or reinforce existing prejudices in society.

Data security: Data security is also an important ethical aspect when using AI for personalization. Organizations must ensure that the data they collect, and use is protected from unauthorized access, theft, or misuse. This includes the use of encryption, secure storage, and access controls to protect data.

Explain ability: Explain ability is an ethical consideration that relates to the transparency of AI algorithms. Companies need to be able to explain how their algorithms work and how they arrive at personalized recommendations or decisions. This is important for both regulatory compliance and building trust with customers.

Fairness: Fairness is an ethical consideration closely related to avoiding bias and discrimination. Businesses need to ensure their AI algorithms are fair, which means they treat all users equally and do not discriminate against any group based on factors like race, gender, or age.

Step-by-Step Instructions: Ethical Considerations in AI Personalization

1. **Establish Clear Ethical Guidelines**

   • Develop comprehensive guidelines that address data privacy, user consent, transparency, and fairness in the use of AI for personalization.

2. **Ensure Transparency in AI Operations**

   • Clearly communicate to users how their data is being used for personalization and the benefits they can expect from it.

3. **Prioritize User Consent and Data Privacy**

   • Implement mechanisms to obtain explicit consent from users for data collection and personalization, ensuring compliance with data privacy laws.

4. **Monitor for Bias and Discrimination**

   • Regularly audit AI algorithms for potential biases or discriminatory practices and take corrective actions, as necessary.

5. **Promote Fairness and Accessibility**

   • Ensure that AI-powered personalization does not disadvantage or exclude any group of users and is accessible to everyone.

6. **Educate Stakeholders about Ethical AI Use**

   • Conduct training and awareness programs for all stakeholders involved in AI personalization to understand and uphold ethical standards.

MEASURING THE ROI OF PERSONALIZATION WITH AI

Personalization has become a crucial part of successful marketing strategies. With the help of AI, companies can now offer their customers highly personalized experiences. However, it is important to measure the ROI of personalization to understand its effectiveness and to optimize investment in AI technologies.

Measuring the ROI of personalization with AI can be challenging as it is difficult to quantify the impact of personalization on customer behavior. However, by analyzing the right data and using the right metrics, organizations can understand the effectiveness of personalization.

One of the most critical metrics to measure the ROI of personalization with AI is the conversion rate. The conversion rate is the percentage of Web site visitors who take a desired action, make a purchase, or fill out a form. By measuring the conversion rate of personalized versus nonpersonalized content, companies can understand the impact of personalization on customer behavior.

A clothing retailer might use AI to personalize product recommendations on its Web site. One could measure the conversion rate of customers who receive personalized recommendations versus those who see generic recommendations. If the conversion rate of personalized recommendations is higher, this indicates that personalization is having a positive impact on customer behavior.

Another important metric to measure the ROI of personalization with AI is customer retention. Engagement refers to the level of interaction that customers have with a brand or product. By analyzing customer retention metrics such as time on site, click-through rates, and social media interactions, businesses can understand the impact of personalization on customer retention.

A hotel chain could use AI to personalize the emails it sends to its customers. They were able to measure the open and click rates of personalized emails compared to nonpersonalized emails. When personalized emails have higher open and click-through rates, it indicates that personalization increases customer retention.

Another important metric to measure the ROI of personalization with AI is customer retention. Customer retention measures the percentage of customers who continue to do business with a company over time. By analyzing customer retention rates for personalized and nonpersonalized experiences, businesses can understand the impact of personalization on customer retention.

Step-by-Step Instructions: Measuring the ROI of AI Personalization

1. **Define Key Performance Indicators (KPIs)**

   • Identify specific KPIs that will measure the success of AI personalization, such as conversion rates, customer engagement, and customer retention.

2. **Set Up Analytics and Tracking**

   • Implement analytics tools and tracking mechanisms to collect data on user behavior, engagement, and conversion metrics.

3. **Conduct A/B Testing**

   • Perform A/B testing to compare the performance of personalized experiences against nonpersonalized ones to directly assess the impact of AI personalization.

4. **Analyze Customer Lifetime Value (CLV)**

   • Calculate the CLV for customers experiencing personalized interactions and compare it to those who do not evaluate long-term fiscal impact.

5. **Assess Customer Satisfaction and Feedback**

   • Use surveys, feedback forms, and sentiment analysis to gauge customer satisfaction with personalized experiences.

6. **Calculate Cost-Benefit Analysis**

   • Analyze the costs associated with implementing AI personalization against the benefits gained in terms of increased revenue and customer engagement.

7. **Regularly Review and Adjust Strategies**

   • Continuously monitor the ROI of AI personalization initiatives and make necessary adjustments to strategies to maximize financial return and customer satisfaction.

An online grocery store might use AI to personalize the product recommendations and discounts it offers its customers. One could measure retention rates of customers who receive personalized recommendations and discounts versus those who see generic recommendations and discounts. If customer retention rates are higher for personalized experiences, this indicates that personalization increases customer retention.

Measuring the ROI of personalization with AI requires analyzing the right data and using appropriate metrics. By measuring metrics like conversion rates, retention, and retention, businesses can understand the impact of personalization on customer behavior and optimize their investment in AI technologies.

Personalization is the process of tailoring experiences to the unique needs, preferences, and characteristics of individual customers. With the advent of AI technologies, personalization has become even more sophisticated and effective, enabling companies to deliver personalized customer experiences at scale.

This chapter began by explaining how AI can be used for customization. AI algorithms can analyze vast amounts of customer data such as purchase history, browsing behavior, demographics, and social media activity to gain insights into customer preferences and behavior. Based on these insights, companies can create personalized experiences such as personalized product recommendations, personalized email campaigns, targeted advertising, and personalized content.

The chapter contained several examples of successful personalization strategies. One example is Netflix, which uses AI algorithms to recommend movies and TV shows to individual users based on their viewing history and preferences. Amazon, which uses AI algorithms to recommend products to customers based on their purchase history and browsing behavior.

Personalization at scale is another important topic covered in this chapter. Automating personalized experiences can be a challenging task, but with AI, companies can create personalized experiences for thousands or even millions of customers at once. AI algorithms can be used to automate customer interactions such as chatbots, voice assistants, and email campaigns to deliver personalized experiences at scale.

The chapter also highlighted ethical considerations in using AI for personalization. One of the main concerns is the potential for biases where AI algorithms can reinforce existing stereotypes and discrimination. To avoid these problems, companies need to ensure their algorithms are transparent, auditable, and free from any form of bias.

The chapter explained how to measure the ROI of personalization with AI. By tracking key metrics like customer satisfaction, engagement, retention, and revenue, businesses can assess the effectiveness of their personalization strategies and make data-driven decisions to improve them.

Chapter 5 of the *AI Marketing Playbook* provided a comprehensive overview of how companies can leverage AI for personalization, including examples of successful strategies, personalization at scale, ethical considerations, and ROI measurement.

CHATBOTS AND ARTIFICIAL INTELLIGENCE-POWERED CUSTOMER SERVICE

This chapter we will discuss the following key topics in detail:

Benefits of using chatbots and AI-based customer service: Explores the various benefits of using chatbots and AI-based customer service. Key benefits include 24/7 availability, faster response times, reduced operational costs, personalized experiences, and improved customer satisfaction.

Examples of successful chatbot implementations: Provides examples of companies that have successfully implemented chatbots to improve their customer service processes. These examples will highlight the different use cases for chatbots, including lead generation, customer support, and sales.

Designing conversational interfaces for chatbots: Discusses key considerations for designing effective conversational interfaces for chatbots. This includes topics like defining the bot personality, creating a seamless user experience, and providing clear navigation options.

Best practices for training chatbots with NLP: Discusses the importance of natural language processing (NLP) in chatbot training and provide best practices for improving its accuracy and effectiveness. This includes topics such as defining bot intent, training with different datasets, and incorporating feedback loops.

The future of AI-based customer service: virtual assistants and voice-activated interfaces: Looks at the future of AI-based customer service and the potential of virtual assistants and voice-activated interfaces. This section also explores the benefits and challenges of these emerging technologies and provides insight into how organizations can prepare for this future.

Overall, this chapter provides a comprehensive overview of chatbots and AI-powered customer service, including the benefits, best practices, and future opportunities in this exciting and rapidly evolving space.

BENEFITS OF USING CHATBOTS AND AI-POWERED CUSTOMER SERVICE

Chapter 6 of *AI Marketing Playbook* covers the topic of using chatbots and AI-powered customer service in marketing. Chatbots and AI-powered customer service have become increasingly popular in recent years as businesses look to streamline their customer service operations and provide better experiences for their customers. This chapter will explore the benefits of using chatbots and AI-powered customer service, including increased efficiency, improved customer experiences, and better data insights.

Increased Efficiency

One of the main benefits of using chatbots and AI-powered customer service is increased efficiency. Chatbots are designed to handle routine tasks and answer frequently asked questions, allowing customer service agents to focus on more complex issues. By automating routine tasks, companies can reduce the number of customer service agents needed and save time and money on training and onboarding.

In addition, chatbots can operate 24/7 and support customers 24/7. This means businesses can respond to customer queries and issues faster, which can result in higher customer satisfaction and retention.

Improved Customer Experiences

Another benefit of using chatbots and AI-powered customer service is improved customer experiences. Chatbots can answer customer inquiries immediately, reduce waiting times, and improve the overall customer experience. Additionally, chatbots can personalize interactions with customers, providing relevant information and recommendations based on their preferences and past interactions.

Additionally, chatbots can be integrated with other communication channels such as social media, email, and messaging apps to provide customers with a seamless experience across all touchpoints. By delivering seamless and personalized experiences, businesses can improve customer satisfaction and loyalty, which can lead to increased sales and revenue.

Better Knowledge of the Data

Chatbots and AI-powered customer service systems can significantly enhance business insights into customer interactions. These technologies not only track and analyze each customer interaction but also provide valuable data on customer behaviors and preferences. Crucially, they identify customer "pain points," which are specific issues or areas of dissatisfaction experienced by customers during their interaction with a service or product. By understanding these pain points, businesses can pinpoint specific areas for improvement in their offerings, tailor their marketing strategies more effectively, and ultimately enhance the overall customer experience by resolving these issues.

Additionally, AI-powered customer service can use machine learning (ML) algorithms to analyze substantial amounts of customer data, giving businesses predictive insights into customer behavior and preferences. With these insights, companies can personalize their marketing messages and offers, improve the effectiveness of their marketing campaigns, and generate more sales.

Profitable

The use of chatbots and AI-supported customer service can be a cost-effective solution for companies. Implementing chatbots and AI-powered customer service can be more economical than hiring and training additional customer service agents. Additionally, chatbots can handle a high volume of inquiries at once, reducing the need for businesses to hire additional customer service representatives during peak hours.

Chatbots and AI-powered customer service can reduce the likelihood of errors and inaccuracies in customer interactions. This can result in fewer customer complaints and lower costs associated with handling those complaints.

Scalable

Chatbots and AI-powered customer service scale to meet the needs of growing businesses. As a business grows, the volume of customer inquiries and interactions can increase, making it difficult for customer service agents to keep up.

In addition, chatbots and AI-powered customer service can be customized to a company's specific needs. By customizing the chatbot to a company's specific needs, businesses can ensure their customers receive the best possible support and experience.

HOW BUSINESSES HAVE IMPLEMENTED CHATBOTS SUCCESSFULLY

Chatbots are becoming increasingly popular among businesses as a tool to provide quick and effective customer support. They are computer programs designed to simulate conversation with human users, and they can be integrated with various platforms like Web sites, mobile apps, and social media platforms to provide customers with instant assistance.

This section will discuss in detail how companies have successfully implemented chatbots and the impact they have on improving customer satisfaction and generating revenue.

E-Commerce and Retail

One of the most important sectors for implementing chatbots is e-commerce and retail. Chatbots are commonly used to help customers navigate the product catalog, search for specific products, and make purchases. They can provide personalized product recommendations, upsell and cross-sell opportunities, and even process payments.

An example of a successful chatbot implementation is H&M, a Swedish multinational clothing retailer. H&M's chatbot on Facebook Messenger helps customers with various tasks, including finding products, checking product availability in nearby stores, and providing personalized style advice. The chatbot uses natural language processing (NLP) to understand customer queries and respond with relevant information. According to H&M, the chatbot resulted in a 70 percent increase in customer retention and a 50% increase in conversions.

Sephora, a cosmetics retailer, uses a chatbot available on Facebook Messenger and Kik and offers customers personalized makeup tips, product recommendations, and beauty tips. The chatbot also allows customers to book in-store appointments, track their loyalty points, and purchase products directly through the chat. Sephora's chatbot resulted in a 10% increase in booking rates and a conversion rate that is 2.5x higher compared to their Web site.

Banking and Finance

Chatbots are also becoming increasingly popular in the banking and finance sectors. They provide customers with instant support, help them manage their finances, and even process transactions.

An example is US-based bank Capital One's chatbot, called Eno, is available on various messaging platforms including SMS, Facebook Messenger, and Amazon Alexa. Eno can help customers with various tasks, for example, checking account balances, paying bills, and even canceling subscriptions. Eno uses ML algorithms to understand customer queries and provide personalized responses. According to Capital One, Eno has handled over 200 million customer interactions and has a customer satisfaction rate of over 90%.

TransferWise, a UK-based money transfer company is available on Facebook Messenger. TransferWise's chatbot helps customers send money to friends and family abroad. The chatbot provides customers with real-time exchange rates, processes payments, and even updates customers on the status of their transfer. TransferWise's chatbot resulted in a 53% increase in customer retention and a 1.5x higher conversion rate compared to their Web site.

BENEFITS OF USING CHATBOTS AND AI-POWERED CUSTOMER SERVICE

Using chatbots and AI-powered customer service offers several key benefits. These tools provide 24/7 availability, ensuring that customers can receive immediate assistance at any time, which significantly enhances customer satisfaction. They also streamline operations by handling routine inquiries efficiently, allowing human agents to focus on more complex issues. Moreover, AI-driven solutions can analyze vast amounts of data to personalize interactions and predict customer needs, leading to more effective and proactive service.

Travel and Hospitality

Chatbots are also commonly used in the travel and hospitality industry to assist customers with various tasks including booking flights, hotels, and restaurants, providing travel recommendations, and even providing concierge services.

An example is Marriott International, a multinational hotel chain. Marriott's chatbot, available on Facebook Messenger and Slack, helps customers book hotel rooms, check in, and even order room service. The chatbot also offers customers travel recommendations and local attractions. According to Marriott, the chatbot resulted in a 400% increase in customer satisfaction and a 20% increase in reservations.

KLM Royal Dutch Airlines has a chatbot, called BlueBot, that is available on various messaging platforms, including Facebook Messenger, WhatsApp, and WeChat. BlueBot helps customers with various tasks including booking flights, checking flight status, and even providing travel recommendations. The chatbot also offers customers information on baggage allowance and check-in procedures. According to KLM, BlueBot has resulted in a 40% increase in customer satisfaction and a 15% increase in customer retention.

Health

Chatbots are also being used in the healthcare industry to give patients instant support, help them manage their medications, and even provide mental health support.

An example is Woebot, a mental health chatbot developed by Stanford University researchers. Woebot provides users with cognitive behavioral therapy (CBT) techniques and personalized mental health support. The chatbot uses NLP and ML to understand user queries and provide relevant responses. According to a study, Woebot led to a significant reduction in symptoms of depression and anxiety.

Your.MD, a health chatbot available on Facebook Messenger and WhatsApp. Your.MD helps users identify symptoms and provides personalized health recommendations. The chatbot uses AI algorithms to analyze user responses and provide accurate health information. Your.MD is proven to provide trusted healthcare advice and has a customer satisfaction rate of over 90%.

To sum up, chatbots are becoming increasingly popular among companies in various industries to provide customers with instant support and improve customer satisfaction. The examples discussed previously illustrate how chatbots can be used effectively to help customers with various tasks, including product recommendations, financial transactions, travel bookings, and even mental health support. As AI technology continues to advance, expect chatbots to become even more mainstream in the business world, offering customers even more personal and efficient support.

Step-by-Step Instructions: Implementing Chatbots for Customer Service

1. **Identify Objectives:**

   • Determine what the chatbot should achieve (e.g., answer FAQs, support ticketing, lead generation).

2. **Choose a Platform:**

   • Select a chatbot platform that best fits technical capabilities and integration needs (e.g., Dialogflow, IBM Watson, Microsoft Bot Framework).

3. **Design the Conversation Flow:**

   • Map out potential dialogues, considering user intents and responses to ensure a natural conversation flow.

4. **Develop and Train the Chatbot:**

   • Use the chosen platform to create the chatbot. Input dialogue scripts and train the bot using NLP to recognize and respond to user queries effectively.

5. **Integrate with Your Systems:**

   • Connect the chatbot to CRM, databases, and other systems to pull in necessary information and deliver more personalized responses.

6. **Test and Refine:**

   • Conduct thorough testing with real users to identify gaps or issues in the conversation flow. Use feedback to refine the chatbot's responses and capabilities.

7. **Deploy and Monitor:**

   • Launch the chatbot on the company Web site, social media, or customer service channels. Continuously monitor its performance and user interactions to make ongoing improvements.

8. **Gather and Analyze Feedback:**

   • Regularly review the chatbot interactions to gain insights into user behavior and frequently asked questions and adjust the chatbot functionalities accordingly.

DESIGNING CONVERSATIONAL INTERFACES FOR CHATBOTS

Designing conversational interfaces for chatbots is a critical aspect of creating successful chatbot experiences. Chatbots are computer programs that simulate human conversation, and they have become increasingly popular in recent years due to advancements in AI and NLP. When it comes to chatbot design, the conversational interface is the key to delivering a positive user experience. This section will discuss the importance of designing conversational interfaces for chatbots and explore best practices for creating effective chatbot experiences.

Why Is Conversational Interface Design Important for Chatbots?

The conversational interface is how users interact with chatbots. It's the primary means by which they ask questions, get answers, and complete tasks. Therefore, the conversational interface is the most critical component of a chatbot design. A well-designed conversational interface can mean the difference between a chatbot that users love and one that frustrates them. The design of the conversational interface is important as it helps chatbots to be easy and intuitive to use. When users interact with a chatbot, they expect it to understand their questions and provide useful and relevant answers. A poorly designed chat interface can lead to misunderstanding, frustration, and user abandonment.

Another reason why conversational interface design is so important is that it helps set the personality and tone of the chatbot. Chatbots can have different personalities, from friendly and helpful to no-nonsense and professional. The conversational interface is where these personalities are expressed and can help users become more engaged with the chatbot.

Best Practices for Designing Conversational Interfaces for Chatbots

Keep it simple

One of the most important principles of conversational interface design is simplicity. Chatbots should be designed with a simple and intuitive interface that is easy to navigate. That means avoiding complex language, convoluted sentence structures, and overly complicated answers.

Use natural language chatbots

Chatbots should be designed to use natural language. That means avoiding forced and robotic responses and instead using language that sounds like it was written by a human. This can help users feel more comfortable and engaged with the chatbot.

Be clear and concise

Another important principle of conversational interface design is clarity. Chatbots must be designed to provide clear and concise answers to user questions. That means avoiding ambiguity and giving users the information they need as quickly as possible.

Integrate images

Visuals can be an effective way to enhance the conversational interface. Chatbots may use images, videos, and other media to provide users with a more engaging and interactive experience. However, it is important to ensure that the images are used appropriately and do not distract from the conversation.

Personalization of use

Personalization is another essential aspect of conversational interface design. Chatbots must be designed to understand user preferences and provide personalized responses and recommendations. This can help users feel more connected to the chatbot and more likely to use it in the future.

Provide feedback

Feedback is critical to the success of any chatbot. Chatbots should be designed to give users feedback after each interaction. This may include confirmation messages, error messages, and other comments to help users understand what's happening and how to proceed.

Test and iterate

It is important to continually test and iterate on chatbots. Chatbots must be developed with analytics and metrics in mind so designers can track user behavior and improve the chat interface over time. By continually testing and iterating on chatbots, designers can ensure they are providing the best possible experience for users.

Designing conversational interfaces for chatbots is a fundamental aspect of creating successful chatbot experiences. By following best practices, for example, by keeping it simple, using natural language, being clear and concise, incorporating images, using personalization, giving feedback and testing, and iterating, designers can create chatbots that are intuitive, engaging, and effective. The conversational interface is key to a positive user experience, and designers need to pay close attention to its design to ensure chatbots are easy to use, intuitive, and useful. This allows them to create chatbots that users love and that bring real value to businesses looking to use AI in their marketing efforts.

Step-by-Step Instructions: Designing Conversational Interfaces for Chatbots

1. **Understand User Needs:**

   • Conduct user research to understand the types of questions and interactions the audience will have with the chatbot.

2. **Define the Chatbot's Purpose:**

   • Clearly outline what the chatbot is designed to do, such as providing customer support, answering FAQs, or guiding users through a process.

3. **Create a Persona for the Chatbot:**

   • Develop a persona that aligns with the brand's voice and tone. This will guide the chatbot's style of communication, making interactions more relatable.

4. **Map Out Conversations:**

   • Design conversation flows that include user queries and chatbot responses. Ensure the conversation paths lead to clear outcomes or solutions for the user.

5. **Develop and Script Dialogues:**

   • Write dialogue scripts for the chatbot that sound natural and engaging, keeping the language simple and clear.

6. **Incorporate Natural Language Understanding (NLU):**

   • Utilize NLU capabilities to allow the chatbot to comprehend and respond to a variety of user inputs and intents effectively.

7. **Design for Clarity and Brevity:**

   • Ensure that the chatbot's messages are concise and to the point, avoiding jargon or complex language that could confuse users.

8. **Test with Real Users:**

   • Conduct user testing to gather feedback on the chatbot's conversational abilities and adjust improve the user experience.

9. **Iterate and Improve:**

   • Regularly update the conversation flows and scripts based on user feedback and changing needs to keep the chatbot effective and relevant.

10. **Ensure Accessibility:**

- Design the chatbot interface to be accessible to all users, including those with disabilities, by following accessibility best practices.

BEST PRACTICES FOR TRAINING CHATBOTS WITH NLP

In recent years, chatbots have become an increasingly popular tool for businesses to improve customer engagement and automate certain processes. However, building a chatbot that can handle complex conversations with customers requires a lot of work and expertise in NLP. This section will discuss the best practices for training chatbots with NLP.

Define the purpose and goals of the chatbot

The first step in creating an effective chatbot is to clearly define its purpose and goals. What should the chatbot do? What goals should it achieve? Should it answer customer questions, provide customer support, or help with sales? By defining the chatbot's purpose and goals, one can ensure that the chatbot is designed to meet the specific needs of their business.

Develop a complete chatbot design

After defining the chatbot's purpose and goals, the next step is to develop a comprehensive chatbot design. This includes deciding on the personality, tone, and communication style of the chatbot. Will the chatbot be friendly and chatty or more formal and professional? Will it use emojis and GIFs or stick with just text communication?

Users must decide on the structure of the chatbot and the flow of the conversation. This includes creating a conversation map that outlines the different paths the chatbot can take based on user input. The conversation card should be designed to guide users to the desired outcome, whether it's answering a question or completing a purchase.

Collect and analyze customer data

To train a chatbot effectively, one needs to understand the needs of their customers. This includes collecting and analyzing customer data such as chat logs, emails, and social media interactions. By analyzing this data, users can identify common customer questions and pain points, which can then be used to train the chatbot to provide better answers.

Use NLP to understand user input

NLP is a key component of chatbot development as it allows the chatbot to understand and interpret user input. NLP algorithms can be trained to identify several types of user input such as questions, statements, and commands. They can also be trained to recognize sentiment, intent, and context, which are critical to providing accurate and relevant answers.

Use ML to continually improve the chatbot

ML algorithms can be used to continually improve chatbot performance over time. By analyzing user interactions and feedback, the chatbot can be trained to provide more accurate and relevant answers. ML can also be used to recognize patterns in user behavior that can be used to optimize the flow and structure of the chatbot conversation.

Thoroughly test the chatbot

Before deploying a chatbot to customers, it's important to test it thoroughly to make sure it works as intended. This includes both manual and automated testing to identify errors or problems. It's also important to test the chatbot with a variety of user input to ensure it can handle a variety of scenarios.

Monitor and improve chatbot performance

Once the chatbot has been deployed, it is important to continuously monitor its performance and make improvements. This includes tracking metrics like user engagement, satisfaction, and conversion rates. By analyzing these metrics, users can identify areas where the chatbot could be improved and make necessary changes.

Building a chatbot with NLP requires a lot of work and expertise. By following these best practices, users can create a chatbot that is tailored to the needs of their business and capable of handling complex conversations with customers. Remember to define the chatbot's purpose and goals, develop a comprehensive chatbot design, gather and analyze customer data, use NLP to understand user input, use ML to continuously improve the chatbot, test the chatbot thoroughly, and monitor and improve its performance over time. By following these best practices, it's possible to create a chatbot that provides a great customer experience and helps a business achieve its goals.

Step-by-Step Instructions: Training Chatbots with NLP

1. **Define Objectives:**

   • Determine the desired achievements of the chatbot, such as customer support, sales, or information provision, to guide the NLP training process.

2. **Gather and Organize Data:**

    • Collect a comprehensive dataset of potential user inquiries, responses, and interactions relevant to the chatbot's objectives.

3. **Preprocess Data:**

    • Clean and organize the collected data, removing irrelevant information and standardizing the text for NLP training.

4. **Develop Training Models:**

    • Use the processed data to create NLP models that can understand and interpret user intent and sentiment.

5. **Train with Contextual Understanding:**

    • Incorporate context-aware algorithms to ensure the chatbot can follow conversation threads and maintain context over multiple interactions.

6. **Implement Intent Recognition:**

    • Utilize intent recognition within NLP to accurately determine what users want from their interactions with the chatbot.

7. **Test and Validate:**

    • Rigorously test the chatbot in various scenarios to ensure it accurately understands and responds to user inputs.

8. **Iterate and Optimize:**

    • Continuously refine the NLP model based on testing feedback and real-world interaction data to improve accuracy and relevancy.

9. **Integrate Continuous Learning:**

    • Implement ML algorithms that allow the chatbot to learn from interactions and improve over time.

10. **Ensure Ethical Use:**

    • Regularly review the chatbot's responses and the data used for training to prevent bias and ensure ethical use of NLP.

THE FUTURE OF AI-POWERED CUSTOMER SERVICE: VIRTUAL ASSISTANTS AND VOICE-ACTIVATED INTERFACES

AI is revolutionizing customer service, and companies are increasingly using AI-based solutions to improve customer interactions, reduce response times and improve customer satisfaction. Two of the most promising technologies in this regard are virtual assistants and speech-enabled interfaces, which have the potential to transform the way customers interact with businesses.

Virtual Assistants

A virtual assistant is an AI-powered program that can interact with customers using a chat interface, voice commands, or both. Virtual assistants can understand natural language queries and provide customers with relevant answers, guidance, or support. These assistants can be integrated into a company's Web site, app or messaging platform and provide 24/7 support and assistance to customers.

One of the main benefits of virtual assistants is their ability to respond to customer inquiries immediately. Traditional customer support methods such as email or phone support can be time consuming and may not always be available. Virtual assistants, however, can provide instant support, making them an ideal solution for time-sensitive requests or urgent issues. The virtual assistants are also scalable. They can handle multiple requests at the same time without requiring additional resources. This can be especially beneficial for companies with a high volume of customer inquiries, as it can reduce the workload on human customer service agents, allowing them to focus on more complex issues.

Virtual assistants not only offer instant support and scalability, but they can also help businesses collect valuable data about their customers. By analyzing customer inquiries and interactions, companies can gain insights into customer needs, pain points, and preferences that can inform product development and marketing strategies.

Voice-Enabled Interfaces

Voice-activated interfaces like Amazon Alexa or Google Home are another exciting development in AI-supported customer service. These interfaces allow customers to use voice commands to interact with businesses, ask questions, make requests, or complete transactions without having to use a keyboard or touchscreen.

Voice-enabled interfaces offer several advantages over traditional customer service methods. First, they're hands-free, allowing customers to interact with businesses while driving, cooking, or doing other tasks. This can be particularly beneficial for businesses that offer services or products that require hands-free operation, such as some automation systems or directions.

Voice-enabled interfaces also provide a more natural and intuitive customer experience than traditional customer service methods. Instead of navigating through complex menus or typing in queries, customers can simply ask a question or request in a conversational tone.

Another benefit of voice-enabled interfaces is their ability to personalize the customer experience. By analyzing customer inquiries and interactions, these interfaces can learn customer preferences and make personalized recommendations, for example, to suggest products or services that may be of interest to the customer.

Step-by-Step Instructions: Integrating Virtual Assistants into Customer Service

1. **Assess Needs and Objectives:**

   • Evaluate the specific customer service needs and objectives of your business to determine how a virtual assistant can best support these goals.

2. **Choose the Right Platform:**

   • Select a virtual assistant platform that aligns with your business needs, considering factors such as scalability, customization, and integration capabilities.

3. **Design the User Experience:**

   • Plan the user interaction flow, ensuring the virtual assistant provides a seamless and intuitive experience across different customer touchpoints.

4. **Develop the Knowledge Base:**

   • Compile a comprehensive knowledge base that the virtual assistant will use to answer queries, including FAQs, product information, and support procedures.

5. **Integrate with Existing Systems:**

   • Connect the virtual assistant with existing customer service, CRM, and data management systems to enable a unified and efficient service experience.

6. **Implement NLP:**

   • Utilize NLP technologies to enhance the virtual assistant's ability to understand and process customer queries accurately.

7. **Train the Assistant:**

   • Conduct extensive training sessions to ensure the virtual assistant can handle a wide range of customer interactions effectively.

8. **Launch a Pilot Program:**

   • Initiate a pilot program to test the virtual assistant's performance in real-world scenarios, allowing for adjustments before full-scale deployment.

9. **Monitor and Analyze Performance:**

   • Continuously monitor the virtual assistant's interactions to assess performance, identify areas for improvement, and gather customer feedback.

10. **Iterate and Improve:**

    • Regularly update the assistant's knowledge base and functionality based on performance data and customer feedback to enhance the overall customer service experience.

THE FUTURE OF AI-POWERED CUSTOMER SERVICE

As AI technology advances, virtual assistants and voice-enabled interfaces are likely to become even more sophisticated, offering businesses new ways to engage with customers and provide personalized support.

One area of AI technology that is expected to see significant growth is NLP. NLP is a computer program's ability to understand and interpret human language, allowing it to analyze customer queries and provide relevant responses. As NLP technology improves, virtual assistants and speech-enabled interfaces are becoming more accurate and effective in understanding customer queries and providing helpful responses.

Another growth area for AI-supported customer service is the use of predictive analytics. *Predictive analytics* involves using data analysis and ML algorithms to identify patterns and trends in customer behavior. By analyzing customer data, companies can anticipate customer needs and provide proactive support, for example by suggesting products or services even before the customer requests them.

Virtual assistants and voice-activated interfaces are two exciting technologies that are transforming the way businesses provide customer service. These AI-powered solutions provide out-of-the-box support, scalability, and personalized experiences, making them an ideal solution for organizations looking to enhance their customer service offerings. As AI technology advances, these solutions will become even more advanced and sophisticated, offering businesses new ways to engage with customers and enhance the customer experience.

While AI-enabled customer service solutions offer many benefits, organizations must also consider the potential risks and challenges associated with these technologies. There is a risk that virtual assistants or voice-enabled interfaces could misinterpret customer requests or provide inaccurate information, potentially damaging the customer experience and undermining trust in the organization.

To mitigate these risks, organizations must ensure they have strong privacy and data security policies in place, as well as comprehensive training and testing programs to ensure virtual assistants and voice-enabled interfaces are accurate and effective. In this way, companies can realize the full potential of AI-powered customer service solutions while maintaining the trust of their customers.

Chapter 6 of the *AI Marketing Playbook* covered the topic of chatbots and AI-powered customer service. The chapter began by discussing the benefits of using chatbots and AI-powered customer service. These benefits include an improved customer experience, reduced customer service costs, increased efficiency and productivity, and the ability to provide 24/7 customer support.

The chapter then provided examples of how companies have successfully implemented chatbots. Clothing company H&M implemented a chatbot that gives customers style recommendations based on their preferences. The airline KLM implemented a chatbot to help customers book flights and provide them with real-time updates on their flights.

The chapter then looked at designing conversational interfaces for chatbots. It explains that conversational interfaces should be designed to mimic human conversation, with clear, concise language and a friendly tone.

Overall, Chapter 6 of the *AI Marketing Playbook* provides a comprehensive overview of the benefits of chatbots and AI-powered customer service, as well as best practices for designing and training chatbots. Additionally, it offers insights into the future of AI-powered customer service, providing businesses with valuable information on how to stay ahead of the curve and providing the best possible customer experience.

IMAGE AND VIDEO RECOGNITION WITH ARTIFICIAL INTELLIGENCE

This chapter delves into how artificial intelligence (AI) can be utilized for recognizing images and videos, and how businesses can leverage this technology for various marketing strategies.

The chapter starts with an introduction to image and video recognition with AI, explaining how AI algorithms can identify and classify images and videos with high accuracy and speed. It also outlines the benefits of using AI for image and video recognition, including enhanced personalization, improved customer experiences, and increased efficiency in marketing campaigns.

Next, the chapter discusses successful examples of image and video recognition strategies implemented by businesses. It highlights how companies like Amazon, Google, and Pinterest have used AI to improve their product recommendations and search functionalities, and how social media platforms like Facebook and Instagram have implemented image recognition for content moderation and ad targeting.

The chapter then explores the various applications of computer vision in marketing. It discusses how businesses can use AI-powered image recognition for image search, visual content analysis, and even customer behavior analysis. It also covers how AI can be used to track and analyze video content, such as advertisements, to optimize marketing strategies and improve engagement.

The next section of the chapter discusses techniques for training image recognition models. It explains how machine learning (ML) algorithms can be trained on large datasets to accurately recognize objects, faces, and scenes in images and videos. It also covers several types of image recognition models, such as convolutional neural networks (CNNs) and object detection models.

The chapter addresses the ethical considerations when using AI for image and video recognition. It explores potential biases and privacy concerns associated with AI-powered image recognition, and how businesses can address these issues through data privacy and security measures.

Chapter 7 of the *AI Marketing Playbook* provides a comprehensive overview of image and video recognition with AI. It covers the benefits, successful examples, applications, training techniques, and ethical considerations associated with this technology, making it a valuable resource for businesses looking to leverage AI for their marketing strategies.

HOW AI CAN BE USED FOR IMAGE AND VIDEO RECOGNITION

Image and video recognition is one of the most popular AI applications in recent years. AI's ability to process massive amounts of visual data in seconds has revolutionized many industries, including marketing. This chapter will go into detail on how AI can be used for image and video recognition in marketing.

The use of AI for image recognition has become increasingly popular in recent years. Image recognition identifies objects or patterns in images, and AI can be trained to recognize objects and patterns with a high degree of accuracy. The applications of image recognition in marketing are wide and varied, from product recognition to image analysis for marketing campaigns.

One of the most common uses of image recognition in marketing is product recognition. AI can be used to recognize specific products in images, which can be useful for tracking product placement and monitoring inventory levels. A retailer could use image recognition technology to monitor the location and availability of products on store shelves. If a product is out of stock or missing, the AI system can pinpoint the problem so store managers can quickly take corrective action.

Another application of image recognition in marketing is sentiment analysis. AI can be trained to recognize emotions and attitudes such as joy, anger, or sadness expressed in images. This information can be used to tailor marketing campaigns to specific emotional responses, for example, using pictures of happy people to promote a product or service.

AI can also be used for image analysis in marketing campaigns. By analyzing images and identifying patterns and trends, marketers can gain valuable insights into customer behavior and preferences. An e-commerce retailer might use image analytics to identify popular trends in product images, for example, color combinations or styles. This information could be used to develop new product lines or marketing campaigns aimed at specific customer preferences.

In addition to image recognition, AI can also be used for video recognition. Video recognition analyzes video content to identify objects, patterns, and actions. This technology is useful for a variety of marketing applications, from video surveillance to video marketing campaigns.

One of the most common uses of video detection in marketing is video surveillance. AI can be used to analyze surveillance camera footage and identify potential threats such as suspicious people or activities. This technology can help improve security measures and protect employees and customers from harm.

Another use of video recognition in marketing is in video marketing campaigns. By analyzing video content, marketers can identify key themes and messages that resonate with customers. This information can be used to develop targeted marketing campaigns that are more likely to increase engagement and sales.

AI is a powerful image and video recognition tool, and its applications in marketing are wide and varied. From product recognition to sentiment analysis, image analysis, and video surveillance, AI can help marketers gain valuable insights into customer behavior and preferences, improve security measures, and design campaigns. As technology advances, expect even more innovative uses of AI in marketing in the years to come.

Step-by-Step Instructions: Implementing AI for Product Recognition in Images and Videos

1. **Define Objectives:** Identify the specific goals for using AI in product recognition. This could include improving online shopping experience, enhancing inventory management, or supporting marketing efforts.

2. **Select the Right AI Technology:** Choose an AI model or service that specializes in image and video recognition. Consider factors like accuracy, processing speed, and the ability to integrate with existing systems.

3. **Gather and Prepare Data:** Collect a diverse set of images and videos featuring the products AI should recognize. Label these assets accurately to train the AI model effectively.

4. **Train the AI Model:** Use the prepared dataset to train the AI model. Ensure that the model can accurately identify various products under various conditions, such as different angles, lighting, and backgrounds.

5. **Test and Validate the Model:** Evaluate the AI model's performance by testing it with a separate set of images and videos. Adjust and retrain the model as needed to improve accuracy and reduce false positives or negatives.

6. **Integrate with Existing Systems:** Once satisfied with the model's performance, integrate it into existing platforms, such as e-commerce sites, inventory management systems, or marketing tools.

7. **Monitor and Update Regularly:** Continuously monitor the AI system's performance and gather feedback from users. Regularly update the model with new data to maintain its accuracy and relevance.

By following these steps, businesses can effectively implement AI for product recognition in images and videos, leading to improved customer experiences and more efficient operations.

SUCCESSFUL IMAGE AND VIDEO DETECTION STRATEGIES

Image and video recognition are among the most promising areas of AI, with significant potential to transform the way marketers approach advertising and customer engagement. Leveraging deep learning algorithms and advanced computer vision techniques, image and video recognition technologies can help businesses automatically analyze visual content, identify objects, and people, and extract valuable information about consumer behavior and experiences.

This section will examine some of the most successful image and video recognition strategies used in marketing today, including object recognition, face recognition, and emotion recognition.

Object Detection

Object recognition is a form of computer vision that allows machines to identify and classify objects in images or videos. It involves training algorithms on large datasets of tagged images, allowing them to recognize specific features and patterns associated with different types of objects.

An example of a successful object recognition strategy in marketing is the use of product recognition in e-commerce. By analyzing product images, retailers can automatically identify specific products and extract metadata such as brand, model, and price to improve the accuracy and efficiency of their product listings.

Amazon's mobile app uses image recognition to help customers find products quickly and easily. The app allows users to photograph a product or scan a barcode, and then provides information about the product, including price, availability, and customer reviews.

Face Recognition

Face recognition is a powerful technology that allows machines to recognize and analyze human faces in images or videos. It detects and maps facial features like eyes, nose, and mouth and compares them to a database of known faces to identify individuals.

An example of facial recognition in marketing is the use of facial recognition technology on social media platforms. Facebook uses facial recognition to automatically tag users in photos, allowing them to easily identify images and share them with their friends and family.

Face recognition is also used in market research to track consumer reactions to products and advertising. By analyzing facial expressions, marketers can gain insight into consumers' emotions and preferences, allowing them to optimize their advertising campaigns and product designs.

Step-by-Step Instructions: Setting Up Visual Search Capabilities

1. **Identify the Scope:** Determine what types of images or products the visual search should focus on. Decide whether it will cover all products or only specific categories.

2. **Choose the Right Technology:** Select a visual search technology or platform that fits e-commerce needs. Consider aspects like accuracy, scalability, and ease of integration with current e-commerce platform.

3. **Prepare Product Catalog:** Ensure that the product catalog is well-organized, and each product image is high-quality and clearly represents the item. This will be crucial for the visual search tool to accurately match user-uploaded images with the products.

4. **Integrate the Visual Search Tool:** Work with the web development team or the visual search provider to integrate the tool into an e-commerce platform. This typically involves API integration or adding a specific code snippet to the site.

5. **Train the AI Model:** If the visual search tool uses AI, it may be necessary to train the model with specific product images so it can accurately recognize and match products in user-uploaded images.

6. **Test the Visual Search Functionality:** Before going live, thoroughly test the visual search feature to ensure it accurately recognizes and suggests products. Check its performance across different product categories and image types.

7. **Launch and Promote:** Once the functionality seems secure, launch the visual search feature on the platform. Promote it to customers through marketing campaigns, tutorials, and highlighting its benefits and ease of use.

8. **Monitor and Optimize:** Continuously monitor the performance of the visual search feature. Collect user feedback and use analytics to understand usage patterns and areas for improvement. Regularly update the product database and refine the AI model to enhance search accuracy and user experience.

By implementing these steps, businesses can successfully integrate visual search capabilities into their e-commerce platforms, providing customers with a more intuitive and efficient way to find products.

Emotion Detection

Emotion recognition is a branch of computer vision that allows machines to analyze human emotions and reactions in images or videos. It involves using ML algorithms to recognize and interpret facial expressions, body language, and other cues associated with various emotional states.

An example of emotion detection in marketing is the use of sentiment analysis in social media monitoring. By analyzing social media posts and comments, businesses can gain insights into consumer sentiment and opinions about their brand, products, and services.

Social media monitoring platform brand watch uses natural language processing and ML algorithms to identify and categorize social media posts based on sentiment. By analyzing the tone and content of these posts, businesses can gain valuable insights into consumer preferences and behavior and adjust their marketing strategies to better meet customer needs.

Another example of emotion recognition in marketing is the use of biometrics to measure consumer responses to advertising. By tracking physiological responses like heart rate, skin conductance, and facial expressions, marketers can gain insight into how consumers are emotionally responding to different types of ads.

Market research company Nielsen uses biometric data to measure the effectiveness of television advertising. By tracking viewers' physiological responses, Nielsen can identify which ads are most effective in eliciting emotional responses and increasing brand loyalty.

Image and video recognition technologies are rapidly changing the way companies approach marketing and customer engagement. By leveraging ML algorithms and computer vision techniques, marketers can gain valuable insights into consumer behavior and preferences to optimize their advertising campaigns and product designs.

Object recognition, face recognition, and emotion recognition are among the most successful image and video recognition strategies used in marketing today. Whether it's improving e-commerce product listings, tracking consumer responses to ads, or measuring sentiment on social media, these technologies help businesses gain competitive advantage by better understanding their customers and providing more personalized and engaging experiences.

However, as with any technology, there are also ethical considerations to consider. Privacy concerns surrounding facial recognition have led to increased scrutiny and regulation in some jurisdictions. As such, organizations need to ensure they use image and video recognition technologies responsibly, with full transparency and in compliance with individuals' privacy laws.

Image and video recognition technologies offer enormous potential for businesses looking to gain deeper insights into consumer behavior and preferences. By leveraging advanced computer vision techniques and ML algorithms, marketers can gain valuable insights and optimize their advertising campaigns and product designs, but, as with any technology, it is important to use these tools responsibly and with due regard to ethical and privacy concerns.

Step-by-Step Instructions: Training AI for Emotion Recognition in Videos

1. **Define Objectives:** Clearly outline what the overall goal is with emotion recognition. Determine whether the focus is on customer feedback, content analysis, or another application.

2. **Gather Data:** Collect a diverse dataset of videos that display a range of emotions. Ensure the dataset includes various demographics, settings, and scenarios to train a robust model.

3. **Annotate Data:** Label the video data with the corresponding emotions. Use clear categories like happiness, sadness, anger, and so on. Consider employing specialists or crowdsourcing platforms for accurate annotation.

4. **Select a Model:** Choose an appropriate AI model for emotion recognition. CNNs and recurrent neural networks (RNNs) are commonly used for video analysis.

5. **Preprocess the Data:** Process the video data to a uniform format suitable for training. This may include resizing frames, normalizing pixel values, and segmenting videos into shorter clips if necessary.

6. **Train the Model:** Feed the processed and annotated video data into the AI model. Use ML techniques to train the model to recognize and classify emotions accurately.

7. **Validate and Test:** Evaluate the model's performance using a separate validation dataset. Adjust parameters and retrain as necessary to improve accuracy and reduce bias.

8. **Implement and Integrate:** Once the model is sufficiently accurate, implement it into the relevant system or platform for sentiment analysis. Ensure seamless integration with existing customer feedback mechanisms or content analysis tools.

9. **Monitor and Refine:** Continuously monitor the AI system's performance in real-world scenarios. Collect feedback and additional data to refine and retrain the model, enhancing its accuracy and reliability over time.

By following these steps, businesses can develop AI systems capable of detecting and analyzing emotions in videos, providing valuable insights for customer sentiment analysis and content optimization.

APPLICATIONS OF COMPUTER VISION IN MARKETING

Computer vision is a powerful technology that has a wide range of applications in marketing. In this section of the *AI Marketing Playbook*, we'll explore some of the keyways in which computer vision is being used to drive marketing efforts.

Image and video recognition for targeted advertising is one of the most powerful applications of computer vision in marketing. By analyzing the content of images and videos, computer vision algorithms can identify the products, brands, and people and use this information to target ads to specific audiences.

If a fashion brand wants to target customers interested in jeans, computer vision algorithms can analyze images and videos of people wearing jeans to identify key characteristics such as color, style, and fit. This information can be used to target ads to customers who are likely to be interested in the same features.

Object recognition for personalized experiences is another application of machine vision in marketing. By using computer vision algorithms to recognize objects such as cars, clothing, or even people, marketers can create personalized experiences tailored to the interests and preferences of individual customers.

For example, a car dealership could use object recognition to identify the make and model of cars customers are interested in and then use that information to create personalized offers and promotions. Similarly, a clothing retailer could use object recognition to identify the style and color of clothing customers are interested in and then use that information to create personalized recommendations and promotions.

Face recognition is another powerful tool that can be used in marketing. By analyzing facial expressions, computer vision algorithms can recognize emotions such as happiness, anger, and sadness, and use this information to understand how customers are responding to products, services, and marketing messages.

For example, a grocery brand could use facial recognition to analyze how customers respond to different tastes and textures and use that information to develop more appealing products. Similarly, a retailer could use facial recognition to analyze how customers react to different product displays, store layouts, and use that information to optimize the customer experience.

Augmented reality (AR) for product viewing is used to create AR experiences that allow customers to view products in real-world environments. By using computer vision algorithms to recognize objects and surfaces in the real world, marketers can create realistic and immersive product visualizations that help customers make more informed purchasing decisions.

For example, a furniture retailer could use AR to show customers what different pieces of furniture would look like in their home. By using computer vision to recognize the size and layout of the space, the retailer was able to create a realistic visualization of how the furniture would fit and look in the space.

Computer vision is a powerful tool that is transforming the way marketers understand and interact with customers. By using computer vision algorithms to analyze images and videos, recognize objects and emotions, and create AR experiences, marketers can create more personalized, engaging, and effective marketing campaigns.

TECHNIQUES FOR TRAINING IMAGE RECOGNITION MODELS

Image recognition models have become essential tools in many industries, including marketing. With the help of deep learning techniques, these models can accurately detect and classify objects in images, which can be used for various purposes such as product recognition, visual search, and image tagging.

This chapter of the *AI Marketing Playbook* will discuss some of the most effective techniques for training image recognition models.

Convolutional Neural Networks (CNNs)

CNNs are a class of deep neural networks designed specifically for image recognition tasks. They consist of multiple layers of convolution filters that can detect local patterns in an image and layers of pooling that can reduce the spatial dimensions of feature maps.

One of the most popular CNN architectures is VGGNet, which has achieved top results in various image recognition benchmarks. VGGNet uses a series of 3x3 convolutional layers, followed by maximum pooling layers and ending with a fully connected layer.

Another popular CNN architecture is ResNet, which introduced the concept of residual connections to overcome the gradient leak problem in deep neural networks. ResNet performed even better than VGGNet on many image recognition tasks.

Learning Transfer

Transfer learning is a technique that consists of using a previously trained model as a starting point for a new task. In image recognition, this means taking a pretrained model, trained on a large dataset like ImageNet, and fitting it to a smaller dataset specific to the new task.

Transfer Learning can save a lot of time and computational resources because the pretrained model has already learned to recognize the basic features of the images. This technique has proven effective in many image recognition tasks, including object detection, segmentation, and classification.

The Inception v3 model trained on ImageNet can be fitted to a fashion image dataset to create a fashion recognition model. Retailers can use it to automatically mark their products with relevant attributes and improve their search and recommendation systems.

Data Increase

Data expansion is a technique that generates new training data by applying random transformations to the original data. This can help increase the size of the training set, reduce overfitting, and improve the model's generalization performance.

Common data enhancement techniques include flipping, rotating, scaling, cropping, and adding noise to images. These transformations can help the model recognize objects in different orientations, sizes, and lighting conditions.

A fashion detection model can be trained on a dataset of product images that have been augmented with random rotations and translations. This can help the model better recognize products from different angles and improve its accuracy on real data.

Learning Together

Ensemble learning is a technique that combines multiple models to improve overall performance. In image recognition, this can be achieved by training multiple models with different architectures or hyperparameters and averaging their predictions.

Ensemble learning can help reduce the variance and bias of individual models and improve their generalization performance. It has proven effective in many image recognition tasks, including object detection and segmentation.

A set of CNN models with different architectures can be used to create a robust product recognition system. This can be used by retailers to automatically recognize and classify their products on real images and improve their inventory management and marketing strategies.

Training image recognition models requires a combination of deep learning techniques, including CNNs, transfer learning, data augmentation, and ensemble learning. By leveraging these techniques, marketers can create powerful image recognition systems that can enhance their product recognition, visual search, and image labeling.

ETHICAL CONSIDERATIONS WHEN USING AI FOR IMAGE AND VIDEO RECOGNITION

When using AI for image and video recognition, it is crucial to consider ethical considerations to ensure that the technology is being used in a responsible and respectful manner. Here are some important ethical considerations to keep in mind:

Bias and Fairness: AI algorithms can be biased when trained on data that is not representative of the population being analyzed. This can lead to unfair and discriminatory results. When an AI algorithm is trained on images of mostly white people, it may have trouble accurately identifying people of other races.

Privacy: When using AI for image and video recognition, it is important to consider the privacy implications of the technology. If the analyzed images or videos contain sensitive information such as medical records or personal data, it may be necessary to obtain the consent of the people in the images or videos.

Consent: In some cases, it may be necessary to obtain the consent of the people in the analyzed images or videos. This is especially important if the images or videos are going to be used for commercial purposes.

Accuracy: The AI algorithms used for image and video recognition may not always be accurate. This can lead to misidentification and other errors. It is important to ensure that technology is used in a way that minimizes these errors.

Transparency: It is important to be transparent about how AI algorithms are used for image and video recognition. This includes being clear about what data is being analyzed and how algorithms are making decisions.

Accountability: When using AI algorithms to make decisions that have real-world consequences, it is important to ensure there is a mechanism to hold those responsible accountable. This includes ensuring there is a way to challenge decisions made by AI algorithms.

Human surveillance: While AI algorithms can be powerful tools for image and video recognition, it's important to remember that they are not infallible. Human oversight is important to ensure technology is used responsibly and ethically.

Examples of Ethical Considerations in AI Image and Video Recognition

- Using AI to analyze images of people without their consent, raising privacy concerns.
- AI algorithms are used to make hiring or lending decisions based on facial recognition, raising concerns about accuracy and bias.
- Using AI to create deepfake videos that can be used to spread misinformation and harm people.
- The use of AI to analyze images and videos in law enforcement may raise concerns about accuracy, bias, and potential privacy breaches.

Ethical considerations are crucial when using AI for image and video recognition. These considerations include ensuring fairness and minimizing bias, respecting privacy, and obtaining consent, ensuring accuracy and transparency, and providing accountability and human oversight. Taking these considerations into account ensures that AI is used responsibly and ethically.

Step-by-Step Instructions: Implementing AI for Enhanced Image and Video Tagging

1. **Define Tagging Requirements:** Identify what types of tags are needed (e.g., objects, people, activities, themes) and establish the tagging criteria to ensure consistency.
2. **Choose an AI Model:** Select an AI model suitable for image and video analysis, such as CNNs for image recognition or deep learning models optimized for video data.
3. **Collect and Prepare Data:** Gather a diverse set of images and videos representative of specific content. Ensure the data is well-organized and of high quality for training the AI model.
4. **Annotate Training Data:** Label the collected images and videos with accurate tags manually to create a training dataset for the AI model. Use detailed and consistent annotations to improve model learning.
5. **Train the AI Model:** Use the annotated dataset to train the AI model, ensuring it learns to recognize and tag the relevant features in images and videos accurately.

6. **Test and Optimize the Model:** Evaluate the model's performance on a separate set of images and videos. Refine and retrain the model as needed to improve accuracy and reduce false positives or negatives.

7. **Integrate with Content Management System (CMS):** Incorporate the trained AI model into a CMS or digital asset management system to automate the tagging process for new content.

8. **Monitor and Update:** Regularly review the AI system's tagging accuracy and update the model with new data or annotations to adapt to evolving content and tagging needs.

9. **User Training and Feedback:** Educate users on how to use the AI-enhanced tagging system effectively and gather feedback to identify any issues or areas for improvement.

10. **Continual Learning:** Implement mechanisms for the AI system to learn from ongoing tagging activities, allowing it to continuously improve and adapt to new content types and tagging requirements.

By following these steps, businesses can implement AI-driven solutions to automate and enhance the image and video tagging process, leading to better content organization and searchability.

SUMMARY

How AI can be used to recognize images and videos. The chapter began by explaining how AI can be used to recognize images and videos. AI can be used to classify images, identify objects, recognize patterns, and analyze video content. AI-powered image and video recognition can help marketers better understand their customers, improve product recommendations, and create more engaging content.

Examples of successful image and video detection strategies: The chapter contained examples of successful image and video detection strategies, such as using AI to recognize logos and branding elements in images and videos. It also discusses how AI-powered image and video recognition can help improve the accuracy of product recommendations, personalize content, and optimize ad targeting.

Applications of computer vision in marketing: The chapter then dealt with the various applications of computer vision in marketing. These applications include facial recognition for personalized experiences, visual search for product discovery, AR for immersive experiences, and object recognition for retail analytics.

Techniques for training image recognition models: The chapter explained how image recognition models can be trained using supervised and unsupervised learning techniques. It also discusses the importance of data quality, feature selection, and model optimization in training accurate image recognition models.

Ethical considerations when using AI for image and video recognition: The chapter concluded by highlighting some ethical considerations when using AI for image and video recognition. These included issues related to privacy, bias and fairness, and transparency in algorithmic decision-making.

Chapter 7 of this book focuses on image and video recognition with AI. The chapter discussed how AI can be used for image and video recognition, provides examples of successful image and video recognition strategies, discusses the applications of computer vision in marketing, techniques for training image recognition models, and ethical considerations when using AI for images and videos.

CHAPTER 8

USING ARTIFICIAL INTELLIGENCE (AI) FOR SOCIAL MEDIA MARKETING

I n this chapter, readers will learn how artificial intelligence (AI) can be used to enhance social media marketing efforts and provide a competitive advantage to businesses.

The chapter begins by discussing the several ways in which AI can be utilized in social media marketing, such as automating tasks, personalizing content, and improving customer engagement. Using machine learning (ML) algorithms and natural language processing (NLP), AI can analyze large amounts of social media data to identify trends, patterns, and insights that can inform marketing strategies.

Next, the chapter provides examples of successful social media marketing campaigns that have incorporated AI. AI-powered chatbots have been used to improve customer service on social media platforms, while personalized content generated by AI has been shown to increase engagement and conversion rates.

The chapter also delves into the role of sentiment analysis in social media marketing. By analyzing the tone and sentiment of social media posts, businesses can better understand customer feedback and tailor their marketing efforts accordingly.

Moreover, the chapter explores the use of predictive analytics in social media marketing. By analyzing historical data and identifying patterns, businesses can make predictions about future customer behavior and adjust their marketing strategies accordingly.

Lastly, the chapter examines the impact of AI on social media advertising. AI-powered tools can help businesses target specific audiences and optimize their ad campaigns for maximum impact.

Overall, Chapter 8 of the book provides a comprehensive overview of how AI can be used to enhance social media marketing efforts, offering practical examples and insights for businesses looking to leverage AI technology in their marketing strategies.

HOW AI CAN BE USED FOR SOCIAL MEDIA MARKETING

AI is revolutionizing the way companies approach marketing. Social media marketing is a key area where AI has been increasingly utilized to help businesses connect with their customers and maximize their social media presence. This section discusses in detail how AI can be used for social media marketing.

The History of AI in Social Media Marketing

Social media marketing has become increasingly important in recent years as companies seek to harness the power of social media to connect with customers and promote their products and services. In the early days of social media marketing, businesses focused on creating content and publishing it on social media platforms in hopes of gaining a following and generating engagement.

As social media platforms became more sophisticated, companies realized that they needed more than simply great content to be successful. They needed to be able to analyze data, spot trends, and understand their audiences to create content that resonated with them.

This is where AI comes in. AI algorithms can analyze massive amounts of data and spot patterns and trends that humans may not be able to see. This has enabled companies to create more targeted social media campaigns, tailored to the interests and behaviors of their customers.

Using AI for Social Media Marketing

There are several ways that AI can be used for social media marketing. The following methods explain different options to implement into your social media marketing strategy.

Social Listening

Social listening involves monitoring social media channels for mentions of a particular brand, product, or service. This allows individuals to keep track of what people are saying about their business and respond to negative comments or criticism.

AI can help automate the social listening process by using NLP algorithms to analyze social media posts and identify sentiments. This allows companies to quickly identify negative comments or complaints and respond to them in a timely manner.

Step-by-Step Instructions for Social Listening with AI

1. **Define Objectives and Key Topics:**

   - Identify desired goals of social listening: brand monitoring, competitor analysis, industry trends, customer sentiment, and so on.
   - List key topics, keywords, brand names, product names, and any relevant hashtags or phrases associated with the brand of choice and its competitors.

2. **Choose the Right AI Social Listening Tool:**

   - Google and select an AI-powered social listening tool that aligns with the project objectives and offers comprehensive monitoring across various social media platforms.
   - Ensure the tool can analyze data in real time, provide sentiment analysis, and detect patterns or trends.

3. **Set Up a Monitoring Dashboard:**

   - Configure the tool to track the identified keywords, phrases, and hashtags.
   - Customize the dashboard to display the metrics and data that are most relevant to project objectives, such as mentioned volume, sentiment analysis, source breakdown, and so on.

4. **Refine the Search with Filters:**

   - Use filters to refine the data by location, language, date range, or specific social media platforms to get more targeted insights.
   - Adjust these filters as needed to focus on emerging trends or specific events related to the specified brand.

5. **Automate Alerts and Notifications:**

   - Set up automated alerts to be notified of unusual spikes in mentions or shifts in sentiment, indicating potential issues or opportunities.
   - Define thresholds for alerts based on the brand's normal social media activity levels.

6. **Analyze Data and Generate Reports:**

   - Regularly review the collected data and generate reports to analyze the performance of the specified brand on social media.
   - Look for insights on customer sentiment, brand health, campaign performance, and competitor activity.

7. Act on Insights:

- Use the insights gained from social listening to inform the marketing strategy, content creation, customer service, and product development.
- Engage with the audience by responding to feedback, joining conversations, and addressing any concerns or questions.

8. Review and Optimize:

- Periodically review the effectiveness of the chosen social listening strategy and adjust the keywords, filters, or tool settings based on the evolving dynamics of social media conversations.
- Stay updated with the latest features of the preferred AI tool to continually enhance social listening capabilities.

By following these steps, one can effectively set up and utilize AI tools for social listening, enabling users to monitor and analyze social media mentions and conversations related to their brand comprehensively.

Content Creation

Creating compelling content is essential to successful social media marketing. However, creating content that resonates with a particular audience can be a challenge.

AI can help by analyzing data about customer behavior and preferences to create personalized content tailored to everyone. Netflix uses AI algorithms to recommend movies and TV shows to users based on their viewing history.

Step-by-Step Instructions: Content Creation and Automation

1. Define Content Goals:

- Establish clear goals to achieve with social media content (e.g., increase brand awareness, drive traffic, generate leads).

2. Select the Right AI Tools:

- Research and choose AI tools that align with content goals. Tools like Hootsuite, Buffer, or Zoho Social can automate scheduling, while AI writers like Jasper or Writesonic can assist in content creation.

3. Set Up the AI Tools:

- Create accounts and configure settings in chosen AI tools. Integrate them with social media accounts to ensure seamless content management.

4. **Develop a Content Strategy:**

   • Plan a content calendar, including the type of content (text, images, videos), topics, and posting frequency. Use AI to analyze trends and audience preferences to inform strategy.

5. **Create Content with AI Assistance:**

   • Utilize AI-driven content creation tools to generate initial drafts, ideas, or images. Customize the content to ensure it aligns with the preferred brand's voice and goals.

6. **Schedule and Automate Posting:**

   • Use the scheduling feature in AI tools to automate the posting of content at optimal times for engagement. Ensure the schedule reflects content strategy and audience's online behavior.

7. **Monitor and Analyze Performance:**

   • Regularly review the performance of automated content using analytics tools. Look for insights on engagement rates, best-performing content types, and audience behavior.

8. **Iterate and Optimize:**

   • Based on performance data, adjust content strategy and automation settings. Experiment with different types of content, posting times, and frequencies to optimize engagement and reach.

By following these steps, users can effectively implement AI-driven systems for creating and scheduling social media content, enhancing the chosen brand's presence and engagement on social platforms.

Chatbots

Chatbots are becoming increasingly popular on social media platforms to provide customer support and engage with customers. Chatbots use AI algorithms to understand natural language and provide automated responses to customer queries.

Chatbots for Customer Interaction: A Guide

1. **Define Objectives and Scope:**

   • *Identify the goals:* Determine what the chatbot should achieve (e.g., answering frequent questions, providing support, facilitating purchases).

• *Establish the scope:* Define the range of topics and services the chatbot will cover.

2. Select the Right Platform:

   • Choose a chatbot development platform based on compatibility with social media channels, required features, and budget.
   • Consider platforms like Chatfuel, ManyChat, or custom solutions if there are specific needs.

3. Design the Conversation Flow:

   • Map out the chatbot's conversation paths, including greetings, common queries, and fallback responses.
   • Use a flowchart to visualize the conversation paths and decision points.

4. Develop and Train the Chatbot:

   • Build the chatbot using the chosen platform, implementing the designed conversation flow.
   • Train the chatbot with a range of inputs to recognize and respond to user queries accurately. Utilize NLP to enhance understanding.

5. Integrate with Social Media Platforms:

   • Connect the chatbot to relevant social media accounts, ensuring it can interact with users through comments, messages, or posts.
   • Follow platform-specific guidelines for integrating chatbots, such as Facebook's Messenger API.

6. Test and Optimize:

   • Conduct thorough testing to ensure the chatbot responds correctly in various scenarios.
   • Collect feedback from test users and adjust improve performance and user experience.

7. Launch and Promote:

   • Deploy the chatbot on social media channels officially.
   • Promote the chatbot through social media posts, Web site, and other marketing channels to encourage user engagement.

8. Monitor and Update Regularly:

   • Regularly review the chatbot's interactions to identify areas for improvement.

- Update the chatbot's responses and conversation flow based on user feedback and changing business needs.

9. Analyze Performance and Gather Insights:

- Use analytics tools to track the chatbot's performance, user engagement, and conversion rates.
- Analyze the data to gain insights into customer behavior and preferences and adjust social media strategy accordingly.

Advertisement

AI algorithms can analyze data about customer behavior and preferences to create targeted advertising campaigns. Facebook uses AI algorithms to target ads to users based on their interests and behaviors.

Influencer Marketing

Influencer marketing involves partnering with social media influencers to promote specific brands or products. AI helps identify influencers who are likely to have the greatest impact on an audience based on their engagement and social media follower rates.

Challenges When Using AI for Social Media Marketing

While AI offers many benefits for social media marketing, there are also some challenges that businesses need to be aware of. Among the many benefits, the following things should be considered as cause for potential issues. These include:

Data Quality: AI

Algorithms rely on data to make decisions. If the data is of inadequate quality or distorted, this can lead to inaccurate results. Companies need to ensure they are using high-quality data to train their AI algorithms.

Privacy Concerns

AI algorithms can collect and analyze large amounts of personal data. This raises privacy and data security concerns. Businesses need to ensure they follow privacy and security best practices to avoid legal or ethical issues.

Cost

Implementing AI for social media marketing can be expensive. Businesses need to weigh the costs against the potential benefits to determine whether the investment is worth it.

AI is changing the way companies approach social media marketing. By using AI algorithms to analyze data and identify patterns and trends, businesses can create more targeted social media campaigns, tailored to their customers' interests and behaviors.

SUCCESSFUL SOCIAL MEDIA MARKETING STRATEGIES

Social media marketing has become an integral part of any modern marketing strategy, with more than four billion people worldwide using social media platforms. However, with so many users and such a vast amount of data, it can be challenging for marketers to keep up with the latest trends, engage their audiences, and drive conversions. This is where AI can play a crucial role in social media marketing.

This section discusses successful social media marketing strategies that use AI. It also provides detailed examples of each strategy to illustrate their effectiveness.

Personalization

Personalization is a crucial aspect of social media marketing. By tailoring content to the interests and preferences of individual users, marketers can increase engagement and increase conversions. However, manually analyzing data to create personalized content can be time-consuming and ineffective. This is where AI can help.

AI algorithms can analyze large amounts of data, such as user behavior and interactions with content, to identify patterns and preferences. Based on this analysis, marketers can create personalized content that resonates with their target audience.

An example of successful personalization using AI is Spotify. Spotify's AI algorithms analyze user behavior such as listening history, search history, and playlists to recommend personalized music. Spotify's Discover Weekly Playlist is a prime example of this. Each week, the algorithm generates a new playlist based on the user's listening history, keeping users engaged and encouraging them to stay on the platform.

Another example of successful personalization using AI is Amazon. Amazon's recommendation system uses AI to analyze user behavior such as search history, purchase history, and recommend personalized products. This has been highly effective as Amazon reports that 35% of their earnings come from their recommendation system.

Chatbots

Chatbots are another effective way to use AI in social media marketing. Chatbots can interact with customers, answer questions, and provide support in real time, which can improve customer satisfaction and increase conversions. However, creating and managing chatbots manually can be time-consuming and complex. This is where AI can help. AI–powered chatbots can use NLP to understand and respond to customer queries just like a human would. This can improve the customer experience, reduce response times, and increase engagement.

An example of a company that has had success with the use of chatbots with AI is H&M. H&M's Facebook Messenger chatbot uses AI to answer customer questions such as product availability and size. The chatbot can also suggest products based on customer preferences and purchase history. This has resulted in a 70% increase in orders placed through the chatbot.

Another example of a company's success with the use of chatbots with AI is Sephora. Sephora's chatbot on Kik uses AI to provide personalized beauty recommendations based on customer preferences and skin type. The chatbot can also help customers find nearby stores and make appointments. This has resulted in an 11% increase in sales at Sephora.

Analysis of Feelings with Sentiment Analysis

Sentiment analysis is the process of using AI to analyze data from social networks such as tweets and posts to determine the sentiment of the content. This can clarify how customers perceive a brand or product and help marketers make informed decisions.

An example of successful sentiment analysis with AI is Airbnb. Airbnb uses sentiment analysis to analyze customer feedback and reviews, which helps the company improve its services and products. Airbnb also uses sentiment analysis to monitor social media platforms for mentions of businesses, allowing them to respond to customer inquiries and feedback in real time.

Another example of successful sentiment analysis with AI is Coca-Cola. Coca-Cola uses sentiment analysis to analyze social media data and identify emerging trends and themes. This helps the company create more relevant and engaging content for their target audience.

AI has become an indispensable tool in social media marketing. By using AI-powered strategies like personalization, chatbots, and sentiment analysis, marketers can improve customer retention, increase conversions, and better understand their audience. Successful examples of these strategies include Spotify's personalized music recommendations, H&M and Sephora's chatbots for customer support and product recommendations, and Airbnb and Coca-Cola's use of sentiment analytics to improve customer satisfaction and create relevant content.

As social media platforms evolve and generate more data, AI will become an even more key component of successful social media marketing strategies. Marketers who adopt AI-powered tools and techniques early on have a competitive advantage when it comes to reaching and connecting with their target audience.

Step-by-Step Instructions: Sentiment Analysis Implementation

1. **Define Objectives:**

    - Determine what the goals are with sentiment analysis (e.g., understanding customer sentiment toward a product, tracking brand reputation, gauging reactions to a marketing campaign).

2. **Choose the Right Tools and Platforms:**

    - Select sentiment analysis tools that best fit the project needs. Options include Brandwatch, Hootsuite Insights, and Talkwalker.
    - Ensure the tool can integrate with specific social media platforms and offers comprehensive analytics features.

3. **Collect and Prepare Data:**

    - Set up the tool to collect relevant data from social media channels. This includes posts, comments, and mentions related to the brand or keywords.
    - Clean the data if necessary to remove irrelevant content or spam.

4. **Configure Sentiment Analysis Parameters:**

    - Define the keywords, phrases, and topics that the sentiment analysis tool will track.
    - Customize the settings to distinguish between positive, negative, and neutral sentiments effectively.

5. **Run the Sentiment Analysis:**

    - Initiate the analysis process within the tool to evaluate the collected social media content.
    - Monitor the tool's performance and adjust the parameters as needed to improve accuracy.

6. **Analyze and Interpret Results:**

    - Review the sentiment analysis results to identify overall trends and patterns in customer sentiment.
    - Look for changes in sentiment over time, differences between platforms, and variations related to specific topics or events.

7. **Take Action Based on Insights:**

    - Use the insights gained from sentiment analysis to inform marketing strategies, product development, and customer service approaches.

- Address negative sentiment by engaging with customers, resolving issues, and making improvements based on feedback.

8. **Report and Share Findings:**

- Compile the results and insights into reports for internal stakeholders.
- Share the findings with relevant departments (e.g., marketing, product development, customer service) to implement necessary changes.

9. **Monitor Continuously:**

- Set up ongoing monitoring to track sentiment over time and detect any sudden changes or emerging trends.
- Regularly update analysis parameters and data collection methods to capture the most relevant and accurate information.

By following these detailed steps, users can effectively implement sentiment analysis in their social media marketing strategy, gaining valuable insights into customer emotions and perceptions that can help shape their business decisions.

THE ROLE OF SENTIMENT ANALYSIS IN SOCIAL MEDIA MARKETING

Social media has become an integral part of our daily lives. People use social media platforms like Facebook, Twitter, Instagram, and LinkedIn to connect with others, share information, and express their opinions. Social media has also emerged as a powerful tool for businesses to reach out to their customers, build brand awareness, and engage with their audience. However, the sheer volume of data generated on social media can be overwhelming for businesses. This is where sentiment analysis comes in.

Sentiment analysis is the process of analyzing social media data to determine the emotional tone behind a piece of content. It helps businesses to gauge how their audience is responding to their brand, products, and services. By analyzing social media data, businesses can gain insights into their audience's opinions, preferences, and behavior, and make informed decisions about their marketing strategies. This section will explore the role of sentiment analysis in social media marketing.

Understand the Audience

One of the key benefits of sentiment analysis is that it helps companies better understand their audience. By analyzing social media data, companies can determine the demographics, preferences, and behavior of their target audience. They can use this information to tailor their marketing strategies to the needs of their target audience. If a company determines that its audience is predominantly female, it can create marketing campaigns that target women. Sentiment analysis also helps businesses identify their audience's pain points and challenges, allowing them to create targeted marketing campaigns that address those issues.

Brand Reputation Monitoring

Another important application of sentiment analysis in social media marketing is brand reputation monitoring. Social media platforms provide a forum for customers to share their positive or negative experiences with a brand. By monitoring social media data, businesses can track what their customers are saying about their brand and products. Users can use sentiment analysis to determine the sentiment behind customer feedback and respond accordingly. If a customer leaves a negative comment about a product, the company can respond with a solution or explanation to address the customer's concerns. By responding to customer feedback in a timely and appropriate manner, companies can build customer trust and loyalty.

Identification of Trends and Opportunities

Sentiment analysis also helps companies identify trends and opportunities in their industry. By analyzing social media data, businesses can identify emerging trends and topics that are popular with their audience. Users can use this information to create content and marketing campaigns that take advantage of these trends. If a company determines that its target audience cares about sustainability, it can create marketing campaigns that promote its green practices. Sentiment analysis also helps companies identify gaps in the market and create new products and services that fill those gaps.

Measurement of Marketing Effectiveness

Sentiment analysis helps companies measure the effectiveness of their marketing campaigns. By analyzing social media data, companies can determine the sentiment behind customer feedback on their marketing campaigns. They can use this information to measure the success of their marketing campaigns and make necessary adjustments. If a marketing campaign receives overwhelmingly negative sentiment, the company can adjust its messaging or targeting to improve the campaign's effectiveness.

Sentiment analysis is a valuable tool for companies looking to leverage social media in their marketing strategies. By analyzing social media data, companies can better understand their target audience, monitor their brand reputation, identify trends and opportunities, and measure the effectiveness of their marketing campaigns. Sentiment analysis enables companies to make informed decisions about their marketing strategies, build customer trust and loyalty, and drive business growth.

PREDICTIVE ANALYTICS AND SOCIAL MEDIA MARKETING

This part of Chapter 8 of the *AI Marketing Playbook* delves into the topic of predictive analytics and social media marketing. Predictive analytics is the process of using data, statistical algorithms, and ML techniques to identify the likelihood of future outcomes based on historical data. Social media marketing, however, is the practice of using social media platforms to promote a product or service.

There was also information about how predictive analytics can be used in social media marketing. This can be done by analyzing social media data to gain insights into customer behavior, preferences, and sentiments. These insights can be used to predict future customer behavior and inform marketing strategies.

One application of predictive analytics in social media marketing is sentiment analysis. Sentiment analysis involves using NLP algorithms to analyze social media posts and determine the sentiment expressed in the text. Sentiment can be classified as positive, negative, or neutral. By analyzing sentiment, marketers can gain insights into customer opinions and feelings about a particular product or brand.

A company might use sentiment analysis to analyze social media posts about a new product release. If the sentiment is overwhelmingly negative, the company might decide to delay the launch or make changes to the product to address the concerns. Contrastingly, if the sentiment is positive, the company might decide to launch the product early or increase marketing efforts.

Another application of predictive analytics in social media marketing is customer segmentation. Customer segmentation involves dividing a customer base into groups based on shared characteristics such as demographics, interests, or behaviors. Predictive analytics can be used to analyze social media data and identify patterns in customer behavior. These patterns can then be used to create customer segments and inform marketing strategies.

A company might use predictive analytics to analyze social media data and identify customers who are most likely to purchase a particular product. The company can then target these customers with personalized marketing messages and offers to increase the likelihood of a purchase.

Predictive analytics can also be used to identify influencers and brand ambassadors. Influencers are individuals with a large following on social media who can promote a product or brand to their followers. Brand ambassadors are individuals who are loyal to a particular brand and are willing to promote the brand to others. Predictive analytics can be used to analyze social media data and identify individuals who are most likely to become influencers or brand ambassadors.

A company will use predictive analytics to analyze social media data and identify individuals who have a large following and frequently post about topics related to the company's products or services. The company can then reach out to these individuals and offer them incentives to become brand ambassadors or influencers.

Predictive analytics can also be used to optimize social media advertising. Social media platforms such as Facebook and Instagram offer advertising options that allow advertisers to target specific audiences based on demographics, interests, and behaviors. Predictive analytics can be used to analyze social media data and identify the most effective targeting options for a particular product or service.

A company that uses predictive analytics to analyze social media data and identify the demographics, interests, and behaviors of customers who are most likely to purchase a particular product. The company can then use this information to create targeted social media ads that are more likely to reach potential customers and result in a purchase.

Predictive analytics can be a powerful tool in social media marketing. By analyzing social media data, marketers can gain insights into customer behavior, preferences, and sentiments. These insights can be used to predict future customer behavior and inform marketing strategies. Applications of predictive analytics in social media marketing include sentiment analysis, customer segmentation, identifying influencers and brand ambassadors, and optimizing social media advertising. By using predictive analytics in social media marketing, companies can improve the effectiveness of their marketing efforts and increase customer engagement and loyalty.

Step-by-Step Guide: Predictive Analytics for Social Media Trends

1. **Define Objectives:**

    • Determine what the goals are with predictive analytics, such as identifying emerging trends, forecasting customer behavior, or optimizing campaign strategies.

2. **Gather and Prepare Data:**

    • Collect historical social media data, including posts, comments, likes, shares, and user demographics.
    • Clean and preprocess the data by removing irrelevant content, correcting errors, and standardizing formats.

3. **Select the Right Tools and Technologies:**

    • Choose analytics tools and software that support predictive modeling and are compatible with specific data sources. Options may include R, Python with libraries (e.g., Pandas and Scikit-learn), or specialized platforms like Hootsuite Insights.

4. Develop Predictive Models:

- Use statistical methods or ML algorithms to analyze historical data and build models that can predict future trends. Common techniques include regression analysis, time series analysis, and neural networks.
- Train models using historical data, ensuring they can accurately forecast future social media behavior.

5. Test and Validate the Models:

- Evaluate the predictive models using a separate dataset to test their accuracy and reliability.
- Use metrics like mean absolute error (MAE), root mean squared error (RMSE), or R-squared to measure performance.

6. Implement the Models:

- Integrate the predictive models into the social media analytics framework to begin forecasting trends and customer behavior.
- Ensure the models can access real-time data feeds for ongoing analysis and prediction.

7. Monitor and Refine:

- Regularly monitor the performance of predictive models and make adjustments as needed to improve accuracy and relevance.
- Update the models with new data and refine algorithms to adapt to changing social media dynamics and customer behaviors.

8. Translate Insights into Action:

- Use the insights gained from predictive analytics to inform social media strategy, content planning, and marketing campaigns.
- Anticipate customer needs, tailor content to emerging trends, and optimize social media presence based on predictive insights.

9. Review and Report:

- Conduct periodic reviews to assess the impact of predictive analytics on social media performance.
- Generate reports and dashboards that summarize predictive insights, trends, and the effectiveness of strategies being used.

By following these steps, users can leverage AI to predict social media trends and customer behaviors, allowing for more strategic planning and proactive decision-making in their social media marketing efforts.

THE IMPACT OF AI ON SOCIAL MEDIA ADVERTISING

Social media advertising has become an essential component of many companies' marketing strategies, and the rise of AI has had a significant impact on the effectiveness and efficiency of these efforts. This section will explore how AI has transformed social media advertising and some of the key examples that illustrate these changes.

Personalization and targeting: One of the key impacts of AI on social media advertising is the ability to personalize ads and target them more effectively. ML algorithms can analyze user data to create detailed customer profiles, including demographics, interests, and purchasing behavior. These profiles can then be used to create highly targeted advertising campaigns that are more likely to resonate with specific audiences.

Facebook uses ML algorithms to analyze user data and create lookalike audiences. These audiences are groups of users who have similar interests and behaviors to existing customers. Advertisers can use these similar audiences to target their ads to the people most likely to be interested in their products or services.

Ad optimization: Another important impact of AI on social media advertising is the ability to optimize ads for better performance. AI algorithms can analyze ad performance in real-time and adjust improve its effectiveness. The AI can adjust ad targeting, bids, and creativity to maximize ad engagement and conversions.

Google Ads uses ML algorithms to automatically optimize ad performance. The platform analyzes ad performance data and makes bid and targeting adjustments to maximize ad conversions. This process is known as smart bidding and has been shown to significantly improve ad performance.

Chatbots and conversational marketing: AI-powered chatbots are becoming increasingly popular in social media advertising. These chatbots can interact with users in real time, answering questions and providing personalized recommendations. Chatbots can be integrated with social media messaging apps like Facebook Messenger, allowing advertisers to interact directly with customers.

Sephora uses a chatbot on Facebook Messenger to provide customers with personalized makeup recommendations. The chatbot asks questions about the user's preferences and makes recommendations based on their answers. This approach has proven to be highly effective, with over 60% of users saying they were happy with the recommendations provided.

Image and video recognition: AI-powered image and video recognition technologies are also having a significant impact on social media advertising. These technologies can analyze visual content to understand its context and meaning, allowing advertisers to create more targeted and personalized advertising campaigns.

Pinterest uses ML algorithms to analyze the visual content of images uploaded by users. This analysis allows the platform to create more accurate and relevant recommendations for users, as well as targeted advertising campaigns for advertisers.

Predictive analytics: AI-powered predictive analytics can analyze large data sets to identify patterns and predict future behavior. This technology can be used in social media advertising to identify potential customers and predict their behavior, allowing advertisers to create more targeted campaigns.

The impact of AI on social media advertising has been significant as technology transforms the way advertisers target, engage with, and convert customers. The ability to personalize and target ads more effectively has resulted in better engagement and conversion rates. AI-powered ad optimization has improved ad performance and reduced costs. Chatbots and conversational marketing have enabled more personalized and engaging interactions with customers.

Predictive analytics have enabled more targeted and personalized advertising campaigns. Predictive analytics has enabled advertisers to identify potential customers and predict their behavior. As AI technology advances, expect even more significant changes to social media advertising in the future. It's important for marketers to stay abreast of these developments and understand how they can leverage AI to create more effective and efficient social media advertising campaigns. By using AI technology, advertisers can create more than personalized and engaging customer experiences, improve ad performance, and get better results from their marketing efforts.

Chapter 8 of the *AI Marketing Playbook* addressed the topic of using AI for social media marketing. In today's digital age, social media has become a crucial platform for businesses to reach their target audience, build brand awareness and connect with customers. AI has revolutionized how companies approach social media marketing, providing them with a wealth of data and insights that can be used to develop more effective strategies.

The chapter began by discussing how AI can be used for social media marketing. AI algorithms can analyze vast amounts of data, including user behavior, demographics, and social media trends, to provide businesses with actionable insights. AI can also be used to automate tasks such as content creation, scheduling, and publishing, which can save companies time and resources. AI-powered chatbots can be used to provide 24/7 customer support and improve customer retention.

An example of successful social media marketing strategies using AI is personalization. AI algorithms can analyze user behavior and preferences to provide users with personalized content and recommendations. This can improve user experience and increase engagement. Netflix uses AI to recommend content to users based on their viewing history, preferences, and behavior.

Another example of successful social media marketing strategies using AI is influencer marketing. AI algorithms can analyze social media data to identify influencers who are having a significant impact on the targeted audience. This can help companies identify the right influencers to work with and develop more effective influencer marketing campaigns.

The chapter also discussed the role of sentiment analysis in social media marketing. Sentiment analysis is the process of analyzing social media data to determine the overall sentiment or opinion about a particular brand, product, or service. AI algorithms can analyze social media data to identify positive and negative sentiments, which can help businesses to understand how their customers feel about their brand and products. This information can be used to develop more effective marketing strategies and improve customer satisfaction.

Predictive analytics is another AI-powered tool that can be used for social media marketing. Predictive analytics uses data, statistical algorithms, and ML techniques to identify patterns and predict future outcomes. In social media marketing, predictive analytics can be used to analyze user behavior and predict future trends. This information can be used to develop more effective marketing strategies and improve customer engagement.

The chapter explored the impact of AI on social media advertising. AI algorithms can analyze social media data to identify the most effective ad placements, target audiences, and ad content. This can help businesses to develop more effective ad campaigns and increase ROI. AI-powered chatbots can also be used to provide personalized advertising experiences to users, which can improve customer engagement and increase conversion rates.

AI has revolutionized the way businesses approach social media marketing. AI-powered tools such as personalization, influencer marketing, sentiment analysis, predictive analytics, and social media advertising have enabled businesses to develop more effective marketing strategies, improve customer engagement, and increase ROI. As AI technology continues to evolve, businesses that embrace AI-powered social media marketing strategies are likely to gain a competitive advantage in the marketplace.

PREDICTIVE ANALYTICS WITH ARTIFICIAL INTELLIGENCE (AI)

This chapter will introduce how artificial intelligence (AI) can be used for predictive analytics, provide examples of successful predictive analytics strategies, cover the basics of predictive modeling with machine learning (ML) algorithms, discuss time series analysis and predictive analytics, and explain the limitations of predictive analytics with AI.

- *How AI can be used for predictive analytics:* Predictive analytics is the practice of using data, statistical algorithms, and ML techniques to determine the likelihood of future outcomes based on historical data. AI can be used to improve the accuracy and speed of predictive analytics by analyzing large amounts of data, spotting patterns, and making predictions.

AI can perform predictive analytics using various techniques such as regression, decision trees, neural networks, and clustering. These techniques are used to identify patterns in data and create predictive models that can be used to predict future outcomes. By using AI, companies can analyze data faster, spot patterns that human analysts might not recognize, and make predictions with greater accuracy.

- *Examples of successful predictive analytics strategies:* There are several examples of successful predictive analytics strategies. Netflix uses predictive analytics to recommend movies and TV shows to its customers based on their viewing history. Amazon also uses predictive analytics to recommend products to customers based on their browsing and purchase history.

Banks and other financial institutions use predictive analytics to detect fraud, assess credit risk and predict customer behavior. Predictive analytics is also used in the healthcare industry to predict disease outbreaks, identify patients at risk of developing certain diseases, and improve treatment outcomes.

- *The basics of predictive modeling with ML algorithms:* Predictive modeling involves the use of statistical algorithms and ML techniques to create predictive models. Predictive models are used to predict future outcomes based on historical data. ML algorithms such as regression, decision trees, and neural networks are used to build predictive models.

In predictive modeling, the first step is to collect and preprocess data. Data preprocessing includes cleaning the data, handling missing values, and converting the data into a format that can be used for modeling. The next step is to choose the appropriate ML algorithm for the problem at hand.

Once the algorithm is selected, the data is divided into training and test datasets. The training set is used to train the model, while the testing set is used to evaluate the model's performance. After training, the model is tested in the test suite to evaluate its performance.

Time series analysis and predictive analysis: Time series analysis is a statistical technique for analyzing time series data. *Time series data* is a sequence of data points collected over time, for example, stock prices, weather data, or Web site traffic. Predictive analytics can be applied to time series data to predict future values.

To carry out time series analyses, the data are first cleaned and preprocessed. The next step is to identify trends, seasonality, and other patterns in the data. Once patterns are identified, a predictive model can be built using ML algorithms such as autoregression, moving average, or exponential smoothing.

Time series analysis and predictive analytics are used in a variety of applications, for example, to predict stock prices, predict demand for products, and predict Web site traffic.

The limitations of AI predictive analytics: Although AI predictive analytics is a powerful tool, it has some limitations. One of the limitations is the quality of the data used for modeling. If the data is inaccurate, incomplete, or biased, the predictive model may not be accurate. Another limitation is the complexity of the model. Complex models can be difficult to interpret and may not generalize well to new data.

Furthermore, predictive models can only predict future outcomes based on historical data. Unanticipated events such as natural disasters or economic downturns could have a material impact on future results that historical data cannot reflect. Predictive models require continuous monitoring and updating to ensure their accuracy and relevance.

Chapter 9 of the *AI for Marketing Playbook* provides an overview of how AI can be used for predictive analytics, examples of successful predictive analytics strategies, the fundamentals of predictive modeling using ML algorithms, time series analysis and predictive analytics, and limitations of predictive analytics with AI. By understanding the possibilities and limitations of AI-powered predictive analytics, companies can make more informed decisions about how to use these technologies to improve their marketing efforts.

HOW AI CAN BE USED FOR PREDICTIVE ANALYTICS

Predictive analytics refers to the use of statistical algorithms and ML techniques to analyze historical data and make predictions about future events or trends. It involves the use of various data mining techniques, statistical modeling, and ML algorithms to analyze data and make predictions. Predictive analytics can be used in a wide range of applications, including marketing, finance, healthcare, and customer service. This section of the *AI Marketing Playbook* will focus on how AI can be used for predictive analytics in marketing.

Marketing is an essential aspect of any business, and predictive analytics can help businesses make data-driven decisions that can help increase revenue, reduce costs, and improve customer satisfaction. AI-powered predictive analytics tools can help marketers gain valuable insights into customer behavior, preferences, and purchasing patterns. By using predictive analytics in marketing, businesses can improve their marketing strategies and better target their audiences.

Types of Predictive Analytics

There are two main types of predictive analytics: descriptive analytics and predictive analytics. *Descriptive analysis* analyzes historical data to gain insight into past events and trends. This type of analysis is useful for understanding what happened in the past and why it happened.

Predictive analytics, however, involves analyzing historical data to make predictions about future events and trends. This type of analysis is useful for identifying patterns and trends in data and making predictions based on those patterns' uses of predictive analytics in marketing

There are various applications of predictive analytics in marketing. Some of the most common are:

- *Customer churn prediction analytics* can be used to predict which customers are likely to churn or end business with a company. By analyzing data about customer behavior, preferences, and buying patterns, companies can identify customers who are at risk of leaving the company and take proactive steps to retain them.

A wireless company might use predictive analytics to identify customers who are likely to switch to a competitor. By analyzing data about customer usage patterns, the company can identify customers who are using their phonEes less, not renewing their contracts, or complaining about service issues. The company can then target those customers with specific offers, discounts, or incentives to entice them to stay.

- *Marketing campaign optimization* predictive analytics can be used to optimize marketing campaigns by identifying the most effective channels, messages and offers. By analyzing data about customer behavior, preferences and reactions to past campaigns, companies can determine which campaigns are most likely to resonate with their target groups.

A clothing retailer could use predictive analytics to determine which products are most popular with its customers. By analyzing sales, returns, and customer feedback data, the retailer can identify which products are most likely to sell and adjust their marketing campaigns accordingly.

- *Personalization of customer experiences:* Predictive analytics can be used to personalize customer experiences by providing personalized recommendations, offers and content. By analyzing data about customer behavior, preferences, and buying patterns, companies can determine which products and services are most relevant to individual customers.

An online retailer could use predictive analytics to recommend products to customers based on their browsing and purchase history. By analyzing customer behavior data, the retailer can identify which products are most likely to appeal to each customer and adjust their recommendations accordingly.

- *Sales forecasting:* Predictive analytics can be used to forecast sales and revenue by analyzing data about past sales, market trends and customer behavior. By using predictive analytics to forecast sales, companies can make more informed decisions about inventory management, staffing, and resource allocation.

A software company might use predictive analytics to forecast sales of its latest product. By analyzing data on previous sales of comparable products, market trends, and customer feedback, the company can forecast how many units of the new product it expects to sell in the next quarter and adjust its production and sales strategies accordingly.

- *Identify cross-sell and up-sell opportunities:* Predictive analytics can be used to identify cross-sell and up-sell opportunities by analyzing data about customer behavior, preferences and buying patterns. By identifying which products and services are most likely to appeal to individual customers, businesses can create targeted offers and promotions to increase sales.

A financial services firm could use predictive analytics to determine which customers are most likely to be interested in its investment services. By analyzing data about customer demographics, income and savings patterns, the company can determine which customers are most likely to be interested in investing and create targeted offers and promotions to encourage them to do so challenges when using AI for predictive analytics in marketing.

While AI-powered predictive analytics tools offer many benefits, there are also some challenges in using these tools in marketing. Some of the most common challenges are:

- *Data quality:* Predictive analytics relies heavily on data, and data quality can significantly affect the accuracy of predictions. If data is incomplete, inaccurate, or out-of-date, predictive analytics models may not be reliable.
- *Privacy and security:* Predictive analytics requires companies to collect and analyze large amounts of data, which can raise privacy and security concerns. Businesses must ensure they collect and store data in accordance with relevant regulations and that they have adequate measures in place to protect customer data from cyber threats.
- *Complexity:* AI-powered predictive analytics tools can be complex and require special skills and experience to use them effectively. Businesses may need to invest in training and development to ensure their marketing teams have the skills and knowledge to use these tools.
- *Cost:* AI-powered predictive analytics tools can be expensive, and organizations may need to invest significant resources to implement these tools effectively. This can be a barrier for small and medium-sized businesses that may not have the resources to invest in these tools.

Predictive analytics is a powerful tool that can help businesses make data-driven marketing decisions. AI-powered predictive analytics tools can help businesses gain valuable insights into customer behavior, preferences, and purchasing behavior that can be used to optimize marketing campaigns, personalize the customer experience, and increase sales. While using AI for predictive analytics in marketing presents some challenges, companies that invest in these tools and overcome these challenges can gain a significant competitive advantage.

SUCCESSFUL PREDICTIVE ANALYTICS STRATEGIES

Predictive analytics is an essential component of AI marketing. It is a type of data analysis that leverages ML and statistical algorithms to predict future events based on historical data. Predictive analytics has been increasingly used by marketers to make informed decisions about their marketing campaigns, including the selection of target audiences, the choice of marketing channels, and the development of content strategies. This chapter will explore successful predictive analytics strategies in the *AI Marketing Playbook*, including case studies and timelines.

Audience Segmentation

One of the most successful predictive analytics strategies is audience segmentation. This strategy involves segmenting the audience into smaller, more specific groups based on their interests, behaviors, demographics, and other factors. By segmenting the audience, one can tailor their marketing messages and campaigns to their specific needs and preferences, resulting in higher engagement and more conversions.

A good example of audience segmentation using predictive analytics is Amazon product recommendations. Amazon uses ML algorithms to analyze customer behavior, including purchase history, browsing history, and search queries, to suggest products they are likely to buy. This approach has been extremely successful for Amazon, increasing sales, retention, and loyalty.

Amazon's product recommendation engine was first introduced in 1999 and has continually improved over the years. Today, Amazon's recommendation engine is one of the most mature and successful examples of predictive analytics in marketing.

Predicting Customer Abandonment

Another successful predictive analytics strategy is predicting customer churn. This strategy involves predicting which customers are most likely to leave a business so proactive steps can be taken to keep them. Predicting customer churn is especially important in industries like telecom, where customers can easily switch providers.

A good example of using predictive analytics to predict customer churn is T-Mobile's Next Best Action program. T-Mobile uses ML algorithms to analyze customer behavior, including usage patterns and payment history, to predict which customers are most likely to leave the company. T-Mobile then takes proactive steps to retain those customers, such as offering discounts or upgrades. This approach was extremely successful for T-Mobile as it reduced churn and increased customer loyalty.

Timeline: T-Mobile's Next Best Action program first launched in 2016 and has continued to improve over the years. Today, T-Mobile's program is one of the most successful examples of predictive analytics in marketing.

Personalization of Content

Another successful predictive analytics strategy is content personalization. This strategy involves tailoring content to the specific interests and likes of the audience, resulting in higher engagement and conversions. Personalization of content can be achieved through a variety of techniques, including recommendations, personalized emails, and targeted advertising on social media.

A good example of content personalization using predictive analytics is Netflix's recommendation engine. Netflix uses ML algorithms to analyze customer behavior, including viewing history and ratings, to suggest content they are likely to enjoy. This approach has been extremely successful for Netflix, increasing customer retention, retention, and loyalty.

Timeline: Netflix's recommendation engine was first introduced in 2006 and has been continually improved over the years. Today, Netflix's recommendation engine is one of the most sophisticated and successful examples of predictive analytics in marketing.

Predictive Scoring of Leads

Another successful predictive analytics strategy is predictive lead scoring. This strategy involves predicting which leads are most likely to become customers, allowing a company to prioritize their sales efforts and resources. Predictive lead scoring can be accomplished through a variety of techniques, including ML algorithms, behavioral scoring, and demographic scoring.

A good example of predictive lead scoring using predictive analytics is HubSpot's lead scoring model. HubSpot uses ML algorithms to analyze customer behavior, including Web site visits, form submissions, and email engagement, to qualify leads based on their likelihood to convert. This approach has been extremely successful for HubSpot, increasing sales productivity and revenue.

Timeline: HubSpot's lead scoring model was first introduced in 2011 and has continually improved over the years. Today, the HubSpot model is one of the most successful examples of predictive analytics in marketing.

Predictive analytics is an essential part of AI marketing. It empowers marketers to make informed decisions about their marketing campaigns, including audience segmentation, churn prediction, content personalization, and predictive lead qualification. These strategies have been successful for companies like Amazon, T-Mobile, Netflix, and HubSpot, resulting in increased sales, retention, and loyalty. Predictive analytics will continue to be a crucial tool for marketers striving to understand their customers and make data-driven decisions about their marketing campaigns.

Step-by-Step Instructions: Setting Up Predictive Analytics with AI

1. **Identify Business Objectives:**

   - Define clear goals and outcomes for predictive analytics. This could range from improving customer retention, forecasting sales, to optimizing marketing campaigns.

2. **Select the Right Tools and Platforms:**

   - Choose predictive analytics software that aligns with business needs, budget, and technical capabilities. Consider tools with AI capabilities, user-friendly interfaces, and integration options.

3. **Data Collection:**

   • Gather historical data relevant to business objectives. This may include sales records, customer interaction logs, social media activity, and so on.

4. **Data Cleaning and Preparation:**

   • Clean the data to remove inconsistencies, duplicates, or irrelevant information. Format and structure the data for analysis, ensuring it's accurate and complete.

5. **Data Analysis and Exploration:**

   • Conduct preliminary analysis to understand trends, patterns, and anomalies in data. This step helps in identifying the key variables that will influence predictive models.

6. **Tool Setup and Configuration:**

   • Install and configure the chosen predictive analytics tool. Set up the environment by importing the cleaned and prepared data.

THE BASICS OF PREDICTIVE MODELING WITH MACHINE LEARNING ALGORITHMS

Predictive modeling is the process of using data and statistical algorithms to make predictions about future events or behaviors. In the context of marketing, predictive modeling can be used to make predictions about consumer behavior, such as whether a customer is likely to make a purchase, churn, or respond to a particular marketing campaign. In this section of Chapter 9 of the *AI Marketing Playbook*, the basics of predictive modeling with machine learning algorithms will be discussed.

Machine learning is a subfield of AI that uses algorithms and statistical models to enable computers to learn from data and make predictions without being explicitly programmed. There are three main types of machine learning algorithms: supervised learning, unsupervised learning, and reinforcement learning. In the context of predictive modeling, the focus will be on supervised learning algorithms.

Supervised learning is a type of machine learning where the algorithm is trained on a labeled dataset, where each data point has a corresponding label or output variable. The goal of supervised learning is to learn a mapping between the input variables and the output variable so that it can make accurate predictions on new, unseen data.

There are several steps involved in building a predictive model with machine learning algorithms:

- *Data collection and preparation:* The first step is to collect and prepare the data for analysis. This includes cleaning and transforming the data, removing missing values, and dealing with outliers. It is important to ensure that the data is representative of the population and that there is no bias in the data.
- *Feature selection and engineering:* The next step is to select the relevant features or variables to be used in the model. Feature selection is important because using too many irrelevant features can lead to overfitting, where the model performs well on the training data but poorly on the new data. Feature engineering involves creating new features or transforming existing features to improve model performance.
- *Model selection and training:* After the data has been prepared and the features have been selected and designed, the next step is to select the appropriate machine learning algorithm for the task at hand. There are many different algorithms to choose from, for example, linear regression, logistic regression, decision trees, random forests, and neural networks. The choice of algorithm depends on the nature of the problem and the data. After selecting the algorithm, the model is trained on the marked dataset using a training algorithm that minimizes the difference between the predicted output and the actual output.
- *Model evaluation and validation:* After training the model, it is important to evaluate its performance against new and invisible data. To do this, the data is divided into training and test sets, with the model being trained on the training set and evaluated on the test set. Model performance is measured using metrics such as accuracy, precision, recall, and F1 score. If the model works well on the test set, it can be used for prediction.
- *Implementation and monitoring:* Once the model is implemented, it is important to monitor its performance over time and update it, as necessary. This includes monitoring the model's inputs and outputs, tracking its accuracy and performance, and retraining the model with new data.

In addition to these steps, there are several best practices to keep in mind when building predictive models with machine learning algorithms:

- *Start with a simple model:* It is important to start with a simple model and gradually increase in complexity as needed. This helps to avoid overfitting and ensures that the model is interpretable.
- *Regularization:* Regularization is a technique used to avoid overfitting by adding a penalty term to the cost function that causes the model to have smaller weights or coefficients. This helps reduce the complexity of the model and improve its generalization performance.

- *Cross-validation:* Cross-validation is a technique used to evaluate model performance on different subsets of data. This requires splitting the data into multiple convolutions and training the model for each convolution while using the rest for validation. This ensures that the model does not overfit a specific subset of the data.
- *Hyperparameter tuning:* Hyperparameters are parameters that are set prior to model training, for example, the learning rate or the number of hidden layers in a neural network. Hyperparameter tuning involves choosing the best set of hyperparameters for the model to optimize its performance.
- *Interpretability:* Interpretability is important in marketing because it allows marketers to understand how the model makes predictions and use those insights to improve their marketing strategies. Techniques such as feature importance analysis, partial dependency graphs, and LIME can be used to interpret model predictions.

Predictive modeling with machine learning algorithms is a powerful tool for marketers to make predictions about consumer behavior and improve their marketing strategies. The process involves multiple steps including data collection and preparation, feature selection and engineering, model selection and training, model evaluation and validation, and implementation and monitoring. Best practices such as starting with a simple model, regularization, cross-validation, hyperparameter tuning, and interpretability can help improve model performance and reliability.

Step-by-Step Instructions: Developing Predictive Models Using Machine Learning

1. **Selecting the Appropriate Algorithm:**

    - Choose a machine learning algorithm that suits business objectives and data characteristics. Common choices include regression models, decision trees, neural networks, and clustering algorithms.

2. **Feature Selection and Engineering:**

    - Identify and select the most relevant features (variables) that influence the predicted outcome. Create new features, if necessary, through processes like feature engineering, to improve model accuracy.

3. **Training the Model:**

    - Use the selected features to train the model. Divide data into training and testing sets. Use the training set to teach the model about the patterns and relationships in the data.

4. **Model Evaluation and Validation:**

   • Test the model using the testing set to evaluate its performance. Assess the model's accuracy, precision, and recall, adjusting model parameters as needed to improve outcomes.

5. **Optimization and Tuning:**

   • Fine-tune the model by adjusting its parameters and retraining it to optimize performance. Use techniques like cross-validation to ensure the model generalizes well to new, unseen data.

6. **Deployment and Monitoring:**

   • Deploy the trained model into the business environment. Regularly monitor its performance, updating and retraining it with new data to maintain its accuracy and relevance.

These steps provide a structured approach to setting up predictive analytics with AI and developing effective predictive models using machine learning in a marketing context.

Time Series Analysis and Predictive Analytics

Time series analysis and predictive analytics are powerful tools used in many industries, including marketing. They allow companies to make informed decisions based on past data and future projections. This section will explore the history, applications, and methods of time series analysis and predictive analytics in marketing.

History of Time Series Analysis

Time series analysis has been around for centuries. The earliest recorded examples of time series data analysis can be found in astronomical observations made by ancient civilizations, such as the Egyptians and Babylonians. These observations were used to predict celestial events and guide agricultural practices.

In the modern era, time series analysis gained popularity in the late nineteenth and early twentieth centuries with the development of statistical methods. One of the pioneers of time series analysis was Sir Francis Galton, who used regression analysis to study meteorological data in the late eighteen hundreds. Other notable statisticians who contributed to the development of time series analysis include Karl Pearson and Ronald Fisher.

The advent of computers in the mid-twentieth century led to the development of more sophisticated time series analysis techniques. In the 1960s and 1970s, advances in computer technology allowed for the development of autoregressive integrated moving average (ARIMA) models, which are still widely used today.

Time Series Analysis in Marketing

Time series analysis is used extensively in marketing to analyze sales data, market trends, and customer behavior. By analyzing historical data, companies can identify patterns and make predictions about future sales and revenue.

One example of the use of time series analysis in marketing is the analysis of sales data for a particular product. By analyzing sales data over time, a company can identify seasonal patterns, such as increased sales during the holiday season. This information can be used to adjust production schedules and marketing campaigns to maximize revenue.

Another example of the use of time series analysis in marketing is the analysis of Web traffic data. By analyzing Web traffic over time, a company can identify patterns in customer behavior, such as peak browsing times and popular pages. This information can be used to optimize Web site design and content to increase engagement and conversions.

Step-by-Step Instruction: Implementing Time Series Analysis for Market Trend Predictions

1. **Understand the Basics of Time Series Analysis:**

   • Learn the key concepts of time series analysis, including trend, seasonality, and noise. Understand how these components influence the data over time.

2. **Collect and Prepare Data:**

   • Gather historical data relevant to the market trend being predicted. Ensure data quality by cleaning and preprocessing the data, such as filling missing values and removing outliers.

3. **Choose the Right Time Series Model:**

   • Select an appropriate time series model based on data characteristics. Common models include ARIMA, seasonal decomposition of time series (STL), and exponential smoothing.

4. **Train and Validate the Model:**

   • Use historical data to train the chosen model. Split the data into training and validation sets to test the model's predictive accuracy and adjust parameters as needed.

5. **Analyze and Interpret the Results:**

   - Evaluate the model's performance using appropriate metrics, like mean absolute error (MAE) or root mean square error (RMSE). Analyze the model's output to identify trends and seasonal patterns.

6. **Implement and Monitor the Model:**

   - Apply the model to forecast future market trends. Regularly monitor its performance and update the model with new data to ensure its accuracy over time.

Predictive Analytics in Marketing

Predictive analytics is a subset of data analytics that uses statistical modeling and machine learning algorithms to make predictions about future events. Predictive analytics is used in marketing to make informed decisions about product development, pricing, and marketing campaigns.

One example of the use of predictive analytics in marketing is the analysis of customer data. By analyzing customer data, such as purchase history and demographics, companies can make predictions about future purchasing behavior. This information can be used to tailor marketing campaigns to specific customer segments and increase the likelihood of conversions. spellings in list headings here.

Another example of the use of predictive analytics in marketing is the analysis of social media data. By analyzing social media data, companies can make predictions about trends and customer sentiment. This information can be used to develop marketing campaigns that resonate with customers and increase brand awareness.

Methods of Time Series Analysis and Predictive Analytics

There are several methods used in time series analysis and predictive analytics, including:

Autoregressive Integrated Moving Average (ARIMA)

   - *ARIMA* is a statistical method used to analyze time series data. ARIMA models can be used to make predictions about future values based on past data. ARIMA models are widely used in marketing to analyze sales data and make predictions about future sales.

Exponential Smoothing (ES)

   - *Exponential smoothing* is a method used to analyze time series data. Exponential smoothing models use a weighted average of past values to make predictions about future values. Exponential smoothing models are commonly used in marketing to analyze sales data and make predictions about future sales.

Regression Analysis

- *Regression analysis* is a statistical method used to analyze the relationship between two or more variables. Regression analysis is commonly used in marketing to analyze the relationship between customer behavior and marketing campaigns or to analyze the relationship between product pricing and sales.

Machine Learning

- *Machine learning* (ML) is a subset of AI that uses algorithms to identify patterns in data. Machine learning algorithms can be used in marketing to make predictions about customer behavior, identify trends, and optimize marketing campaigns.

Time series analysis and predictive analytics are powerful tools that can help companies make informed decisions based on past data and future projections. These tools are widely used in marketing to analyze sales data, customer behavior, and market trends. By using these methods, companies can optimize their marketing campaigns, increase revenue, and stay ahead of the competition.

The Limitations of Predictive Analytics with AI

- *Predictive analytics:* This is a vital aspect of AI marketing, providing insights into future events, behaviors, and outcomes. However, there are several limitations to predictive analytics, which could undermine the efficacy of AI marketing strategies. This section of Chapter 9 of the *AI Marketing Playbook* will explore these limitations and provide examples to illustrate their impact.
- *Limited data availability and quality:* Predictive analytics requires vast amounts of data to be analyzed, and the accuracy of the predictions is directly proportional to the quality of the data. If the data available is limited or of inadequate quality, predictive analytics models will struggle to produce accurate predictions. A retail store may struggle to predict demand for a new product if they only have limited sales data or if the data is riddled with errors. Similarly, a marketing campaign may fail to predict customer behavior accurately if the data used is biased, incomplete, or inconsistent.
- *Inability to account for human behavior:* Predictive analytics is based on historical data, which assumes that the future behavior of individuals will remain consistent with past patterns. However, human behavior

is unpredictable and influenced by a range of factors such as emotions, external events, and personal circumstances. A customer may have purchased a product in the past but may not do so in the future due to a change in their financial situation or a shift in their priorities. This means that predictive analytics cannot always account for the impact of human behavior on future outcomes, making it less reliable in some cases.

- *Complex models and algorithms:* Predictive analytics models are complex and require specialized skills to build and maintain. This means that small and medium-sized businesses may struggle to afford the necessary technology and talent to use predictive analytics effectively. Additionally, models and algorithms may be too complex to explain to stakeholders, leading to mistrust and lack of adoption. This limitation means that predictive analytics may not be accessible to all businesses, giving larger companies with more resources an unfair advantage.

- *Limited accuracy and reliability:* Predictive analytics models may produce inaccurate or unreliable predictions due to several factors, including errors in the data used, incorrect assumptions made during modeling, and unforeseen changes in the environment. A weather forecasting model may predict sunny weather but end up with a sudden thunderstorm. Additionally, some models may produce overfitting, where they are too closely aligned with the data used during the modeling process, resulting in a lack of generalizability to new data. This limitation means that businesses may make decisions based on inaccurate predictions, leading to costly mistakes.

- *Ethical considerations:* Predictive analytics relies heavily on personal data, which raises ethical concerns about privacy and data protection. If data is not handled ethically, it may result in a loss of trust between businesses and customers, leading to reputational damage. Additionally, some predictive analytics models may produce biased predictions due to the inclusion of biased data or algorithmic biases. An HR model may unfairly disadvantage certain groups of job applicants, leading to discrimination. This limitation means that businesses must be ethical in their use of predictive analytics to avoid reputational and legal consequences.

While predictive analytics is a crucial aspect of AI marketing, it has its limitations. These limitations include limited data availability and quality, an inability to account for human behavior, complex models and algorithms, limited accuracy and reliability, and ethical considerations. Businesses must be aware of these limitations and take steps to mitigate their impact, such as investing in high-quality data, building ethical models, and continuously monitoring and refining their predictive analytics strategies.

Step-by-step Guide: Overcoming Limitations of Predictive Analytics

1. **Acknowledge the Limitations:**

   • Understand that predictive analytics relies on historical data and assumptions about future trends, which may not always hold true due to unforeseen events or changes in the market.

2. **Ensure Data Quality:**

   • Invest in the collection and maintenance of high-quality data. Regularly review and cleanse the data to reduce errors, biases, and inconsistencies.

3. **Handle Model Complexity:**

   • Choose models that balance accuracy and interpretability. Avoid overly complex models that are hard to understand and maintain. Use regularization techniques to prevent overfitting.

4. **Test and Validate Models Thoroughly:**

   • Use cross-validation and back testing to test the model's performance on unseen data. Adjust the model as necessary to improve its predictive power.

5. **Monitor and Update Models Regularly:**

   • Continuously monitor the model's performance over time. Update the model with new data and adjust its parameters to adapt to changes in the underlying patterns.

6. **Consider Ethical and Legal Implications:**

   • Be mindful of the ethical and legal considerations of using predictive analytics, especially regarding privacy, consent, and data protection. Ensure compliance with relevant laws and regulations.

Chapter 9 of the *AI Marketing Playbook* covered two main topics: *natural language processing* and *recommendation systems*. A detailed summary of each topic follows and an explanation how they were covered in the chapter.

Natural Language Processing

The chapter started by introducing natural language processing (NLP) as a subset of AI that deals with the interaction between computers and human languages. It explains that NLP involves a range of techniques for analyzing and understanding human language, such as text mining, sentiment analysis, and topic modeling.

The chapter then went into more detail about each of these techniques. Text mining, it explains, involves using NLP algorithms to extract useful information from large volumes of unstructured text data.

Sentiment analysis, on the other hand, is the process of using NLP to determine the emotional tone of a piece of text, such as whether it is positive, negative, or neutral. Topic modeling, the chapter explains, is a technique for identifying themes or topics within a large set of text data.

The chapter also covered some of the key applications of NLP in marketing. It explains how NLP can be used to analyze customer feedback and reviews, which can help businesses identify common themes and areas for improvement. It also discusses how NLP can be used to analyze social media data, which can provide insights into consumer sentiment and help businesses identify influencers and brand ambassadors.

The chapter then went on to discuss some of the challenges associated with NLP, such as the difficulty of interpreting sarcasm and irony in text. It also discusses the importance of data privacy and ethical considerations when using NLP techniques.

Overall, the chapter provided a comprehensive overview of NLP and its applications in marketing. It covers the key techniques and challenges associated with NLP and provides real-world examples of how businesses are using NLP to gain insights into consumer behavior.

Recommendation Systems

The second topic covered in this chapter is recommendation systems. The chapter starts by explaining that recommendation systems are a type of AI algorithm that suggests products or services to users based on their previous behavior or preferences.

The chapter then went into more detail about the two main types of recommendation systems: collaborative filtering and content-based filtering. Collaborative filtering, the chapter explains, involves analyzing the behavior of similar users to make recommendations. Content-based filtering, however, involves analyzing the characteristics of items to make recommendations.

The chapter also covered some of the key challenges associated with recommendation systems. It explains that recommendation systems can suffer from the "cold start" problem, which occurs when there is insufficient data to make accurate recommendations for new users or items. The chapter also discusses the challenge of balancing personalization with serendipity, or the ability to recommend items that a user may not have thought of on their own.

The chapter then went on to provide real-world examples of how recommendation systems are being used in marketing. It discusses how Netflix uses a recommendation system to suggest movies and TV shows to users based on their viewing history. It also discusses how Amazon uses a recommendation system to suggest products to users based on their browsing and purchasing history.

The chapter concluded by discussing some of the ethical considerations associated with recommendation systems. It explains that recommendation systems can reinforce biases if they are not designed and trained carefully, and that there is a risk of creating filter bubbles if users are only exposed to content that aligns with their existing preferences.

Overall, this chapter provided a comprehensive overview of recommendation systems and their applications in marketing. It covers the key types of recommendation systems and the challenges associated with them and provides real-world examples of how businesses are using recommendation systems to improve the customer experience. It also discusses the ethical considerations associated with recommendation systems, highlighting the importance of responsible AI practices in marketing.

EMAIL MARKETING WITH ARTIFICIAL INTELLIGENCE (AI)

E mail marketing is a critical component of digital marketing, as it allows businesses to communicate with their audience and customers directly. With the help of artificial Intelligence (AI), businesses can optimize their email marketing campaigns to drive more engagement, conversions, and revenue.

Ways AI Can Be Used for Email Marketing

- *Segmentation:* AI algorithms can analyze customer data and segment audiences based on factors such as demographics, behavior, interests, and past interactions. This helps businesses tailor their emails to specific groups of people, which can increase open rates, click-through rates, and conversions.
- *Personalization:* AI can help companies personalize email content by dynamically generating subject lines, headlines, and even the body of the email based on individual customer data, preferences, and behavior. This makes the email more relevant and engaging for the recipient, which can result in higher engagement rates and conversions.
- *Optimization:* AI algorithms can analyze email performance data and use predictive analytics to optimize email campaigns. AI can suggest the best time to send emails, the optimal frequency of emails, and the most effective email content based on past performance data.
- *Testing:* AI can help companies test different email variants and automatically select the best-performing version. This helps companies optimize their email campaigns without having to manually analyze performance data.

Examples of Successful Email Marketing Strategies with AI

- *Spotify:* Spotify uses AI to personalize its email campaigns based on user listening behavior. They send personalized playlists and recommendations based on the user's preferred genres and artists, helping to increase engagement and loyalty.
- *Airbnb:* Airbnb uses AI algorithms to personalize its email content based on a user's search and booking history. This helps Airbnb send more targeted and relevant emails, which can increase engagement and bookings.
- *Grammarly:* Grammarly uses AI to personalize its email subject lines based on recipient typing behavior. This helps increase the open and engagement rate of emails.

Techniques to Optimize Email Subject Lines with AI

- *Predictive analytics:* AI algorithms can analyze performance data from past emails and predict the best-performing subject lines for future emails.
- *A/B testing:* AI can help companies test different subject lines and automatically select the best-performing version based on past performance data.
- *Personalization:* AI can help businesses generate personalized subject lines based on customer data and behavior, which can increase open and engagement rates.

Personalization of Email Content with AI

- *Dynamic content generation:* AI algorithms can analyze customer data and generate personalized email content based on individual preferences, behavior, and past interactions.
- *Product recommendations:* AI can recommend products or services to individual customers based on their browsing history, purchase history, and preferences.
- *Behavior triggers:* AI can automatically send personalized emails based on customer behavior, for example, abandoned cart reminders or personalized recommendations.

Measuring Email Marketing Effectiveness with AI

- *Predictive analytics:* AI algorithms can analyze past email performance data and predict the expected results of future email campaigns.
- *A/B testing:* AI can help companies test different email variants and automatically select the best-performing version based on past performance data.

- *Key performance indicators:* AI can track and analyze email key performance indicators (KPI) such as open rates, click rates, and conversion rates to measure the effectiveness of email campaigns.

AI can improve email marketing campaigns by optimizing segmentation, personalization, optimization, and testing. Successful email marketing strategies that use AI include personalizing email content and subject lines based on customer data, behavior, and preferences. Techniques for optimizing email subject lines with AI include using predictive analytics, A/B testing, and personalization. Personalizing email content with AI can be achieved through dynamic content generation, product recommendations, and behavioral triggers. Measuring the effectiveness of email marketing with AI can be done through predictive analytics, A/B testing, and performance metrics such as open rates, click-through rates, and conversion rates.

HOW AI CAN BE USED FOR EMAIL MARKETING

Email marketing has been around for decades, and it remains one of the most effective marketing channels for businesses of all sizes. In recent years, the use of AI in email marketing has become increasingly popular, providing marketers with more accurate data and insights to optimize their campaigns. AI can be used for email marketing in several ways, including personalization, segmentation, and predictive analytics. This chapter will discuss in detail how AI can be used for email marketing.

Personalization

- *Personalization:* This is a crucial aspect of email marketing because it enables companies to send targeted messages to their subscribers, thereby increasing the chances of conversion. AI can be used to personalize email marketing campaigns in several ways, such as product recommendations, subject lines, and content.
- *Product recommendations:* With AI, companies can use data to analyze customer behavior and preferences and recommend products that the customer is most likely to buy. This can be done by analyzing the customer's previous purchases, browsing history, and search queries. By recommending products that customers are interested in, companies can increase customer loyalty and sales.
- *Subject lines:* AI can be used to analyze subject lines and determine which are most likely to generate higher open rates. By analyzing past email campaigns, the AI can identify which subject lines performed best and generate new subject lines based on that data. This allows businesses to send emails with subject lines that are more likely to grab the recipient's attention.

- *Content:* AI can also be used to personalize email content. AI can analyze the recipient's preferences and create content tailored to their interests. By using data to personalize email content, businesses can increase engagement and conversion rates.

Segmentation

- *Segmentation:* This is the process of dividing email lists into smaller groups based on certain criteria. By segmenting email lists, businesses can send more targeted messages to specific groups of subscribers, thereby increasing the chances of conversion. AI can be used to segment email lists in a variety of ways, including demographics, behavior, and engagement.
- *Demographics:* AI can analyze demographics such as age, gender, and location to build targeted email lists. By segmenting email lists based on demographics, businesses can send more relevant messages to specific groups of subscribers.
- *Behavior:* AI can also be used to build email lists based on customer behavior, such as past purchases, browsing history, and search queries. By analyzing customer behavior, companies can send targeted messages to subscribers who have shown interest in a specific product or service.
- *Engagement:* AI can analyze customer engagement with email campaigns, for example, open rates, click rates and conversion rates to build targeted email lists. By segmenting email lists by engagement, businesses can send more targeted messages to subscribers who are most likely to convert.

Step-by-Step Instructions

1. **Collect data:** Gather customer data from CRM, social media interactions, Web site analytics, and other touchpoints.
2. **Analyze data:** Use AI tools to analyze the data and identify patterns in customer behavior, preferences, and demographics.
3. **Create segments:** Based on the analysis, create segments of the audience with similar characteristics or behaviors.
4. **Customize campaigns:** Tailor email content for each segment by specifically addressing their unique challenges and concerns, known as 'pain points'.
5. **Monitor and Adjust:** Regularly review the performance of each segment and refine segmentation strategy accordingly.

Predictive analytics

- *Predictive analytics:* This is the process of using data, statistical algorithms, and machine learning (ML) techniques to determine the likelihood of future outcomes. AI can be used for predictive analytics in email marketing to determine which subscribers are most likely to convert and which campaigns are most likely to succeed.

• *Identify high-quality subscribers:* AI can analyze customer data to determine which subscribers are most likely to convert. By identifying high-quality subscribers, businesses can send targeted messages to those subscribers, increasing the chances of conversion. Predicting campaign success: AI can analyze past email campaigns to determine which campaigns are most likely to be successful in the future. By using predictive analytics to identify successful campaigns, businesses can optimize their campaigns for better results.

AI can be used for email marketing in a variety of ways, including personalization, segmentation, and predictive analytics. By using AI to personalize email content, segment email lists, and analyze customer behavior and engagement, businesses can increase engagement and conversion rates. AI can also be used for predictive analytics to determine which subscribers are most likely to convert and which campaigns are most likely to succeed. By using AI in email marketing, businesses can optimize their campaigns to deliver better results and increase customer retention and sales.

However, it is important to note that AI is not a panacea and must be used in conjunction with human intelligence and creativity. AI can provide valuable insights and data, but it's up to marketers to use that data to create effective email marketing campaigns.

Overall, using AI in email marketing is a powerful tool that can help businesses achieve better results, but it must be used responsibly and in conjunction with other marketing strategies. As AI technology continues to advance, expect even more innovative uses of AI in email marketing and other marketing channels.

EXAMPLES OF SUCCESSFUL EMAIL MARKETING STRATEGIES THAT USE AI

Email marketing has long been a staple of digital marketing, allowing businesses to reach their customers and prospects directly through their inboxes. However, with the rise of AI, email marketing has become even more effective and personalized. This chapter will explore successful email marketing strategies that use AI, including their history, benefits, and how they work.

Personalization

One of the key benefits of AI in email marketing is personalization. With the ability to collect and analyze vast amounts of data, AI can create highly targeted and personalized emails for each recipient. By using AI to segment an email list based on factors such as demographics, behavior, and preferences, one can send personalized emails that are more likely to be opened and engaged with.

History: Personalization has been a part of email marketing for a long time, but the rise of AI has made it much more effective. In the early days of email marketing, personalization was limited to simple things like addressing the recipient by name. Today, AI-powered personalization can take many forms, including dynamic content, product recommendations, and personalized subject lines.

Example: Amazon is a great example of a company that uses AI-powered personalization in their email marketing. They use data from customer behavior, such as past purchases and browsing history, to make personalized product recommendations in their emails. If a customer has been browsing for running shoes, Amazon might send them an email with recommended running shoes that are like the ones they have viewed or purchased in the past.

Step-by-Step Instructions: Personalization of Email Content with AI

1. **Integrate Data Sources:** Ensure all customer data sources are integrated into an AI platform to get a unified view of each customer.
2. **Set Personalization Goals:** Define what personalization means for campaigns, whether it's product recommendations, content, or offers.
3. **Implement AI Algorithms:** Utilize AI to analyze individual customer data and predict preferences and behaviors.
4. **Generate Personalized Content:** Create dynamic email content that changes based on the customer's profile and behavior.
5. **Test and Optimize:** Continuously test different personalization strategies and use AI insights to optimize the content.

Predictive Analytics

Another way that AI can be used in email marketing is through predictive analytics. By analyzing data on customer behavior, such as past purchases, browsing history, and email engagement, AI can predict what products or services a customer is most likely to be interested in. This allows users to send highly targeted and relevant emails that are more likely to result in conversions.

History: Predictive analytics has been used in email marketing for several years, but the rise of AI has made it much more effective. In the past, predictive analytics was limited to simple rules-based algorithms. Today, AI-powered predictive analytics can analyze vast amounts of data and make highly accurate predictions about customer behavior.

Example: Netflix is a notable example of a company that uses predictive analytics in their email marketing. They use data on customer viewing behavior to predict what shows and movies a customer is most likely to be interested in. They then send personalized emails with recommendations based on these predictions. If a customer has been watching a lot of romantic comedies, Netflix might send them an email with recommendations for other romantic comedies that they might enjoy.

Step-by-Step Instructions for Predictive Analytics in Email Marketing

1. **Define Desired Goals**

   • Determine desired achievements with predictive analytics, like enhancing open rates, conversion rates, or customer retention.

2. **Data Collection and Aggregation**

   • Collect data from various sources, including customer purchase history, Web site behavior, and email interactions, ensuring it's integrated into a single system.

3. **Analyze and Segment**

   • Use predictive analytics tools to analyze the data, identify patterns, and segment the audience based on predicted behaviors or preferences.

4. **Create Targeted Campaigns**

   • Design targeted email campaigns for the identified segments, ensuring the content is relevant to each group.

5. **Deploy and Monitor**

   • Launch the campaigns and monitor their performance, adjusting strategy based on real-time insights to meet objectives.

6. **Refine and Repeat**

   • Continuously improve the approach based on campaign results and evolving data insights to enhance future predictive analytics efforts in email marketing.

Automated Emails

Another way that AI can be used in email marketing is through automation. By using AI-powered automation tools, users can send targeted emails based on customer behavior, such as abandoned carts, product recommendations, and follow-up emails. This allows them to send the right message at the right time, without having to manually send each email.

History: Automated emails have been used in email marketing for several years, but the rise of AI has made them much more effective. In the past, automated emails were limited to simple triggers, such as a customer abandoning their cart. Today, AI-powered automation can analyze customer behavior and send highly targeted emails based on that behavior.

Example: Sephora is a fitting example of a company that uses automated emails in their email marketing. They use AI-powered automation to send targeted emails based on customer behavior, such as abandoned carts and product recommendations. If a customer abandons their cart, Sephora might send them an email with a reminder to complete their purchase, along with a personalized product recommendation based on their browsing history.

Step-by-Step Instructions for Automated Emails

1. **Find Behaviors to Automate**

   • Identify customer behaviors that will trigger automated emails, such as cart abandonment or product browsing without purchase.

2. **Automation Tools**

   • Select and implement an AI-driven email automation tool that aligns with systems and data.

3. **Install Email Templates**

   • Develop customized templates for different automated email scenarios, tailored to the triggering behavior.

4. **Define Triggers and Workflows**

   • Set up triggers in the automation tool to initiate the sending of automated emails based on identified customer behaviors.

5. **Testing and Optimization**

   • Conduct tests to ensure automated emails are functioning as intended and make adjustments based on the feedback.

6. **Launch and Monitor**

   • Deploy automated email campaigns, continuously monitor their performance, and make ongoing adjustments to improve interaction and conversion rates.

Dynamic Content

AI can be used to create dynamic content in email marketing. *Dynamic content* is content that changes based on the recipient's behavior or preferences, allowing companies to send more personalized and relevant emails. By using AI to analyze customer data, one can create dynamic content that is tailored to each recipient, increasing engagement and conversions.

History: Dynamic content has been used in email marketing for several years, but the rise of AI has made it much more effective. In the past, dynamic content was limited to simple rules-based algorithms. Today, AI-powered dynamic content can analyze vast amounts of data and create highly personalized content in real-time.

Example: The clothing company, ASOS, is a great example of a company that uses AI-powered dynamic in their email marketing. They use data on customer behavior, such as past purchases and browsing history, to create personalized emails with dynamic content. They might send an email with a selection of dresses that are tailored to the recipient's preferences, based on their browsing history and past purchases.

Step-by-Step Instructions for Dynamic Content

1. **Identify Data Sources**

   • Compile information from customer behavior, purchase history, and Web site interactions to form the basis for dynamic content.

2. **Segment the Audience**

   • Utilize AI to analyze the data and segment the audience according to their behaviors and preferences.

3. **Define Content Variations**

   • Develop targeted offers, articles, and product recommendations for each segment.

4. **Integrate Dynamic Content in Emails**

   • Select an email marketing platform that supports dynamic content and establish rules or algorithms to insert relevant content for each segment in the emails.

5. **Test and Optimize**

   • Perform A/B testing to compare dynamic content with static content and use the results to enhance the content and segmentation strategy.

6. **Launch and Monitor**

   • Dispatch emails with dynamic content to evaluate engagement and conversion rates, continually adjusting the strategy based on customer feedback and behavior.

Benefits of AI in Email Marketing

There are many benefits to using AI in email marketing, including:

- *Increased personalization:* AI allows users to create highly personalized emails that are tailored to each recipient, increasing engagement and conversions.
- *Improved targeting:* By using AI to segment the email list, one can send targeted emails to specific groups of customers, increasing the effectiveness of their campaigns.
- *Enhanced automation:* AI-powered automation allows users to send targeted emails based on customer behavior, without having to manually send each email.
- *Real-time analysis:* AI can analyze customer data in real-time, allowing users to make changes to their email campaigns on the fly.

AI has revolutionized email marketing, allowing businesses to create highly personalized and targeted campaigns that are more effective than ever before. By using AI-powered personalization, predictive analytics, automated emails, and dynamic content, businesses can increase engagement and conversions, while also saving time and resources. As AI continues to evolve, expect to see even more innovative and effective email marketing strategies in the future.

TECHNIQUES FOR OPTIMIZING EMAIL SUBJECT LINES WITH AI

Email marketing has long been a staple of digital marketing strategies, and optimizing email subject lines is one of the keyways to ensure that emails are opened and read. In recent years, advances in artificial intelligence (AI) have made it easier to optimize subject lines using data and ML techniques. This chapter will discuss techniques for optimizing email subject lines with AI, including using natural language processing (NLP) and predictive analytics.

NLP

NLP is a subfield of AI that focuses on understanding and analyzing human language. NLP can be used to optimize email subject lines by analyzing the language and syntax of successful subject lines to identify patterns and trends that can be applied to future subject lines.

One way that NLP can be used is by analyzing the sentiment of subject lines. Positive sentiment is often associated with higher open rates, so using words that evoke positive emotions can be effective. A subject line like "Don't miss out on this amazing offer!" has a positive sentiment and may be more effective than a more neutral subject line like "Check out our latest deals."

NLP can also be used to analyze the structure of subject lines. Research has shown that shorter subject lines tend to have higher open rates. NLP can be used to identify shorter subject lines that are still engaging and attention-grabbing.

Additionally, NLP can be used to analyze the use of punctuation, capitalization, and other elements of syntax to identify patterns that are associated with higher open rates.

Predictive Analytics

Another way that AI can be used to optimize email subject lines is through predictive analytics. Predictive analytics uses ML algorithms to analyze data and make predictions about future outcomes. In the context of email marketing, predictive analytics can be used to analyze data on past email campaigns and identify patterns that are associated with higher open rates.

One way that predictive analytics can be used is by analyzing the behavior of individual subscribers. If a subscriber consistently opens emails with subject lines that include certain keywords or phrases, the predictive analytics algorithm can be trained to identify those patterns and suggest similar subject lines for future emails.

Predictive analytics can also be used to analyze data on larger groups of subscribers. If a company has a large database of subscriber data, predictive analytics can be used to the characteristics of subscribers who are most likely to open emails and identify patterns that can be applied to future campaigns. This could include demographic information such as age, gender, and location, as well as information on subscriber behavior such as the time of day that emails are opened.

Examples

To illustrate these techniques, the following examples demonstrate how AI can be used to optimize email subject lines, enhancing engagement through precision and relevance. These strategies not only increase open rates but also ensure the content is tailored to the audience's preferences and behaviors.

Example 1: Using NLP to Analyze Sentiment

A clothing retailer is preparing to launch a new line of summer dresses and wants to create a subject line that will generate excitement and encourage subscribers to click through to the Web site. They use NLP to analyze the sentiment of past successful subject lines and identify words and phrases that are associated with positive emotions. They decide to use the subject line "Get ready for summer with our stunning new dresses!" which has a positive sentiment and includes keywords that are associated with summer and excitement.

Example 2: Using NLP to Analyze Structure

A software company is preparing to send out a newsletter to their subscribers and wants to create a subject line that will grab their attention without being too long. They use NLP to analyze the structure of past successful subject lines and identify patterns that are associated with higher open rates. They decide to use the subject line "Boost your productivity with these tips!" which is short and attention-grabbing while still conveying the value of the content in the newsletter.

Example 3: Using predictive analytics to analyze subscriber behavior

A fitness company wants to create a subject line for their weekly newsletter that will appeal to subscribers who are interested in yoga. They use predictive analytics to analyze data on past campaigns and identify patterns among subscribers who have opened emails with subject lines related to yoga. They discover that subscribers who have opened these emails are more likely to be women aged 25–40 and live in urban areas. They decided to use the subject line "Find your Zen with our new yoga classes" which targets this specific demographic and includes keywords that are associated with yoga and relaxation.

Overall, optimizing email subject lines with AI can be a powerful way to improve the effectiveness of email marketing campaigns. By using NLP and predictive analytics techniques, companies can analyze data on past campaigns and identify patterns that are associated with higher open rates. This can lead to more engaging and effective subject lines that generate more clicks and conversions.

Step-by-Step Instructions for Optimizing Email Subject Lines with AI:

1. **Analyze Historical Data**

   • AI should analyze past email campaign data to identify which types of subject lines have historically performed well.

2. **Implement NLP for Sentiment Analysis**

   • Apply NLP to determine the sentiment of successful subject lines, guiding the creation of new ones.

3. **Use Predictive Analytics**

   • Utilize predictive analytics to predict how different subject line variations may perform, based on historical data.

4. **Create and Test Variations**

   • Develop various subject line options based on AI analysis and conduct A/B testing to identify which yield the best open rates.

5. **Optimize Based on Performance**

   • Refine and enhance future campaign subject lines using insights gained from testing.

6. Continuous Learning and Adaptation

- Persistently analyze new data and update AI models to advance subject line optimization over time.

PERSONALIZING EMAIL CONTENT WITH AI

This section of Chapter 10 of the *AI Marketing Playbook* delves into the topic of personalizing email content using AI. Personalization is a critical element of modern marketing strategies, as it enables businesses to connect with their customers on a more personal level, increasing engagement and driving more conversions. AI can help marketers achieve this level of personalization by analyzing vast amounts of customer data and generating tailored content that speaks directly to each individual customer.

The section explores the different ways AI can be used to personalize email content, the benefits of personalization, and some examples of successful implementations of AI-powered email personalization.

Why Personalize Email Content?

Email marketing has been a staple of digital marketing for decades. However, the rise of social media and other digital channels has led some to question whether email is still an effective marketing tool. The truth is, email is still one of the most effective ways to reach customers, with a much higher return on investment than many other channels.

However, email marketing is only effective if the emails resonate with the recipients. In other words, the emails must be relevant and interesting to the individual customer. This is where personalization comes in.

Personalization involves tailoring the content of an email to the recipient's interests, behaviors, and preferences. This can be achieved by analyzing customer data, such as purchase history, browsing behavior, and demographic information. With this data, marketers can create highly targeted email campaigns that are more likely to engage the recipient and drive conversions.

Benefits of Personalization

There are many benefits to personalizing email content with AI. Some of the most notable include:

- *Increased engagement:* Personalized emails are more likely to capture the recipient's attention and lead to higher engagement rates. When the content is relevant and interesting to the recipient, they are more likely to read the email and take action.
- *Improved conversions:* Personalization can also lead to higher conversion rates. By tailoring the content to the recipient's interests and preferences, marketers can create email campaigns that are more likely to drive sales.

- *Better customer relationships:* Personalization can help build stronger relationships with customers by showing them that the business understands their needs and preferences. This can lead to increased loyalty and repeat business.
- *More efficient marketing:* Personalization can also lead to more efficient marketing campaigns. By targeting only those customers who are most likely to be interested in a particular product or service, marketers can save time and resources while still achieving their marketing goals.

How AI Can Personalize Email Content

AI can help personalize email content in several ways. Some of the most common methods include:

- *Predictive analytics:* Predictive analytics involves using ML algorithms to analyze customer data and predict which products or services a customer is most likely to be interested in. This information can then be used to create personalized email campaigns that are more likely to resonate with the recipient.
- *NLP:* NLP involves using AI to understand and analyze human language. NLP can be used to analyze customer feedback, social media posts, and other forms of customer communication to gain insights into their interests and preferences.
- *Content creation:* AI can also be used to create personalized content for email campaigns. This can include product recommendations, personalized offers, and other tailored messaging.
- *Behavioral analysis:* Behavioral analysis involves analyzing a customer's online behavior to gain insights into their interests and preferences. This data can then be used to create personalized email campaigns that are more likely to engage the recipient.

Examples of AI-Powered Email Personalization

Many businesses have already implemented AI-powered email personalization with enormous success. Here are a few examples:

- *Spotify:* Spotify uses AI to create personalized playlists for each user based on their listening history. They also send out personalized emails with music recommendations based on the user's listening history and preferences. This personalization has led to increased user engagement and retention.
- *Amazon:* Amazon uses AI to personalize email content based on a user's browsing and purchase history. They send out personalized product recommendations and offers, increasing the likelihood of repeat purchases.
- *Netflix:* Netflix uses AI to personalize email content based on a user's viewing history. They send out personalized recommendations for new

shows and movies based on the user's interests, increasing user engagement and retention.

- *Sephora:* Sephora uses AI to personalize email content based on a user's past purchases and browsing history. They send out personalized product recommendations and offers, which has led to increased customer loyalty and repeat purchases.

In each of these examples, AI is used to analyze customer data and create personalized email campaigns that are tailored to each individual recipient. This leads to higher engagement, better customer relationships, and increased sales and revenue.

Personalizing email content with AI is a powerful tool for modern marketers. By analyzing customer data and creating tailored content, businesses can engage with their customers on a more personal level, leading to increased engagement and conversions. The benefits of personalization are clear, and many businesses have already seen great success with AI-powered email personalization. As technology continues to advance, expect to see even more sophisticated and effective personalization techniques in the future.

Step-by-Step Instructions for Personalizing Email Content with AI

1. **Collect Customer Data**

   - Compile comprehensive data on customers, including demographic details, purchase history, and online behavior.

2. **Integrate AI Tools**

   - Utilize AI tools to analyze the collected data, revealing insights and patterns.

3. **Segment the Audience**

   - Based on AI analysis, segment the audience into groups with similar interests and behaviors.

4. **Create Personalized Content**

   - Develop content tailored for each segment, aligning with their interests and preferences.

5. **Automate Email Personalization**

   - Employ email marketing software with AI capabilities to automatically insert personalized content in emails for each segment.

6. Test and Optimize

- Personalize content, conduct A/B testing to gauge effectiveness, and refine to improve engagement and conversion rates.

7. Monitor and Adapt

- Continuously use AI to fine-tune content and segmentation, enhancing personalization in email campaigns over time.

MEASURING THE EFFECTIVENESS OF EMAIL MARKETING WITH AI

Email marketing has been one of the most popular forms of digital marketing for decades. However, with the increasing amount of data available, marketers are constantly looking for ways to improve their email marketing campaigns to achieve better results. Artificial intelligence (AI) has emerged as a powerful tool in this regard. AI can analyze massive amounts of data and help marketers understand what works and what doesn't work in their email marketing campaigns. This chapter will discuss how AI can be used to measure the effectiveness of email marketing campaigns.

History of Email Marketing

Email marketing has been around since the inception of the Internet, but it was not until the late 1990s that businesses started using email marketing as a marketing tool. The first email marketing campaign was sent in 1978 by Gary Thuerk, a marketer at Digital Equipment Corporation. Thuerk sent an email promoting DEC's computers to 400 users on the ARPANET (the precursor to the Internet). The campaign generated $13 million in sales, which was a massive success at that time.

Over the years, email marketing has evolved, and marketers have developed various strategies to make their campaigns more effective. With this evolution, it's important to note that email marketing has also become more challenging as people's inboxes are flooded with hundreds of emails every day. Marketers need to create campaigns that stand out and capture their target audience's attention.

Measuring the Effectiveness of Email Marketing with AI

Measuring the effectiveness of email marketing campaigns is essential to understand whether they are achieving their intended objectives or not. AI can help marketers measure the effectiveness of their campaigns in several ways, including the following types.

Predictive Analytics

Predictive analytics is a subset of AI that uses ML algorithms to analyze data and make predictions about future events. Marketers can use predictive analytics to predict the success of their email marketing campaigns. They can use predictive analytics to identify the best time to send emails, the subject lines that are most likely to be opened, and the content that is most likely to be engaged with.

Tools like IBM Watson Marketing Insights and Salesforce Einstein can help marketers analyze their email campaigns and predict their success. These tools can analyze massive amounts of data, including customer behavior, historical data, and campaign performance, to provide actionable insights that can help marketers optimize their email campaigns.

Personalization

Personalization is a critical factor in the success of email marketing campaigns. AI can help marketers personalize their emails based on individual customer preferences and behaviors. Marketers can use AI to analyze customer data, including purchase history and browsing behavior, to create personalized product recommendations.

Tools like Persado and Phrasee can help marketers create personalized email subject lines and body copy that resonates with their target audience. These tools use NLP algorithms to analyze customer data and create personalized email content.

A/B Testing

A/B testing is a customary practice in email marketing, where marketers test different versions of emails to determine which one performs better. AI can help marketers optimize their A/B testing by analyzing massive amounts of data to determine which variables have the most significant impact on email performance. AI can analyze the impact of different subject lines, call-to-action (CTA) buttons, and email layouts on email performance.

Tools like Optimizely and Adobe Target can help marketers optimize their A/B testing by analyzing data and providing insights on which variables have the most significant impact on email performance.

Sentiment Analysis

Sentiment analysis is a technique used to determine the emotions associated with a particular piece of content. AI can help marketers analyze customer sentiment about their email campaigns by analyzing customer feedback, including email replies and social media mentions.

Tools like Hootsuite Insights and NetBase Quid can help marketers analyze customer sentiment about their email campaigns. These tools use NLP algorithms to analyze text data and determine the sentiment associated with it. This information can help marketers identify areas of improvement in their email campaigns and adjust their strategies accordingly.

Conversion Rate Optimization

Conversion rate optimization (CRO) is a process of optimizing a Web site or landing page to increase the likelihood of visitors taking a specific action, such as making a purchase or filling out a form. AI can help marketers optimize their email campaigns for conversion by analyzing customer behavior and providing insights on which variables have the most significant impact on conversion rates.

Tools like Optimizely and Adobe Target can also be used to optimize email campaigns for conversion. These tools use ML algorithms to analyze customer behavior and provide insights on which variables have the most significant impact on conversion rates.

AI can be a powerful tool for measuring the effectiveness of email marketing campaigns. AI can help marketers predict the success of their campaigns, personalize their emails, optimize their A/B testing, analyze customer sentiment, and optimize their campaigns for conversion. Marketers who use AI to measure the effectiveness of their email campaigns can gain valuable insights that can help them improve their campaigns and achieve better results. As AI continues to evolve, expect to see even more innovative solutions for measuring the effectiveness of email marketing campaigns.

Step-by-Step Instructions for Measuring the Effectiveness of Email Marketing with AI

1. **Define Key Metrics**

   • Determine the KPIs for email campaigns, such as open rate, click-through rate, and conversion rate.

2. **Implement AI Analytics Tools**

   • Deploy AI-powered tools to analyze these KPIs, offering detailed insights into campaign performance.

3. **Conduct Predictive Analysis**

   • Use predictive analytics to project future campaign performance and pinpoint areas for improvement.

4. **Execute A/B Testing**

   • Test various elements of email campaigns, like subject lines, content, and timing, to identify the most effective strategies.

5. **Optimize for Conversion**

   • Utilize insights from AI analysis and A/B testing to enhance email campaigns and achieve higher conversion rates.

6. Continuous Improvement

- Regularly revise and update AI models and strategies based on the latest data and performance trends to improve email marketing's effectiveness.

Chapter 10 of the *AI Marketing Playbook* discussed the use of AI in email marketing, including its benefits and effective strategies for implementation.

The chapter began by explaining how AI can be used to optimize email marketing by improving subject lines, personalizing content, and measuring its effectiveness. AI algorithms can help marketers analyze customer data and behavior to create more targeted and relevant emails that are more likely to be opened and clicked.

One example of AI in email marketing is the use of predictive analytics to determine which customers are most likely to purchase certain products or services. This can be done by analyzing their past purchases, browsing behavior, and other data points, and using this information to create personalized email campaigns that are tailored to their specific interests and needs.

Another successful email marketing strategy that uses AI is the use of dynamic content, which allows marketers to create multiple versions of an email with different content, images, and offers based on customer data. This can help to increase engagement and drive conversions by delivering more relevant content to each individual recipient.

AI can also be used to optimize email subject lines by analyzing past email performance and using ML algorithms to predict which subject lines are most likely to be opened and clicked. This can help marketers to create more compelling and effective subject lines that are more likely to capture the attention of their target audience.

Personalizing email content with AI can also be a highly effective strategy. By using customer data and behavior to create more targeted and relevant content, marketers can increase engagement and drive conversions. This can include personalized product recommendations, customized offers, and targeted messaging based on customer preferences and behavior.

Measuring the effectiveness of email marketing with AI can be done by analyzing key metrics such as open rates, click-through rates, conversion rates, and revenue generated. By using ML algorithms to analyze this data, marketers can gain valuable insights into the performance of their email campaigns and use this information to optimize future campaigns for better results.

The use of AI in email marketing can help marketers to create more targeted, personalized, and effective campaigns that deliver better results and drive higher engagement and conversions. By using machine ML algorithms to analyze customer data and behavior, marketers can create more relevant content and optimize email campaigns for maximum impact.

The use of AI in email marketing is a powerful tool that can help marketers to deliver more personalized and relevant content, improve engagement and conversions, and optimize email campaigns for maximum impact. By leveraging predictive analytics, dynamic content, and ML algorithms, marketers can create more effective email campaigns that deliver better results and drive business growth. It is essential for marketers to continue to stay updated on the latest trends and developments in AI and email marketing to stay ahead of the competition and drive success in their business.

CHAPTER 11

SEARCH ENGINE OPTIMIZATION (SEO) WITH ARTIFICIAL INTELLIGENCE (AI)

C hapter 11 of the *AI Marketing Playbook* delves into the exciting world of search engine optimization (SEO) and how artificial intelligence (AI) is transforming this field. In this chapter, readers will learn how AI can be used to optimize their Web site for search engines and help to achieve higher rankings in search results. The chapter will also explore some successful SEO strategies that use AI, techniques for keyword research with AI, optimizing content for search engines with AI, and the future of SEO with AI, including voice search and natural language processing (NLP), as outlined in the following summaries.

How AI Can Be Used for SEO

Search engines use complex algorithms to determine the relevance and value of a Web site, and to rank it in search results. These algorithms are constantly evolving, making it difficult for marketers to keep up with the latest SEO techniques. This is where AI can help. AI-powered tools and techniques can analyze large volumes of data and help marketers identify the most effective SEO strategies. Here are some ways in which AI can be used for SEO:

- *Content optimization:* AI-powered content optimization tools can analyze Web site content and identify areas that need improvement. They can suggest changes to headlines, meta tags, and content structure to make it more search engine friendly.
- *Link building:* AI can help identify high-quality Web sites for link building purposes. These tools can analyze the backlinks of top-ranking Web sites and provide recommendations for high-quality Web sites that individuals can approach for link building.

- *Keyword research:* AI can help to identify the most relevant keywords for a Web site by analyzing search queries and Web site content. AI-powered tools can also suggest related keywords and long-tail keywords that can help improve search engine rankings.
- *User behavior analysis:* AI can help one understand how users interact with a Web site and what they are looking for. This information can be used to optimize Web site content and improve the user experience.

Examples of Successful SEO Strategies that Use AI

Here are some examples of successful SEO strategies that use AI:

- *IBM Watson:* IBM Watson is a cognitive computing system that can analyze large volumes of data and provide insights into SEO. It can identify the keywords that are most likely to drive traffic to a Web site and suggest changes to Web site content to improve search engine rankings.
- *Yoast SEO:* Yoast SEO is a WordPress plugin that uses AI to optimize Web site content for search engines. It analyzes Web site content and provides suggestions for improving SEO, such as adding keywords, optimizing images, and improving readability.
- *BrightEdge:* BrightEdge is an AI-powered SEO platform that helps businesses improve their search engine rankings. It provides insights into Web site performance, keyword performance, and competitive analysis.

Techniques for Keyword Research with AI

Keyword research is an essential part of any SEO strategy. Here are some techniques for keyword research with AI:

- *Use AI-powered tools:* There are many AI-powered keyword research tools available that can help you identify the most relevant keywords for a Web site. These tools can analyze search queries, Web site content, and user behavior to provide insights into the keywords that are most likely to drive traffic to a particular Web site.
- *Analyze competitor keywords:* AI-powered tools can analyze the keywords used by competitors and provide insights into the keywords that are most effective for a particular industry.
- *Use NLP:* NLP is a branch of AI that can analyze text and identify the meaning of words and phrases. By using NLP, a user can identify long-tail keywords and related keywords that can help improve their search engine rankings.

Optimizing Content for Search Engines with AI

Here are some techniques for optimizing content for search engines with AI:

- *Use AI-powered content optimization tools:* AI-powered content optimization tools can analyze Web site content and suggest changes to improve search engine rankings. These tools can suggest changes to headlines, meta tags, and content structure to make it more search engine friendly.
- *Use NLP:* NLP can also be used to optimize content for search engines. By analyzing text and identifying the meaning of words and phrases, NLP can help users identify the most relevant keywords for their content and optimize it accordingly.
- *Optimize for voice search:* With the rise of voice assistants like Siri and Alexa, optimizing content for voice search is becoming increasingly important. AI-powered tools can help users identify the most common voice search queries and optimize their content to provide answers to these queries.

The Future of SEO with AI: Voice Search and NLP

The future of SEO is closely tied to the development of AI and its applications in NLP and voice search. Here are some ways in which AI is expected to shape the future of SEO:

- *Voice search:* With the increasing popularity of voice assistants, voice search is expected to become a major player in SEO. AI-powered tools can help identify the most common voice search queries and optimize content to provide answers to these queries.
- *NLP:* As AI becomes more advanced, NLP is expected to become more sophisticated. This will allow search engines to better understand the meaning of words and phrases, making it easier to identify the most relevant content for search queries.
- *Personalization:* AI can also be used to personalize search results based on individual user preferences and behavior. This can improve the user experience and lead to higher engagement and conversions.

AI is transforming the field of SEO and providing marketers with powerful tools to improve their Web site rankings and drive traffic to their Web site. By using AI-powered tools and techniques, marketers can identify the most effective SEO strategies, conduct keyword research, optimize content for search engines, and stay ahead of the latest SEO trends. As AI continues to evolve, the future of SEO is expected to become even more exciting, with new opportunities for personalization, voice search, and NLP.

HOW AI CAN BE USED FOR SEO

SEO is the practice of optimizing a Web site to rank higher in search engine results pages (SERPs). It involves a variety of techniques, including keyword research, on-page optimization, link building, and content creation.

SEO is essential for any business that wants to drive traffic to their Web site and increase their online visibility. However, the process of SEO can be time-consuming and complicated. This is where AI can come in to help streamline and enhance the SEO process.

AI has the potential to revolutionize the SEO industry by providing insights and data-driven solutions that can help businesses stay ahead of the competition. This chapter will explore how AI can be used for SEO, including its benefits, challenges, and potential applications.

Benefits of AI for SEO

- *Automated keyword research:* One of the essential elements of SEO is keyword research, which involves identifying the keywords that the target audience is using to search for particular products or services. AI-powered tools can automate this process by analyzing search queries and identifying relevant keywords and phrases. This not only saves time but also ensures that users are targeting the right keywords.
- *Content creation:* Content is the foundation of any successful SEO strategy, and AI-powered tools can help generate high-quality content that resonates with the target audience. AI-powered tools can analyze search data, social media trends, and user behavior to generate content ideas and even create entire articles.
- *NLP:* NLP is a branch of AI that enables machines to understand human language. NLP can be used to analyze the text on a Web site and identify areas for improvement. NLP-powered tools can identify duplicate content, broken links, and other issues that can negatively impact a Web site's SEO.
- *Personalization:* Personalization is becoming increasingly important in the world of SEO. By analyzing user data, AI-powered tools can deliver personalized content and search results that are tailored to each user's interests and preferences. This can lead to higher engagement and better SEO results.
- *Link building:* Link building is a crucial element of SEO, but it can be time-consuming and challenging. AI-powered tools can automate the process of finding high-quality links by analyzing Web sites and identifying relevant opportunities. This not only saves time but also ensures that users are building high-quality links that will positively impact their SEO.

Challenges of AI for SEO

- *Complexity:* AI is a complex and rapidly evolving field, and implementing AI-powered SEO strategies can be challenging. It requires specialized knowledge and expertise, and businesses may need to invest in training or hiring new talent.

- *Cost:* Implementing AI-powered SEO strategies can be expensive, especially for small businesses. AI-powered tools can be costly, and businesses may need to invest in hardware, software, and other infrastructure to support AI-powered SEO initiatives.
- *Data privacy:* AI-powered tools rely on data, and businesses need to ensure that they are collecting and processing data in compliance with data privacy regulations. This can be challenging, especially with the increasing number of data privacy regulations around the world.
- *Bias:* AI-powered tools are only as good as the data they are trained on. If the data is biased or incomplete, the AI-powered tools may produce biased results. It is essential to ensure that the data used to train AI-powered SEO tools is diverse and unbiased.

Applications of AI for SEO

- *Voice search optimization:* With the rise of voice assistants like Siri and Alexa, voice search is becoming increasingly popular. AI-powered tools can help optimize Web sites for voice search by analyzing natural language queries and optimizing content accordingly.
- *Image and video SEO:* AI-powered tools can analyze images and videos on a Web site and identify areas for improvement. AI-powered tools can analyze image alt tags, file names, and captions to ensure that they are optimized for SEO. AI-powered tools can also analyze video transcripts and identify relevant keywords that can improve video SEO.
- *Predictive analytics:* AI-powered tools can analyze user data and predict search trends, allowing businesses to stay ahead of the competition. Predictive analytics can also help businesses identify areas for improvement and make data-driven decisions.
- *Local SEO:* Local SEO is becoming increasingly important, especially for small businesses. AI-powered tools can help businesses optimize their local SEO efforts by analyzing local search queries and identifying relevant keywords and phrases.
- *Content optimization:* AI-powered tools can analyze content on a Web site and identify areas for improvement. AI-powered tools can analyze the readability of content, identify keyword stuffing, and even provide suggestions for improving content structure.

AI has the potential to revolutionize the SEO industry by providing data-driven solutions that can help businesses stay ahead of the competition. AI-powered tools can automate time-consuming tasks, generate high-quality content, and provide personalized search results. However, implementing AI-powered SEO strategies can be challenging and expensive, and businesses need to ensure that they are collecting and processing data in compliance with data privacy regulations. Nonetheless, the benefits of AI for SEO are significant, and businesses that embrace AI-powered SEO strategies are likely to see significant improvements in their online visibility and search engine rankings.

SUCCESSFUL SEO STRATEGIES THAT USE AI

SEO is an ever evolving and complex field that has a significant impact on a business's online presence. With the advancement of AI technology, many businesses have started leveraging AI-powered SEO strategies to enhance their digital marketing efforts. This chapter discusses successful SEO strategies that use AI and provides examples of how businesses have implemented them.

Content Optimization Using AI

Content is the backbone of SEO. With AI-powered content optimization, businesses can produce high-quality content that resonates with their audience and ranks higher on SERPs. AI algorithms can analyze the content and suggest ways to improve it, including keyword optimization, readability, and relevance. One of the best examples of content optimization using AI is Grammarly. Grammarly uses AI algorithms to analyze and suggest improvements to the content's grammar, readability, and clarity. With its ability to learn and adapt to individual writing styles, it has become a valuable tool for bloggers, content writers, and digital marketers.

AI-Powered Keyword Research

Keyword research is the foundation of SEO. It helps businesses identify the right keywords that their audience is searching for and target them in their content. AI-powered keyword research tools can help businesses find new and relevant keywords that they may not have considered before. One such tool is SEMrush. It uses AI to analyze search queries, identify trends, and suggest new keyword ideas. SEMrush's Keyword Magic Tool helps businesses find keywords that their competitors are using and identify low-competition keywords that they can target.

Voice Search Optimization Using AI

With the rise of voice assistants like Alexa, Siri, and Google Assistant, voice search optimization has become a crucial aspect of SEO. AI-powered voice search optimization tools can help businesses optimize their content for voice search queries. These tools can analyze the conversational nature of voice searches and suggest long-tail keywords that businesses can target in their content. One such tool is AnswerThePublic. It uses AI algorithms to analyze search queries and generate a list of questions related to a particular topic. By optimizing content for these questions, businesses can improve their chances of appearing in voice search results.

Predictive Analytics Using AI

Predictive analytics is a powerful AI technology that can help businesses make data-driven decisions. In SEO, predictive analytics can help businesses identify trends, anticipate changes in search engine algorithms, and make strategic decisions to improve their online presence. One of the best examples of predictive analytics in SEO is Google Analytics. Google Analytics uses AI algorithms to analyze Web site traffic and provide insights into user behavior, demographics, and interests. This information can help businesses optimize their content and improve their Web site's user experience.

AI-Powered Link Building

Link building is an essential part of SEO. It involves getting high-quality links from other Web sites that point back to the specified Web site. AI-powered link building tools can help businesses identify relevant Web sites to target for link building campaigns. These tools can analyze Web site content, backlink profiles, and authority to identify potential link building opportunities. One such tool is BuzzStream. It uses AI to analyze Web site content and suggests personalized outreach emails that can help businesses build high-quality backlinks.

Using AI for link-building can streamline the process and make it more effective. Below is an outline of a structured approach to using AI tools for link-building, from researching prospects to creating personalized outreach.

Step-by-Step Guide for Using AI for Link Building

Step 1: Define Goals and Target Audience

- **Objective Setting**: Decide what the desired goals are for the link-building campaign, such as improving SEO rankings, increasing Web site traffic, or enhancing brand visibility.
- **Audience Identification**: Use AI to analyze the current customer base and Web site visitors to identify the characteristics of the target audience. Tools like Google Analytics and AI-powered customer segmentation platforms can be beneficial here.

Step 2: Identify Potential Link Opportunities

- **Competitor Analysis**: Use AI tools to analyze competitors' backlinks. Tools like Ahrefs, SEMrush, or Moz can show users where their links are coming from, helping you identify potential link-building opportunities.
- **Content Gap Analysis**: Deploy AI to conduct a content gap analysis between your Web site and your competitors' Web site. This can highlight topics they cover that you don't, presenting opportunities for creating content that attracts backlinks.

Step 3: Create High-Quality, Link-Worthy Content

- **Content Creation**: Use AI-powered content creation tools (like Jasper, formerly known as Jarvis) to generate articles, blogs, or other types of content that are original, informative, and engaging.
- **Content Optimization**: Apply AI tools for SEO optimization to ensure content ranks well on search engines, making it more likely to attract backlinks naturally.

Step 4: Build a Prospect List for Outreach

- **Prospect Finding**: Leverage AI tools to find Web sites, blogs, and influencers that are relevant to your niche. Tools like BuzzSumo can help identify potential link-building partners by analyzing content popularity and influencer engagement.
- **Prospect Prioritization**: Use AI to prioritize prospects based on their domain authority, relevance to your niche, and the likelihood of linking back to your content.

Step 5: Personalize Outreach

- **Email Crafting**: Employ AI-powered writing assistants to help craft personalized outreach emails. These tools can suggest personalized opening lines or comment on a recent article the prospect published, making your outreach more likely to receive a positive response.
- **Follow-Up Automation**: Utilize AI-driven CRM tools to automate follow-up emails, ensuring you remain persistent in outreach efforts without coming off as spammy.

Step 6: Monitor and Analyze Results

- **Backlink Monitoring**: Use backlink tracking tools to monitor the backlinks that have been acquired. This helps in understanding the impact of link-building efforts on the SEO performance.
- **Campaign Analysis**: Implement AI analytics tools to measure the success of your link-building campaign against your initial objectives. Analyze what worked and what didn't to refine the strategy for future campaigns.

Step 7: Adjust and Improve Continuously

- **Iterative Learning**: Use insights gained from AI analytics to continuously refine link-building strategy. This includes improving content, targeting better prospects, and personalizing outreach further.

Additional Tips:

- **AI Ethics and Transparency**: Always be transparent about using AI in content creation and outreach efforts where necessary.
- **Compliance with Webmaster Guidelines**: Ensure that your use of AI for link-building complies with search engine webmaster guidelines to avoid penalties.

Using AI in link-building strategy can significantly enhance efficiency and effectiveness. By following these steps and continuously refining the approach based on AI-driven insights, one can achieve better results and a stronger online presence.

Remember, effective link building is about quality over quantity. It's important to focus on building genuine relationships and providing value through content and interactions. ChatGPT can provide valuable insights and ideas, but the actual implementation requires a personalized and strategic approach.

Image Optimization Using AI

Images play a crucial role in SEO. They help break up content, make it more engaging, and provide additional information to search engines. AI-powered image optimization tools can help businesses optimize their images for search engines by analyzing the images' alt text, file size, and quality. One such tool is TinyIMG. It uses AI algorithms to compress images without losing quality, optimize alt text, and improve image file names, all of which can help businesses improve their Web site's load speed and overall, SEO.

AI-powered SEO strategies are transforming the way businesses approach SEO. By leveraging AI technologies like content optimization, keyword research, voice search optimization, predictive analytics, link building, and image optimization, businesses can enhance their online presence and improve their Web site's rankings on SERPs. Successful implementation of AI-powered SEO strategies can lead to increased: Web site traffic, higher engagement rates, and improved business outcomes. As AI continues to advance, it will undoubtedly play an increasingly significant role in SEO, and businesses that adopt AI-powered SEO strategies today will be better equipped to stay ahead of the competition tomorrow.

TECHNIQUES FOR KEYWORD RESEARCH WITH AI

Keyword research is a critical aspect of any successful marketing strategy. It involves identifying the phrases or words that potential customers use when searching for products or services in a particular industry. Keyword research helps to optimize Web sites, create relevant content, and attract more organic traffic. With the advent of AI, keyword research has become more accessible, efficient, and effective. This section of the *AI for Marketing Playbook* discusses various techniques for conducting keyword research with AI.

- *Natural language processing (NLP):* NLP is a technique that AI uses to understand human language. NLP algorithms analyze text and identify patterns, relationships, and sentiments. NLP can be useful for keyword research because it can help identify keywords that customers use to describe products or services. It can also identify long-tail keywords, which are longer and more specific phrases that customers use when searching for products or services. NLP can analyze customer reviews, social media posts, and online forums to identify the most popular keywords used by customers in your industry.

- *Image and video recognition:* Image and video recognition is another AI technique that can be used for keyword research. AI algorithms can analyze images and videos to identify objects, people, and even emotions. This technique is particularly useful for identifying visual keywords that customers use when searching for products or services. If a company is selling a product that is popular among athletes, image recognition can identify the most common sports or activities associated with that product. This information can be used to create relevant content and optimize the Web site for those keywords.

- *Sentiment analysis:* Sentiment analysis is a technique that AI uses to understand the emotions and attitudes expressed in text. Sentiment analysis algorithms analyze customer reviews, social media posts, and online forums to identify positive or negative sentiment toward a particular brand or industry. This technique can be used to identify keywords that are associated with positive sentiment, such as "excellent customer service" or "high-quality products." It can also help identify negative keywords that customers associate with an industry, such as "poor quality" or "bad customer service."

- *Competitor analysis:* Competitor analysis is an essential aspect of keyword research. AI can be used to analyze a competitor's Web site, content, and social media profiles to identify the keywords they are targeting. This information can be used to identify gaps in strategy and find new keywords to target. AI algorithms can also analyze competitor's backlinks to identify the most valuable keywords for an industry.

- *Keyword clustering:* Keyword clustering is a technique that involves grouping similar keywords together. AI algorithms can analyze substantial amounts of data to identify keywords that are related to each other. This technique can be useful for identifying long-tail keywords that customers use when searching for specific products or services. By grouping similar keywords together, one can create more relevant content and optimize their Web site for a wider range of keywords.

- *Voice Search Optimization:* With the rise of voice assistants such as Siri, Alexa, and Google Assistant, voice search optimization has become an essential aspect of keyword research. AI can analyze voice searches to identify the most popular keywords used by customers when using voice assistants. Voice searches are often more conversational and longer than text searches, so AI algorithms can identify long-tail keywords that are specific to voice searches.

• *Predictive Keyword Analysis:* Predictive keyword analysis is a technique that uses AI to predict the most popular keywords for a particular industry in the future. AI algorithms can analyze data trends, customer behavior, and industry developments to identify emerging keywords. This technique can be useful for identifying new keywords to target before competitors do.

AI has revolutionized keyword research by providing marketers with powerful tools to identify the most relevant and profitable keywords for their industry. Techniques such as NLP, image and video recognition, sentiment analysis, competitor analysis, keyword clustering, voice search optimization, and predictive keyword analysis can help you conduct more efficient and effective keyword research. By leveraging AI, one can gain a deeper understanding of their target audience, identify new opportunities, and optimize their Web site and content for the keywords that matter most. However, it's important to remember that AI is not a replacement for human insight and expertise. It's essential to combine AI with personalized knowledge and experience to develop a comprehensive and effective keyword research strategy.

OPTIMIZING CONTENT FOR SEARCH ENGINES WITH AI

Optimizing content for search engines is a crucial component of any digital marketing strategy. With the increasing popularity of AI in the marketing world, it is now possible to use AI-powered tools and techniques to optimize content for search engines. This chapter will explore the numerous ways AI can be used to optimize content for search engines.

Understanding AI and Search Engines

Before diving into the ways AI can optimize content for search engines, it is essential to understand the relationship between AI and search engines. AI refers to the ability of machines to perform tasks that typically require human intelligence, such as language understanding, reasoning, and learning. Search engines, on the other hand, use algorithms to analyze and rank Web pages based on relevance and other factors.

AI can help search engines better understand Web content by analyzing and processing vast amounts of data, including text, images, and videos. It can also help search engines identify patterns and trends in search queries, making it easier to deliver relevant results to users.

Using AI to Optimize Content for Search Engines

Now that readers have a basic understanding of AI and search engines, it's time to explore how AI can be used to optimize content for search engines.

Keyword Research

Keyword research is an essential component of any SEO strategy. It involves identifying the keywords and phrases that users are searching for and incorporating them into one's content. AI-powered tools can help identify keywords and phrases that are relevant to that particular content and are likely to rank well on search engines. These tools use NLP to analyze search queries and identify relevant keywords and phrases.

The tool Ahrefs uses AI to analyze search queries and identify related keywords and phrases. It also provides information on keyword difficulty and search volume, making it easier to choose the right keywords for particular content.

Step-by-Step Guide for Using AI for Keyword Research

Step 1: Define SEO Goals

- **Objective Setting**: Clearly outline what the desired achievement is with SEO efforts, such as increasing organic traffic, improving search engine rankings, or boosting conversion rates.
- **Target Audience Identification**: Use AI to analyze existing Web site data to identify target audience's preferences, behaviors, and search patterns.

Step 2: Conduct Keyword Research

- **AI-Powered Keyword Discovery**: Utilize AI-powered keyword research tools (like SEMrush, Ahrefs, or Moz) to find relevant keywords and phrases. These tools can suggest keywords based on search volume, difficulty, and relevance tocontent.
- **Search Intent Analysis**: Apply AI to analyze the search intent behind the keywords. Understanding whether users are seeking information, looking to make a purchase, or comparing products is crucial for tailoring your content.

Step 3: Analyze Competitors

- **Competitor Identification**: Use AI to identify main competitors based on shared keywords and industry relevance.
- **Content and SEO Strategy Analysis**: Deploy AI tools to analyze competitors' content, backlink profiles, and overall, SEO strategy. This can uncover gaps in strategy and opportunities for improvement.

Step 4: Optimize Content Strategy

- **Content Gap Analysis**: Implement AI to perform a content gap analysis between your site and those of your competitors. This helps in identifying topics that are underexplored on your Web site.

- **AI-Generated Content Ideas**: Leverage AI tools to generate content ideas and headlines that are optimized for search intent and keyword relevance.

Step 5: Create and Optimize Content

- **AI-Assisted Content Creation**: Use AI writing assistants to create or improve content that is engaging, informative, and optimized for SEO.
- **On-Page SEO Optimization**: Apply AI tools for on-page optimization, including optimizing titles, meta descriptions, and headers for targeted keywords. These tools can also suggest internal linking opportunities.

Step 6: Monitor SEO Performance

- **AI Analytics Tools**: Utilize AI-driven analytics tools to monitor your Web site's SEO performance. Track rankings, organic traffic, and other key performance indicators (KPIs) to gauge the success of your efforts.
- **Adjust Based on Insights**: Use the insights gained from AI analytics to continuously refine your SEO strategy, focusing on areas that need improvement.

Step 7: Backlink Analysis and Outreach

- **AI-Powered Backlink Analysis**: Use AI tools to analyze backlink profile and those of competitors. Identify high-quality backlink opportunities.
- **Outreach Strategy**: Implement AI to help craft personalized outreach emails for link-building opportunities, making requests more likely to be accepted.

Additional Tips:

- **Stay Updated on AI Trends**: SEO and AI technologies evolve rapidly. Stay informed about the latest AI tools and best practices in SEO to keep strategy effective.
- **Ethical Considerations**: Use AI responsibly, ensuring that the content remains ethical, transparent, and provides real value to the audience.
- Incorporating AI into SEO research and strategy can provide a competitive edge, making processes more efficient and uncovering opportunities one might not find otherwise. By following these steps and continuously learning from AI-generated insights, users can optimize their Web site's SEO performance and achieve online visibility goals.

Remember, SEO is an ongoing process, and strategies should be adjusted over time based on performance and changing search engine algorithms. ChatGPT can provide valuable insights and suggestions, but it's also important to stay informed with the latest SEO trends and best practices.

CONTENT CREATION

Creating high-quality content that is optimized for search engines is crucial for improving your Web site's ranking. AI-powered content creation tools can help you create content that is relevant, engaging, and optimized for search engines.

One example of an AI-powered content creation tool is Articoolo. This tool uses AI to generate high-quality articles based on keywords and phrases. It analyzes the context of the keywords and creates unique, relevant content that is optimized for search engines.

Step-by-Step Instructions for Using AI for Content Creation

Using ChatGPT for content creation involves leveraging its capabilities to generate ideas, structure content, and produce drafts that can be refined and tailored to specific needs. Here's a step-by-step guide to utilizing ChatGPT effectively for this purpose:

1. Define Your Content Objectives

Purpose and Audience: Identify the purpose of content (inform, persuade, entertain) and the target audience.

Key Topics: Determine the topics or themes the content will cover.

2. Brainstorming Ideas with ChatGPT

Topic Suggestions: Ask ChatGPT for content ideas or topics related to a particular field.

Angle and Perspective: Discuss different angles or perspectives to approach that particular topic.

3. Creating an Outline

Structure Request: Request ChatGPT to create an outline for content, including introduction, main points, and conclusion.

Subtopics: Identify key subtopics to be included and ask ChatGPT to structure these within that content.

4. Drafting Content

Initial Draft: Ask ChatGPT to generate a draft based on the outline. This can be a section-by-section approach.

Expand and Elaborate: Request elaboration on specific points or ask for additional details to flesh out sections.

5. Incorporating SEO (if applicable)

Keyword Integration: If the content is for online purposes, integrate relevant keywords. Users can ask ChatGPT for suggestions.

SEO-Friendly Content: Request tips or strategies for making the content SEO-friendly.

6. Adding Creativity

Creative Elements: Ask for creative elements like metaphors, anecdotes, or stories relevant to the topic.

Style and Tone: Discuss and define the style and tone suitable for the target audience and purpose.

7. Editing and Refining

Grammar and Style Checks: Use ChatGPT to review the content for grammatical errors or stylistic improvements.

Feedback: Ask ChatGPT for feedback on how the content can be improved.

8. Formatting and Presentation

Formatting Tips: Get tips on formatting content for better readability and engagement.

Visual Elements: Discuss ideas for accompanying visuals, like images or infographics, if applicable.

9. Call to Action (if applicable)

Crafting a CTA: If the content has a specific goal (like sales, sign-ups), ask for help in creating an effective call-to-action.

10. Final Review

Read Through: Do a final read-through of the content to ensure it flows well and meets all objectives.

Adjustments: Make any final adjustments based on a review.

11. Using Feedback for Improvement

Gathering Feedback: After publishing or sharing the content, gather feedback.

Iterative Improvement: Use this feedback for future content creation, discussing improvements with ChatGPT.

12. Staying Current and Relevant

Trends and Updates: Regularly consult ChatGPT about the latest trends in content creation and updates in a particular field to keep content relevant.

Remember, while ChatGPT can significantly aid in the content creation process, the finishing touch and human judgment are crucial to ensure the content aligns with goals, voice, and audience expectations.

Content Optimization

Optimizing content for search engines involves making sure it is structured and formatted correctly and contains the right keywords and phrases. AI-powered content optimization tools can help to optimize content for search engines by analyzing the structure, formatting, and content of a Web site.

The tool Clear scope uses AI to analyze a Web site's content and provide suggestions on how to improve it. It analyzes the content and compares it to the top-ranking content for the same keywords, providing suggestions on how to improve the content's relevance and structure.

Image and Video Optimization

Images and videos can play a significant role in improving a Web site's ranking on search engines. AI-powered tools can help optimize images and videos for search engines by analyzing the content and providing suggestions on how to improve their relevance and structure.

The tool Google Vision uses AI to analyze images and provide information on the content of the image. It can identify objects, people, and text in images, making it easier to optimize them for search engines.

AI-powered tools and techniques can be an asset for optimizing content for search engines. They can help with keyword research, content creation, content optimization, and image and video optimization. As AI continues to evolve, expect to see more innovative ways to optimize content for search engines. By leveraging AI-powered tools and techniques, marketers can improve their Web site's ranking on search engines and attract more traffic to their site.

Using AI for video and image optimization can significantly enhance the visual content's performance, making it more engaging for viewers and more likely to rank well on search engines. Here's a step-by-step guide to leveraging AI for optimizing videos and images.

Step-by-Step Instructions for Using ChatGPT for Video and Image Optimization

Step 1: Define Your Objectives

- *Objective Setting:* Identify what desired goals of your visual content, whether it's increasing engagement, improving SEO rankings, or enhancing user experience on your Web site.
- *Target Audience Analysis:* Use AI to analyze the audience's preferences, helping to tailor the visual content to their interests and behaviors.

Step 2: Optimize Visual Content for SEO

- *AI-Powered Keyword Research:* Utilize AI tools for keyword research specific to the visual content. Apply these keywords strategically in image descriptions, alt tags, video titles, and descriptions.
- *Content Tagging and Classification:* Implement AI to automatically tag and categorize the visual content, making it more discoverable both on the site and in search engine results.

Step 3: Image Optimization

- *AI-Driven Image Enhancement:* Use AI tools to automatically adjust the brightness, contrast, saturation, and sharpness of all images, improving their quality without manual editing.
- *Compression and Resizing:* Employ AI to compress and resize images without significant loss in quality, ensuring the Web site's load time is optimized.
- *Custom Thumbnail Creation:* Leverage AI to generate eye-catching, relevant thumbnails for videos, increasing click-through rates from search results.

Step 4: Video Optimization

- *AI-Enhanced Editing:* Utilize AI-powered video editing tools to improve lighting, stabilize shaky footage, and enhance overall video quality.
- *Automated Subtitling and Transcription:* Use AI to generate accurate subtitles and transcripts for videos, making them accessible to a wider audience and improving SEO.
- *Content Analysis for Engagement:* Apply AI to analyze video content, identifying elements that drive engagement and suggesting improvements for future videos.

Step 5: Personalization and A/B Testing

- *AI-Powered Personalization:* Use AI to personalize visual content displayed to different segments of the audience based on their preferences and past interactions.
- *Automated A/B Testing:* Leverage AI tools to conduct A/B tests on different versions of the images and videos, including variations in titles, descriptions, and thumbnails, to see what performs best.

Step 6: Monitor Performance and Gain Insights

- *Performance Tracking:* Utilize AI-driven analytics tools to track how the visual content performs across different platforms, analyzing metrics such as views, engagement rates, and conversion rates.
- *Insights and Improvements:* Use AI to analyze performance data, providing actionable insights for improving future video and image content.

Step 7: Ensure Accessibility and Compliance

- *Accessibility Features:* Apply AI to ensure visual content is accessible to all users, including those with disabilities, by automatically generating alt text for images and captions for videos.

- *Compliance Checks:* Use AI tools to ensure visual content complies with regulations and platform-specific guidelines, reducing the risk of it being flagged or removed.

Additional Tips:

- *Stay Informed on AI Developments:* The field of AI is rapidly evolving. Stay updated on new tools and techniques for optimizing video and image content.
- *Ethical Considerations:* Be mindful of privacy and ethical considerations when using AI, especially in personalization and data analysis.

By following these steps and leveraging AI in your video and image optimization efforts, one can significantly improve the visibility, engagement, and performance of their visual content across various platforms.

THE FUTURE OF SEO WITH AI: VOICE SEARCH AND NLP

SEO is a crucial aspect of digital marketing that has evolved considerably over the years. With the advent of AI, the landscape of SEO is changing once again. AI-powered technologies such as voice search and NLP are driving the future of SEO. This section will explore how AI is impacting SEO, particularly in the context of voice search and NLP.

Voice Search

Voice search is a rapidly growing trend that is transforming the way people search for information online. As per ComScore, by 2020, 50% of all online searches will be conducted via voice search. With voice assistants like Siri, Alexa, and Google Assistant, users can search for information, set reminders, and perform a host of other tasks without having to type anything. As such, voice search is becoming an increasingly popular way for people to interact with technology.

For SEO, this means that businesses need to start optimizing their Web sites and content for voice search. Voice search queries tend to be longer and more conversational than text-based queries, which means that traditional SEO strategies may not work as effectively for voice search. Here are some tips for optimizing for voice search:

- *Use natural language:* As voice searches tend to be more conversational, businesses should optimize their content for natural language queries. This means using long-tail keywords and focusing on the intent behind the search query.
- *Focus on local SEO:* Voice searches often have a local intent, such as "Find a coffee shop near me." As such, businesses should focus on optimizing their local SEO to ensure that they appear in local search results.

- *Optimize for featured snippets:* Featured snippets are the answer boxes that appear at the top of search results. Voice assistants often read out the featured snippet as the answer to a voice search query. As such, businesses should optimize their content to appear in featured snippets.
- *Optimize for mobile:* Voice searches are often performed on mobile devices, so businesses should ensure that their Web sites are optimized for mobile.
- *Create FAQ pages:* Voice assistants often use FAQ pages to answer voice search queries. Businesses should create FAQ pages that are optimized for voice search queries.

NLP

NLP is an AI-powered technology that enables machines to understand and interpret human language. NLP is already being used in various applications, including chatbots, virtual assistants, and voice search. With NLP, machines can understand the context and intent behind a user's search query, which means that businesses need to start optimizing their content for NLP.

Here are some tips for optimizing for NLP:

- *Focus on intent:* NLP focuses on the intent behind a user's search query. Businesses should optimize their content for the user's intent, rather than just the keywords they use.
- *Use semantic search:* Semantic search is a search technique that focuses on the meaning behind a user's search query, rather than just the keywords. Businesses should optimize their content for semantic search to ensure that it is relevant and valuable to users.
- *Use structured data:* Structured data is a way of organizing information on a Web site so that machines can understand it better. Businesses should use structured data to ensure that their content is easily understood by machines.
- *Use conversational language:* NLP is all about understanding natural language. Businesses should use conversational language in their content to make it easier for machines to understand.
- *Use sentiment analysis:* Sentiment analysis is a technique that uses NLP to determine the sentiment behind a user's search query. Businesses can use sentiment analysis to understand the emotions behind their customers' search queries and optimize their content accordingly.

AI-powered technologies such as voice search and NLP are changing the landscape of SEO. Businesses that want to stay ahead of the curve need to start optimizing their content for these technologies. Optimizing for voice search means focusing on natural language, local SEO, featured snippets, mobile optimization, and creating FAQ pages. Optimizing for NLP means focusing on intent, semantic search, structured data, conversational language, and sentiment analysis.

The future of SEO with AI is exciting, and businesses that embrace these technologies will have a competitive advantage. AI-powered technologies are making it easier for businesses to understand their customers' needs and preferences and provide them with relevant and valuable content. As such, businesses that invest in AI-powered SEO strategies will be better equipped to provide their customers with the best possible experience and drive business growth.

SEO has been a crucial aspect of digital marketing for years now. SEO is the process of optimizing Web site content and structure to improve a Web site's visibility and ranking on SERPs. Over time, search engines have become more complex, and SEO has evolved from simple keyword stuffing to an intricate process that requires a deep understanding of user intent, semantic search, and a range of other factors that affect ranking. This chapter will explore how AI is being used in SEO to improve the efficiency and effectiveness of the process.

AI can be used to improve SEO in several ways. One of the most significant benefits of AI is its ability to analyze and process vast amounts of data quickly and accurately. This makes it possible to extract insights that would be difficult or impossible for humans to identify manually. Here is some ways AI can be used in SEO:

- *Content optimization:* AI can analyze existing content and suggest changes to improve its relevance, readability, and keyword density. It can also suggest related keywords and topics that can be added to the content to make it more comprehensive and valuable to users.
- *Keyword research:* AI can analyze search engine data to identify new and emerging keywords that can be used to improve ranking and attract more traffic to a Web site. This can help businesses stay ahead of the curve and adapt their content to the changing search landscape.
- *Competitive analysis:* AI can analyze competitor Web sites and identify their strengths and weaknesses. This can help businesses identify opportunities for improvement and develop strategies to outperform their competitors.
- *Natural language processing (NLP):* AI can analyze user search queries and understand their intent, context, and language nuances. This can help businesses create content that better matches user intent and improve their chances of ranking for relevant keywords.

Many businesses have already started using AI to improve their SEO strategies. Here are some examples of successful AI-powered SEO strategies:

- *Airbnb:* Airbnb uses AI to optimize its content for search engines. It uses a machine learning (ML) model to analyze user search queries and identify the most relevant keywords and topics. This has helped Airbnb improve its ranking and attract more traffic to its Web site.

- *HubSpot:* HubSpot uses an AI-powered content optimization tool called "Content Strategy." This tool analyzes existing content and suggests changes to improve its relevance, readability, and keyword density. It also suggests related keywords and topics that can be added to the content to make it more comprehensive and valuable to users.
- *Rank Brain:* Rank Brain is an AI-powered algorithm used by Google to analyze user search queries and understand their intent. It uses NLP to match user queries with relevant content and improve the accuracy of search results.

Techniques for keyword research with AI Keyword research is an essential aspect of SEO. AI can help businesses identify new and emerging keywords that can be used to improve their ranking and attract more traffic to their Web site. Here are some techniques for keyword research with AI:

- *Natural language processing (NLP):* NLP is a technique used to analyze user search queries and understand their intent, context, and language nuances. This can help businesses identify keywords that match user intent and create content that better meets their needs.
- *Topic modeling:* Topic modeling is a technique used to identify the most relevant topics related to a particular keyword or query. This can help businesses create comprehensive content that covers all aspects of a particular topic and attracts more traffic to their Web site.
- *Keyword clustering:* Keyword clustering is a technique used to group related keywords into clusters. This can help businesses identify keyword themes and create content that covers all aspects of a particular theme.

Optimizing content for search engines with AI can help businesses optimize their content for search engines in several ways. Here are some techniques for optimizing content with AI:

- *Content optimization tools:* AI-powered content optimization tools can analyze existing content and suggest changes to improve its relevance, readability, and keyword density. These tools can also suggest related keywords and topics that can be added to the content to make it more comprehensive and valuable to users.
- *Image and video optimization:* AI can analyze images and videos and suggest changes to improve their relevance and keyword density. This can help businesses improve the visibility of their multimedia content on search engines.
- *Voice search optimization:* As more people use voice search to find information online, businesses need to optimize their content for voice search. AI can analyze user voice queries and identify the most relevant keywords and topics that can be used to optimize content for voice search.

The future of SEO with AI: Voice search and NLP As AI continues to evolve, the future of SEO is likely to be shaped by two key trends: voice search and NLP. Here are some ways these trends are likely to impact SEO in the future:

- *Voice search:* As more people use voice search to find information online, businesses will need to optimize their content for voice search. This will require a deep understanding of user intent, NLP, and the ability to create content that matches the way people speak.
- *Natural language processing (NLP):* As search engines become more sophisticated, they will rely more heavily on NLP to understand user search queries and match them with relevant content. This will require businesses to create content that is optimized for natural language and that reflects the way people speak.

AI is rapidly transforming the way SEO is done. By leveraging the power of AI, businesses can improve their ranking, attract more traffic to their Web site, and create content that better meets the needs of their users. From content optimization to keyword research, AI is being used in a variety of ways to improve the efficiency and effectiveness of SEO. As AI continues to evolve, expect to see even more exciting developments in the world of SEO.

USING ARTIFICIAL INTELLIGENCE FOR CONTENT MARKETING

The following list includes a breakdown of the topics covered in this chapter:

- *How AI can be used for content marketing:* AI can be used to improve various aspects of content marketing, including content ideation, creation, personalization, and measurement. By using AI technologies, marketers can automate routine tasks, gain insights into their audience behavior, and optimize their content marketing efforts for better results.
- *Examples of successful content marketing strategies with AI:* Several companies have successfully used AI in their content marketing campaigns. Coca-Cola's "Share a Coke" campaign used AI to customize custom name tags to increase engagement and social sharing. Sephora, a cosmetics brand, uses AI chatbots to provide customers with personalized recommendations based on their skin type, preferences, and purchase history.
- *The role of AI in idea generation and content creation:* AI can help content creators generate the latest ideas by analyzing data from various sources such as social media, search trends and customer feedback. Users can also help with the creation process by suggesting titles, images, and keywords that will resonate with their audience.
- *Personalization of content for different audience segments with AI:* AI can help marketers personalize content for different segments of their audience by analyzing their behavior, preferences, and demographics. This may include tailoring the tone, language, and format of the content to the needs and interests of the target audience.

- *Measuring content marketing effectiveness with AI:* AI can give marketers real-time insights into the performance of their content marketing efforts. This includes tracking metrics like engagement rates, conversion rates, and customer lifetime value, as well as identifying patterns and trends that may inform future content marketing strategies.

Overall, AI can be a valuable tool for content marketers looking to streamline their efforts, deliver personalized experiences to their audience, and drive better results.

HOW AI CAN BE USED FOR CONTENT MARKETING

AI has revolutionized the world of marketing, including content marketing. This section will discuss in detail how AI can be used for content marketing.

Content Creation

One of the main ways AI can be used in content marketing is through content creation. AI-powered content creation tools can help create a variety of content formats, such as articles, blogs, social media posts and even videos.

These AI-powered tools can create content based on specific keywords, subject matter, and even tonality and writing style. By using these tools, users can create a massive amount of content in a short amount of time, which can be incredibly helpful in scaling content marketing efforts.

AI in Content Marketing: Step-by-Step Instructions for Content Creation

1. **Identify Content Goals:**

   - Define the objectives of the content marketing strategy, such as brand awareness, lead generation, or thought leadership.
   - Align these goals with the type of content to be created.

2. **Keyword and Subject Research:**

   - Use AI-powered tools to conduct research on trending keywords, topics, and questions in a particular industry.
   - Identify gaps in existing content that specific marketing efforts could fill.

3. **AI Tool Selection and Setup:**

   - Choose an AI-powered content creation tool that best fits specific needs based on features such as language generation, tone analysis, and style customization.
   - Set up the tool with specified content parameters, including keywords, desired tone, and content format.

4. **Content Generation:**

- Input research findings into the AI tool to generate content drafts.
- Allow the tool to create initial versions of articles, blog posts, social media updates, or video scripts.

5. **Quality Check and Editing:**

- Review and edit the AI-generated content to ensure it aligns with the brand's voice and editorial guidelines.
- Make adjustments to enhance readability, engagement, and SEO.

6. **Content Optimization:**

- Use additional AI tools to optimize content for search engines and user engagement.
- Analyze and incorporate optimal content structures, meta tags, and semantic keywords.

7. **Multimedia Integration:**

- If the content format allows, use AI to create or suggest images, infographics, or video content that complements the text.
- Integrate these multimedia elements to increase the appeal and effectiveness of the content.

8. **Publishing and Distribution:**

- Utilize AI to determine the best channels and times for publishing the content.
- Automate the content distribution process across selected platforms.

9. **Performance Monitoring and Analytics:**

- Implement AI tools to track the performance of the content.
- Analyze metrics such as engagement, lead generation, and conversions.

10. **Iterative Improvement:**

- Use the insights gathered from AI analytics to continuously improve content.
- Adapt a strategy and creation process based on data-driven feedback.

Content Optimization

Another way AI can help with content marketing is by optimizing content. AI-powered tools can analyze content and provide suggestions on how to optimize it for better performance. This includes analyzing the content's readability, keyword density, and overall structure.

By optimizing content, users can increase your visibility in search engines and make it more attractive to their target audience. This can lead to higher engagement rates, more traffic to their Web site, and better conversions.

Personalization

AI can also be used to personalize content. By analyzing user data such as search history, browsing behavior and social media activity, AI-powered tools can create personalized content for individual users.

This can help one provide more relevant content to their audience, which can improve engagement rates and lead to more conversions. Personalization also helps build stronger relationships with customers by showing them an understanding of their needs and interests.

Content

AI can also help with content distribution. AI-powered tools can analyze user behavior and preferences to identify the best channels to distribute content. This includes identifying the most effective social media platforms, email marketing campaigns, and even paid advertising channels.

By using AI to optimize your content delivery strategy, users can ensure their content reaches the right audience at the right time, increasing the likelihood of engagement and conversions.

AI-Powered Content Distribution: Step-by-Step Instructions

1. **Tool Integration and Data Collection:**

   • Integrate AI-powered analytics tools with content management systems.
   • Collect data on user interactions, preferences, and engagement across channels.

2. **Channel Analysis:**

   • Use AI to analyze the effectiveness of various distribution channels including social media, email, and paid ads.
   • Determine which channels resonate most with the target audience.

3. **Content Strategy Optimization:**

   • Apply AI insights to tailor content distribution strategy.
   • Choose the most effective platforms for each type of content based on AI recommendations.

4. Timing and Scheduling:

- Leverage AI to determine the optimal times for content posting when audience engagement is highest.
- Schedule content releases across platforms accordingly.

5. Performance Monitoring:

- Continuously monitor how distributed content performs on each channel.
- Use AI tools to track engagement metrics such as likes, shares, and comments.

Content Analysis

AI can be used for content analysis. AI-powered tools can analyze the content's performance, including engagement rates, traffic, and conversion rates. By analyzing this data, one can gain insight into the strengths and weaknesses of their content and make data-backed decisions to improve their content marketing strategy.

AI can be used in a variety of ways for content marketing, including content creation, optimization, personalization, distribution, and analytics. By using AI-powered tools, one can improve the effectiveness of their content marketing efforts, increase engagement rates, and drive more conversions.

AI-Powered Content Analysis: Step-by-Step Instructions

1. Engagement Tracking:

- Implement AI tools to measure engagement rates on content.
- Track key performance indicators like page views, bounce rates, and social shares.

2. Content Effectiveness Evaluation:

- Analyze traffic and conversion rates related to content.
- Use AI to assess which pieces of content are driving results and contributing to specific goals.

3. Insight Extraction:

- Extract actionable insights on content performance including what themes, formats, and topics perform best.
- Identify trends and patterns in audience behavior in response to content.

4. **Strategy Refinement:**

   - Apply the insights gained from AI analysis to refine content marketing strategy.
   - Make informed decisions on content creation, publication, and promotion.

5. **A/B Testing:**

   - Use AI to design and execute A/B tests on content.
   - Optimize headlines, images, and call-to-actions based on test outcomes.

6. **Content Update and Repurposing:**

   - Based on AI insights, update existing content to improve performance.
   - Repurpose high-performing content into different formats for broader distribution.

SUCCESSFUL CONTENT MARKETING STRATEGIES THAT USE AI

Content marketing is a crucial component of any modern marketing strategy, as it allows businesses to engage with potential customers by providing valuable and informative content. In recent years, artificial intelligence (AI) has emerged as a powerful tool for optimizing content marketing strategies. This section of the *AI Marketing Playbook* will explore some successful content marketing strategies that use AI, providing in-depth examples and historical context.

   - *Personalization* is one of the most effective ways to engage with customers and build lasting relationships. By tailoring content to individual users based on their interests and behaviors, businesses can provide a more relevant and engaging experience. However, manually curating personalized content for each user can be time-consuming and expensive. This is where AI comes in.

AI-powered personalization algorithms can analyze substantial amounts of data, such as users' browsing history, social media activity, and purchase behavior, to provide personalized content recommendations in real-time. Netflix's recommendation algorithm uses machine learning (ML) to analyze users' viewing histories and provide personalized movie and TV show recommendations.

Another example of AI-powered personalization is Amazon's recommendation engine. When users browse Amazon's Web site, they are presented with a range of products that are tailored to their interests and past purchases. Amazon's recommendation engine uses ML algorithms to analyze users' browsing and purchase behavior, as well as factors such as price, popularity, and product availability, to provide personalized recommendations.

- *Content Creation Creating:* High-quality content is a time-consuming and resource-intensive process. However, AI-powered content creation tools can help businesses to streamline this process and produce content at scale. One example of an AI-powered content creation tool is Wordsmith, which uses natural language generation (NLG) technology to automatically generate written content based on predefined templates and data sources.

The Associated Press uses Wordsmith to automatically generate news articles about corporate earnings reports. The tool analyzes the financial data and generates a written article that summarizes the key findings, which is then published on the AP's Web site.

Another example of AI-powered content creation is Canva's design tool, which uses ML to suggest design elements such as fonts, colors, and images based on the content of the design. This tool allows users to create high-quality designs quickly and easily, without requiring extensive design experience.

- *SEO Optimization:* Search engine optimization (SEO) is a crucial component of any content marketing strategy, as it helps businesses to rank higher in SERPs and drive organic traffic to their Web site. However, optimizing content for SEO can be a complex and time-consuming process, as it involves analyzing keywords, optimizing on-page elements such as meta descriptions and headers, and building high-quality backlinks.

AI-powered SEO tools can help businesses to streamline this process and optimize their content more effectively. MarketMuse uses AI to analyze the content of a Web site and identify gaps and opportunities for optimization. The tool provides recommendations for optimizing on-page elements such as meta descriptions and headers, as well as suggestions for creating the latest content to target specific keywords.

Another example of AI-powered SEO is BrightEdge, which uses ML to analyze SERPs and identify opportunities for optimization. The tool provides recommendations for optimizing on-page elements, building backlinks, and creating content that is optimized for specific keywords.

- *Social Media Marketing:* Social media is a powerful tool for engaging with customers and building brand awareness. However, managing multiple social media accounts and creating engaging content can be a time-consuming and resource-intensive process. AI-powered social media tools can help businesses to streamline this process and optimize their social media marketing efforts.

Hootsuite uses AI to analyze social media conversations and identify trends and insights. The tool provides recommendations for creating content that is relevant and engaging to users, as well as scheduling posts and tracking social media metrics such as engagement and reach.

Another example of AI-powered social media marketing is Lumen5, which uses AI to automatically generate video content from written articles or blog posts. The tool analyzes the content and creates a video that is optimized for social media platforms such as Facebook, Instagram, and Twitter.

- *Predictive Analytics:* Predictive analytics is a powerful tool for understanding customer behavior and predicting future trends. By analyzing large amounts of data, such as customer demographics, purchase history, and Web site interactions, businesses can gain insights into their customers' needs and preferences.

AI-powered predictive analytics tools can help businesses to streamline this process and provide more accurate predictions. Salesforce's Einstein AI uses ML to analyze customer data and provide insights into customer behavior and preferences. The tool can predict which customers are most likely to make a purchase, as well as which products they are most likely to be interested in.

Another example of AI-powered predictive analytics is IBM Watson Analytics, which uses natural language processing (NLP) technology to analyze customer data and provide insights into customer behavior and preferences. The tool can identify trends and patterns in customer behavior, as well as provide recommendations for optimizing marketing strategies based on these insights.

AI is a powerful tool for optimizing content marketing strategies. From personalization to SEO optimization, AI-powered tools can help businesses to streamline their content creation process and provide a more engaging and relevant experience to their customers. By leveraging AI, businesses can gain insights into their customers' needs and preferences, as well as predict future trends and behaviors. As AI technology continues to evolve, it is likely that people will see even more innovative content marketing strategies that leverage the power of AI.

THE ROLE OF AI IN CONTENT IDEATION AND CREATION

Artificial Intelligence (AI) has revolutionized various industries, and content creation is not an exception. Content ideation and creation is a crucial aspect of marketing, branding, and communication. AI has the potential to transform content ideation and creation by making it easier, more efficient, and more effective. This section will explain in detail the role of AI in content ideation and creation.

Content Ideation

Content ideation is the process of generating ideas for content. It is a crucial aspect of content creation as it determines the quality and effectiveness of the content. Traditional content ideation methods involve brainstorming, researching, and analyzing data. However, AI can provide a more efficient and effective way of generating ideas.

AI-powered content ideation tools can analyze vast amounts of data, identify trends, and generate ideas based on the data. Tools like BuzzSumo and SEMrush can analyze social media and search engine data to generate content ideas that are likely to perform well. These tools can also analyze competitors' content and identify gaps that can be exploited to generate unique and valuable content.

AI-powered content ideation tools can also analyze user behavior and preferences to generate personalized content ideas. Netflix uses AI to analyze user data and generate personalized recommendations for movies and TV shows. Similarly, AI-powered content ideation tools can analyze user data and generate personalized content ideas for brands and businesses.

AI-powered content ideation tools can also generate ideas based on NLP and ML algorithms. Tools like Google's AI Writer and Copy.ai can generate headlines, introductions, and even full articles based on keywords and prompts.

Content Creation

Content creation is the process of producing content based on the ideas generated during the ideation phase. Traditional content creation methods involve writing, designing, and producing content manually. However, AI can provide a more efficient and effective way of creating content.

AI-powered content creation tools can automate the content creation process by generating text, images, and videos based on data and algorithms. Tools like Artisto and Prisma can transform images into artistic styles using deep learning algorithms. Similarly, tools like Lumen5 and Wave.video can generate videos based on text and images using AI-powered algorithms.

AI-powered content creation tools can also generate text-based content using NLP and ML algorithms. Tools like Grammarly and Hemingway can analyze text and suggest improvements in grammar, readability, and style. Similarly, tools like Wordsmith and Quill can generate personalized content based on user data and preferences.

AI-powered content creation tools can also assist human content creators by automating repetitive tasks. Tools like Yoast and SEMrush can automate SEO optimization tasks like keyword research and optimization. Similarly, tools like Grammarly and Hemingway can automate the editing and proofreading tasks, allowing content creators to focus on higher-level tasks like strategy and creativity.

Benefits of AI in Content Ideation and Creation

- *Increased efficiency:* AI-powered content ideation and creation tools can automate repetitive tasks, allowing content creators to focus on higher-level tasks like strategy and creativity. This increases the efficiency and productivity of content creation.
- *Improved quality:* AI-powered content ideation and creation tools can analyze vast amounts of data and generate personalized content based on user data and preferences. This improves the quality and relevance of the content.
- *Cost-effective:* AI-powered content ideation and creation tools can reduce the cost of content creation by automating repetitive tasks and improving the efficiency of the content creation process.
- *Scalability:* AI-powered content ideation and creation tools can generate large volumes of content quickly and efficiently. This makes it possible to scale content creation without compromising quality.
- *Competitive advantage:* AI-powered content ideation and creation tools can provide a competitive advantage to brands and businesses by generating unique and valuable content that stands out from the competition.
- *Personalization:* AI-powered content ideation and creation tools can generate personalized content based on user data and preferences, improving user engagement and satisfaction.

Challenges of AI in Content Ideation and Creation

- *Quality control:* AI-powered content creation tools may generate low-quality or irrelevant content, requiring human oversight and intervention.
- *Bias:* AI-powered content ideation and creation tools may be biased toward certain demographics or preferences, leading to a lack of diversity and inclusivity in the content.
- *Intellectual property:* AI-powered content creation tools may generate content that infringes on copyright and intellectual property laws, requiring legal oversight.
- *Technical complexity:* AI-powered content ideation and creation tools require technical expertise and resources, making it difficult for small businesses and individuals to adopt.

AI has the potential to transform content ideation and creation by making it more efficient, effective, and personalized. AI-powered content ideation and creation tools can analyze vast amounts of data, generate personalized content, and automate repetitive tasks, improving the efficiency and quality of content creation. However, there are also challenges, including quality control, bias, intellectual property, and technical complexity. As AI technology continues to evolve, it is essential to balance the benefits and challenges of AI in content ideation and creation to ensure that the content created is of high quality, diverse, and inclusive.

Step-by-Step Instructions for The Role of AI in Idea Generation and Content Creation

1. **Define Content Goals**

    • Set specific objectives for content, like enhancing brand awareness, increasing traffic, or generating leads, to steer the idea generation process.

2. **Choose AI Tools for Idea Generation**

    • Go for AI tools capable of analyzing data from social media, search trends, and customer feedback to generate content ideas. Tools like BuzzSumo, SEMrush, and Ahrefs can indicate popular topics and uncover gaps in a specific industry.

3. **Generate Ideas Using AI**

    • Employ the selected AI tools to suggest topics, headlines, or content outlines based on their data analysis.

4. **Validate and Refine Ideas**

    • Evaluate the AI-generated ideas, refining them to align with content strategy and objectives, considering audience relevance, brand alignment, and market trends.

5. **Create Content with AI Assistance**

    • Utilize AI-based writing aids like Grammarly, Hemingway, or other AI writing assistants to help in drafting, editing, and optimizing the content for readability and SEO.

6. **Optimize Content for SEO**

    • Apply AI-powered SEO tools to enhance the content's search engine visibility, receiving guidance on keywords, content readability, and SEO improvement tips.

7. **Publish and Monitor Performance**

    • Release the AI-enhanced content and employ analytics tools to track its performance, monitoring engagement, traffic, and conversion metrics to gauge content effectiveness.

8. Iterate and Improve

- Continually refine content strategy based on the collected data. Use AI to analyze feedback and performance trends, consistently enhancing and optimizing the content creation process.

PERSONALIZING CONTENT FOR DIFFERENT AUDIENCE SEGMENTS WITH AI

In the modern digital age, businesses and organizations have a wealth of information at their disposal about their customers and target audiences. By leveraging this data and using artificial intelligence (AI) tools, businesses can personalize their content for different audience segments to improve engagement, increase conversions, and drive revenue.

In this chapter, we'll explore the concept of personalizing content for different audience segments with AI, discussing what it is, why it's important, and how businesses can go about implementing it.

What is Personalizing Content for Different Audience Segments with AI?

Personalizing content for different audience segments with AI involves tailoring the content that a business creates and distributes to specific groups of people based on a variety of factors, such as their age, gender, location, interests, purchase history, and more.

AI tools can analyze large sets of data to identify patterns and make predictions about what types of content will resonate with different audience segments. This can include everything from the language used in marketing materials to the images and videos that are included in ads.

The goal of personalizing content in this way is to make it more relevant and engaging for different groups of people, increasing the likelihood that they will take the desired action, whether that's making a purchase, filling out a form, or simply spending more time on a Web site.

Why is Personalizing Content with AI Important?

There are several key reasons why personalizing content for different audience segments with AI is becoming increasingly important for businesses.

First, customers today have come to expect a personalized experience when interacting with brands online. With so much competition and so many options available, customers are more likely to engage with businesses that make an effort to understand and cater to their individual needs and preferences.

In fact, a survey by Epsilon found that 80% of consumers are more likely to do business with a company if it offers a personalized experience. Additionally, 90% of consumers say that they find personalization appealing.

Second, personalizing content can lead to higher conversion rates and increased revenue. By delivering more targeted and relevant content to different audience segments, businesses can increase the likelihood that those people will take the desired action, whether that's making a purchase or signing up for a newsletter.

A study by HubSpot found that personalized calls-to-action (CTAs) resulted in a 202% higher conversion rate than generic CTAs. Similarly, a study by Monette found that personalization can lead to a 20% increase in sales.

Personalizing content with AI can help businesses improve their overall marketing and sales strategies. By analyzing data about customer behavior and preferences, businesses can identify trends and insights that can inform future marketing campaigns and product development efforts.

How to Personalize Content for Different Audience Segments with AI

Now that it's been established what personalizing content for different audience segments with AI is and why it's important, it's time to dive into how businesses can go about implementing it. Here are a few key steps:

Step 1: Identify Audience Segments

The first step in personalizing content with AI is for users to identify the different audience segments that they want to target. This could include groups of people who share certain demographic characteristics, such as age, gender, or location, as well as those who have demonstrated specific interests or behaviors, such as previous purchases or Web site interactions.

Once users have identified these different segments, they can begin collecting data about them in order to better understand the target audience's needs and preferences.

Step 2: Gather and Analyze Data

The next step is to gather and analyze data about different audience segments. This could include a variety of different types of data, such as demographic information, purchase history, Web site behavior, and social media interactions.

There are a variety of different tools and platforms that businesses can use to collect and analyze this data, including customer relationship management (CRM) systems, marketing automation platforms, and social media monitoring tools.

Once the data has been collected, one can use AI-powered tools such as ML algorithms to analyze it and identify patterns and trends that can inform content personalization efforts.

Step 3: Create Personalized Content

The next step is to use the insights gained from the data analysis to create personalized content for each audience segment. This could include everything from email marketing campaigns to social media ads to Web site landing pages.

When creating this content, it's important to tailor it to the specific needs and preferences of each audience segment. This could include using language that resonates with a particular demographic group, or using images and videos that align with their interests and preferences.

Step 4: Test and Refine

It's important to test and refine content personalization efforts over time. This could involve A/B testing different versions of content with different audience segments to see which performs best, or gathering feedback from customers to understand how they are responding to personalized content.

By continually testing and refining your content personalization strategies, one can improve the effectiveness of the personalization over time and continue to drive engagement and revenue for your business.

Personalizing content for different audience segments with AI is a powerful way for businesses to improve engagement, increase conversions, and drive revenue. By using AI-powered tools to analyze data and create targeted, relevant content for each audience segment, businesses can create a more personalized and effective customer experience.

While implementing content personalization strategies may require a significant investment of time and resources, the benefits can be significant, including increased customer loyalty, higher conversion rates, and improved marketing and sales strategies. As such, businesses that are looking to stay competitive in today's crowded digital marketplace should consider leveraging AI to personalize their content and better connect with their target audiences.

Step-by-Step Instructions for Personalizing Content for Different Audience Segments with AI

1. **Identify Audience Segments**

   • Start by categorizing an audience based on demographics, behavior's, interests, and purchase history. Use AI tools to analyze customer data and identify distinct patterns and preferences for segmentation.

2. **Collect and Analyze Data**

   • Gather data from CRM systems, Web site analytics, social media interactions, and email campaigns. Employ AI-powered tools to deeply analyze this information, uncovering the unique characteristics and behaviors of each segment.

3. **Define Personalization Goals**

   • Establish clear objectives for personalization, such as enhancing engagement, boosting conversion rates, or fostering customer loyalty.

4. **Develop Personalized Content Strategies**

   • Utilize the insights from the data analysis to create tailored content strategies for each audience segment, including the type of content, messaging, tone, and preferred delivery channels.

5. **Implement AI-driven Personalization**

   • Use AI tools to automate the personalization process, enabling real-time dynamic content adjustments based on individual user behavior and interaction history.

6. **Execute and Distribute Content**

   • Distribute personalized content through selected channels, such as email, social media, and Web sites, ensuring it aligns with the interests and needs of each segment.

7. **Monitor and Analyze Performance**

   • Track the performance of personalized content using analytics tools, focusing on key metrics like engagement rates, conversion rates, and return on investment (ROI) to evaluate the success of personalization efforts.

8. **Refine and Optimize**

   • Continuously improve strategy based on performance data, employing AI to test various content variations and optimize approaches for the maximum impact of personalized content.

MEASURING THE EFFECTIVENESS OF CONTENT MARKETING WITH AI

Content marketing is a vital aspect of any digital marketing strategy that involves creating and sharing valuable, relevant, and consistent content to attract and retain a clearly-defined audience—and, to drive profitable customer action. As content marketing becomes more widespread, marketers must find ways to measure the effectiveness of their efforts to justify the investment and optimize their campaigns for better results.

Artificial Intelligence (AI) can be a valuable tool for measuring the effectiveness of content marketing. AI-powered analytics and tracking tools can help marketers analyze and interpret vast amounts of data from various sources, including social media, Web site analytics, customer feedback, and search engine data. This chapter will discuss how AI can help measure the effectiveness of content marketing in detail.

Understanding Content Marketing

Content marketing is a strategic approach that involves creating and distributing valuable, relevant, and consistent content to attract and retain a clearly defined audience. The goal of content marketing is to drive profitable customer action by creating trust and loyalty with the audience.

The content created in content marketing can take many forms, including blog posts, videos, infographics, social media posts, podcasts, and more. The content is designed to provide value to the audience, educate, entertain, and solve problems. When executed correctly, content marketing can generate significant benefits for businesses, including increased Web site traffic, better search engine rankings, more social media engagement, and improved brand recognition.

Measuring the Effectiveness of Content Marketing

The effectiveness of content marketing can be measured in many ways. Some common metrics include Web site traffic, social media engagement, email subscribers, lead generation, and sales. However, to accurately measure the effectiveness of content marketing, it's important to track and analyze multiple metrics.

One of the challenges of measuring the effectiveness of content marketing is the sheer volume of data generated. There are many sources of data, including Web site analytics, social media analytics, email marketing analytics, and more. Marketers must analyze and interpret this data to make informed decisions about their content marketing strategy.

How AI Can Help Measure the Effectiveness of Content Marketing

AI-powered analytics and tracking tools can help marketers measure the effectiveness of content marketing by analyzing vast amounts of data and providing actionable insights. AI can help marketers make sense of complex data sets, identify patterns, and predict trends.

Here is some ways AI can help measure the effectiveness of content marketing:

1. Sentiment Analytics

AI-powered sentiment analysis tools can help marketers analyze customer feedback, social media posts, and other forms of user-generated content to determine how customers feel about their brand, products, and services. This can help marketers identify areas for improvement and adjust their content marketing strategy accordingly.

2. Personalization

AI-powered personalization tools can help marketers deliver more personalized content to their audience. By analyzing customer data and behavior, AI can help marketers tailor content to specific audience segments, improving engagement and conversion rates.

3. Content Optimization

AI-powered content optimization tools can help marketers improve their content's performance by analyzing Web site analytics, user behavior, and search engine data. By analyzing this data, AI can identify areas where content can be improved, such as headlines, meta descriptions, and content structure.

4. Predictive Analytics

AI-powered predictive analytics tools can help marketers predict future trends and outcomes based on historical data. This can help marketers optimize their content marketing strategy by identifying which types of content are most likely to perform well with their audience.

5. Natural Language Processing (NLP)

AI-powered NLP tools can help marketers analyze and understand customer feedback, social media posts, and other forms of user-generated content. NLP can help marketers identify common themes, sentiment, and other important insights that can inform their content marketing strategy.

Challenges of Using AI for Measuring the Effectiveness of Content Marketing

While AI can be a powerful tool for measuring the effectiveness of content marketing, there are also some challenges to consider. Here are a few:

1. Quality of Data

AI is only as good as the data it analyzes. If the data is inaccurate or incomplete, the insights generated by AI may not be accurate or useful. Marketers must ensure that the data they are collecting is of high quality and relevant to their content marketing strategy.

2. Integration

AI-powered analytics tools must be integrated into existing marketing systems and workflows to be effective. This can be a challenge, as different tools and platforms may have different data formats and requirements. Marketers must ensure that their AI-powered tools are properly integrated with their existing systems to maximize their effectiveness.

3. Cost

AI-powered analytics tools can be expensive, especially for smaller businesses with limited budgets. Marketers must weigh the costs of implementing AI-powered tools against the potential benefits they may provide.

4. Privacy Concerns

AI-powered tools that analyze customer data must be implemented with privacy concerns in mind. Marketers must ensure that they are collecting and analyzing customer data in a responsible and ethical way that respects customer privacy.

Measuring the effectiveness of content marketing is critical for optimizing strategy and justifying investment in content marketing. AI-powered analytics and tracking tools can help marketers make sense of the vast amounts of data generated by content marketing efforts, providing insights into audience sentiment, personalization, content optimization, predictive analytics, and NLP.

While there are some challenges to implementing AI-powered tools, the benefits they can provide are significant. By using AI to measure the effectiveness of content marketing, marketers can improve their content strategy, increase engagement and conversion rates, and drive business results.

Chapter 12 of the *AI Marketing Playbook* explored numerous ways in which AI can be used for content marketing. It highlights the importance of content marketing in today's digital age and how AI can help marketers create and distribute effective content.

The chapter discussed how AI can be used to automate the content creation process, analyze data to better understand audience behavior and preferences, and personalize content to engage different audience segments. AI-powered tools like NLP and ML algorithms can help marketers create compelling content that resonates with their target audience.

The chapter also provided several examples of successful content marketing strategies that use AI, such as the "Predictive Personalization" approach used by Netflix and the "AI Writing Assistant" tool used by Grammarly. These strategies highlight how AI can help marketers identify patterns and trends in audience behavior and use that information to create more personalized and effective content.

The chapter discussed the role of AI in content ideation and creation. AI-powered tools like content recommendation engines can help marketers identify relevant topics and keywords for their content, while NLP algorithms can assist with the writing process by suggesting ways to improve readability and tone.

The chapter then delved into the importance of personalizing content for different audience segments with AI. Personalization helps marketers create more relevant and engaging content, which can improve customer loyalty and retention. AI-powered tools like recommendation engines and chatbots can help marketers personalize content based on factors like location, device, and behavior.

The chapter explored how AI can be used to measure the effectiveness of content marketing. AI-powered analytics tools can provide insights into audience engagement and help marketers optimize their content for better results.

These tools can also help marketers track the success of their content across multiple channels and platforms.

Overall, Chapter 12 of the *AI Marketing Playbook* provided a comprehensive overview of how AI can be used to enhance content marketing strategies. By leveraging the power of AI, marketers can create more compelling and effective content that resonates with their target audience and drives business results.

Marketing Automation with Artificial Intelligence (AI)

Marketing automation is the process of using technology to automate repetitive marketing tasks, such as lead generation, lead nurturing, and customer engagement. By incorporating AI into marketing automation, businesses can streamline their marketing efforts and create more personalized and effective marketing campaigns.

One of the primary benefits of using AI in marketing automation is that it can help businesses analyze large amounts of data and make data-driven decisions. AI algorithms can analyze customer behavior and demographics to identify patterns and preferences, allowing businesses to tailor their marketing messages to specific audiences.

Some examples of successful marketing automation strategies that use AI include:

- *Chatbots:* AI-powered chatbots can be used to provide customer support and answer frequently asked questions, freeing human resources for more complex questions.
- *Predictive lead scoring:* AI algorithms can analyze customer data to predict which leads are most likely to convert, allowing sales teams to focus their efforts on the most promising leads.
- *Personalized content recommendations:* AI-powered content recommendation engines can analyze user behavior and preferences to suggest relevant content, thereby increasing engagement and conversions.
- *Automated email campaigns:* AI can be used to personalize email campaigns, email subject and email content based on time and frequency, increasing absorption, open and click-through rates.

When it comes to automating lead scoring and nurturing with AI, companies can use techniques like predictive modeling and machine learning algorithms to analyze customer data and identify the most promising leads. By automating lead management with personalized messaging and content, businesses can increase customer retention and improve conversion rates.

In automated email campaigns and drip marketing, AI can be used to analyze customer behavior and preferences to personalize email content, subject lines and send times. By automating these campaigns, businesses can save time and resources by delivering targeted and effective messages.

However, there are also challenges and limitations associated with using AI for marketing automation. One of the challenges is the need for high-quality data to train AI algorithms, as inaccurate or incomplete data can lead to incorrect predictions and recommendations. Additionally, there is a risk of over-reliance on automation, which can lead to a loss of personalization and human touch in marketing campaigns.

Overall, while there are challenges and limitations to using AI for marketing automation, the benefits of increased efficiency, personalization, and effectiveness make it an invaluable tool for today's marketers.

AI-powered chatbots can be used for customer service. Discuss how individuals can use AI to automate marketing.

Artificial Intelligence (AI) has transformed the marketing landscape in recent years by providing a powerful marketing automation tool. With the advent of AI, marketers can now analyze big data and automate routine marketing tasks so they can make more informed decisions and improve overall performance. This essay provides an overview of AI in marketing automation, its history, examples, and how it can be incorporated into an AI-powered marketing textbook.

AI has been a buzzword for decades, but it's only been a few years since AI and machine learning (ML) became widespread in the marketing world. In 2017, the technical research and consulting firm, Gartner, predicted that by 2020, 85% of customer interactions would happen without human intervention. The rise of AI in marketing automation is the result of several factors, including the growing availability of data, the need for customization, and the ability to automate repetitive tasks.

The use of AI in marketing automation began with chatbots using natural language processing (NLP) to understand and answer customer questions. Chatbots can be integrated into Web sites, social media platforms, and messaging apps, providing businesses with a convenient and cost-effective way to interact with their customers. In recent years, AI has also been used for personalization, predictive analytics, and marketing automation.

There are many ways to use AI in marketing automation. Following are some of the most popular use case examples:

- *Personalization:* AI can be used to create highly personalized marketing campaigns by analyzing customer data, behavior, and preferences. Netflix uses AI algorithms to recommend movies and TV shows to users based on their viewing history.

- *Predictive analytics:* AI can analyze customer data to predict future behavior and trends. This information can be used to create more targeted and effective marketing campaigns. Amazon uses AI to predict what products customers are likely to buy next and sends them personalized recommendations.
- *Chatbots:* AI-powered chatbots can be used to provide instant customer support and answer frequent questions. They can also be used to guide customers through the sales process and make recommendations based on their preferences.
- *Lead scoring:* AI can analyze customer behavior to determine which leads are most likely to convert. This information can be used to prioritize sales efforts and improve conversion rates.
- *Marketing automation:* AI can automate routine marketing tasks such as sending emails, scheduling social media posts, and creating reports. This frees up marketers' time to focus on more strategic tasks.

To incorporate AI into the marketing playbook, businesses should follow these steps:

- *Identify business objectives:* Start by identifying the business objectives to be achieved through AI. This could be improving customer engagement, increasing sales, or reducing costs.
- *Collect data:* Collect relevant data from various sources such as customer interactions, sales data, and Web site analytics. This data will be used to train AI algorithms and create personalized marketing campaigns.
- *Choose the right AI tool:* Choose the right AI tool based on business objectives and data. If one wants to automate routine marketing tasks, they could use a marketing automation platform like Marketo or HubSpot. If one wants to create personalized campaigns, they could use an ML platform like Google Cloud or Amazon SageMaker.
- *Train AI algorithms:* Train AI algorithms using data to create personalized campaigns, predict customer behavior, and automate routine tasks.
- *Analyze results:* Analyze the results of AI-powered marketing campaigns to measure their effectiveness. Use this data to optimize campaigns and improve ROI.

AI has become an essential tool for marketing automation, providing businesses with the ability to analyze large amounts of data, automate routine tasks, and create highly personalized marketing campaigns. With the increasing availability of data and the need for personalization, AI is expected to continue to transform the marketing landscape in the coming years.

In summary, AI has revolutionized marketing automation, providing businesses with the ability to make more informed decisions and improve their overall effectiveness. AI can be used for personalization, predictive analytics, chatbots, lead scoring, and marketing automation. To incorporate AI into the marketing playbook, businesses should identify their business objectives, collect relevant data, choose the right AI tool, train AI algorithms, and analyze the results of their campaigns. By following these steps, businesses can leverage the power of AI to create more effective and efficient marketing campaigns.

Step-by-Step Instructions for Implementing AI-Powered Chatbots

1. **Define the Chatbot's Purpose:** Establish clear objectives for the chatbot, such as lead generation or customer support. This will guide the design and functionality of the chatbot.

2. **Select a Suitable Platform:** Choose a chatbot platform that aligns with business needs. Consider factors like integration capabilities, ease of use, and the type of engagement desired (Web site, social media, messaging apps).

3. **Design the Chatbot's Conversation Flow:** Develop the dialogue flow of the chatbot, including the questions it will ask and the answers it will provide. This is crucial for creating a seamless and effective user experience.

4. **Deploy the Chatbot Across Platforms:** Integrate the chatbot into the Web site, social media pages, or messaging applications, depending on the best place to engage with users.

5. **Train the Chatbot with AI:** Utilize AI to enable the chatbot to understand and respond to user queries effectively. This involves programming the chatbot to learn from interactions and improve its responses over time.

6. **Test and Refine the Chatbot:** Before fully launching, test the chatbot to identify any issues or areas for improvement. Make necessary adjustments to ensure it functions correctly and meets user needs.

7. **Monitor and Evaluate Performance:** Regularly analyze the chatbot's interactions with users to assess its performance. Use insights from this data to make ongoing enhancements, ensuring the chatbot continues to meet its objectives effectively over time.

SUCCESSFUL MARKETING AUTOMATION STRATEGIES THAT USE AI

Marketing automation has been a game changer for businesses, helping them streamline their marketing processes and reduce manual workloads. With the integration of AI, marketing automation strategies have become even more effective, enabling businesses to personalize their marketing efforts, optimize their campaigns, and generate higher revenue.

Here are Some Examples of Successful Marketing Automation Strategies that Utilize AI

- *Personalized email campaigns:* Email marketing is still a powerful tool for businesses, and personalized email campaigns have been proven to generate higher open and click-through rates. With the help of AI, businesses can personalize their email campaigns based on a recipient's behavior, preferences, and demographics.

E-commerce companies like Amazon use AI-powered algorithms to recommend products to customers based on their purchase history and browsing behavior. This type of personalized marketing not only increases the chances of a sale, but it also enhances customer experience by showing them products that they are more likely to be interested in.

- *Chatbots for customer support:* Chatbots are a popular marketing automation tool that can be used for customer support, lead generation, and even sales. With AI, chatbots can be programmed to provide personalized recommendations, answer frequently asked questions, and even help customers complete transactions.

H&M, the Swedish clothing company, uses a chatbot on its Facebook Messenger to provide personalized style recommendations to customers. By analyzing a customer's preferences, the chatbot can suggest outfits and clothing items that are likely to appeal to them.

- *Predictive analytics for lead scoring:* Lead scoring is a crucial part of the sales process, as it helps businesses identify which leads are most likely to convert into customers. With AI-powered predictive analytics, businesses can analyze large amounts of data to identify patterns and predict which leads are more likely to convert.

HubSpot, a marketing automation platform, uses AI-powered predictive lead scoring to help businesses prioritize their sales efforts. The platform analyzes data from a company's Web site, social media, and other sources to identify leads that are most likely to convert into customers, allowing businesses to focus their efforts on those leads.

- *Dynamic content personalization:* Dynamic content personalization involves using AI to customize content based on a recipient's preferences, behavior, and demographics. This can be done through personalized product recommendations, targeted advertising, and even customized landing pages.

Netflix uses AI-powered algorithms to personalize its content recommendations for each user. By analyzing a user's viewing history, ratings, and other data points, Netflix can suggest content that is more likely to be of interest to them.

- *Predictive content creation:* Predictive content creation involves using AI to analyze data and predict which content is most likely to be successful. This can include predicting which blog topics will generate the most traffic, which social media posts will receive the most engagement, and even which email subject lines will generate the most opens.

IBM's Watson Content Hub uses AI to analyze data from a company's Web site, social media, and other sources to predict which content is most likely to be successful. By using this data to guide content creation, businesses can improve their content marketing efforts and generate higher engagement.

Marketing automation strategies that utilize AI are becoming increasingly popular and effective. By personalizing marketing efforts, optimizing campaigns, and predicting customer behavior, businesses can generate higher revenue and provide better customer experiences. The above examples of successful marketing automation strategies are just a few of the many ways that AI can be used to improve marketing efforts.

TECHNIQUES FOR AUTOMATING LEAD SCORING AND NURTURING WITH AI

Lead scoring and nurturing are critical components of a successful marketing strategy. Lead scoring is the process of ranking and assigning a score to leads based on their level of engagement and readiness to buy. *Lead nurturing* is the process of developing relationships with leads by providing them with relevant information and personalized communication to move them further down the sales funnel. However, these processes can be time-consuming and complex, which is where AI comes in. This chapter will explore the techniques for automating lead scoring and nurturing with AI.

Step 1: Define the Ideal Customer Profile (ICP)

The first step in automating lead scoring and nurturing with AI is to define the ideal customer profile (ICP). This includes identifying the characteristics of the target audience such as demographics, firmographics, behavior, and other relevant information. By creating a detailed ICP, an individual can narrow down their focus and ensure that they are targeting the right leads.

Step 2: Identify Key Buying Signals

Once the ICP has been identified, the next step is to identify the key buying signals that indicate a lead's level of engagement and readiness to buy. These signals can include Web site behavior, email engagement, social media activity, and other actions that demonstrate interest in the product or service. By tracking these signals, one can score leads based on the level of engagement and prioritize them accordingly.

Step 3: Use AI-Powered Lead Scoring Models

AI-powered lead scoring models use machine learning algorithms to analyze large amounts of data and identify patterns that indicate a lead's level of engagement and readiness to buy. These models can consider a variety of factors such as Web site behavior, email engagement, social media activity, and other relevant data points. By using AI-powered lead scoring models, one can automate the lead scoring process and ensure that the sales team is focusing on the most qualified leads.

Step 4: Use AI-Powered Lead Nurturing Tools

AI-powered lead nurturing tools use machine learning algorithms to personalize communication with leads based on their behavior and preferences. These tools can automatically send personalized emails, chat messages, and other communications to leads based on their level of engagement and readiness to buy. By using AI-powered lead nurturing tools, one can automate the lead nurturing process and ensure that their leads are receiving the right information at the right time.

Step 5: Integrate AI-Powered Tools into the CRM

To fully automate lead scoring and nurturing with AI, it is essential to integrate AI-powered tools into a customer relationship management (CRM) system. This allows users to track lead behavior and engagement across multiple channels and automate communication based on the lead's level of engagement and readiness to buy. By integrating AI-powered tools into the CRM, one can streamline their lead management process and ensure that their sales team has access to the most up-to-date information about leads.

Step 6: Monitor and Optimize AI-Powered Lead Scoring and Nurturing

The last step in automating lead scoring and nurturing with AI is to monitor and optimize the system over time. This involves analyzing data, testing different approaches, and refining AI-powered models and tools to ensure that they are delivering the best results. By continuously monitoring and optimizing AI-powered lead scoring and nurturing, one can improve conversion rates and drive more revenue for their business.

Automating lead scoring and nurturing with AI can be a game-changer for marketing strategy. By defining the ICP, identifying key buying signals, using AI-powered lead scoring models and lead nurturing tools, integrating these tools into your CRM, and monitoring and optimizing the system over time, a user can streamline their lead management process and drive more revenue for their business.

THE ROLE OF AI IN AUTOMATED EMAIL CAMPAIGNS AND DRIP MARKETING

Email marketing is an essential aspect of digital marketing, and it has remained so over the years. With the advent of AI, marketers can now leverage the power of machine learning algorithms to improve the effectiveness of their email campaigns. AI can help marketers create automated email campaigns that deliver personalized messages to their target audience, thereby increasing engagement and conversions. This chapter will explore the role of AI in automated email campaigns and drip marketing and how businesses can use AI to improve their email marketing efforts.

Automated Email Campaigns

An automated email campaign is a series of prewritten emails that are sent automatically to subscribers based on specific triggers. The triggers can be anything from a new subscriber signing up for a newsletter to a customer making a purchase. Automated email campaigns are an effective way to nurture leads and convert them into customers. They are also a wonderful way to keep customers engaged and informed about a particular brand.

With AI, businesses can create more effective automated email campaigns by using machine learning algorithms to analyze customer behavior and create personalized messages. AI can help businesses identify the most effective subject lines, images, and calls-to-action to use in their emails. AI can also help businesses determine the best time to send emails based on the recipient's behavior, such as when they are most likely to open an email or make a purchase.

To create an automated email campaign, businesses need to follow these steps:

- *Define the goal of the campaign:* The first step is to determine the goal of the campaign. Is it to promote a new product or service, nurture leads, or retain customers?
- *Define the trigger:* The trigger is what initiates the email campaign. It could be anything from a new subscriber signing up for a newsletter to a customer making a purchase.
- *Create a series of emails:* The next step is to create a series of emails that will be sent out automatically to subscribers. These emails should be personalized and relevant to the recipient's interests.
- *Use AI to personalize emails:* AI can be used to analyze customer behavior and personalize emails based on their interests and behavior.
- *Test and optimize:* The last step is to test and optimize the automated email campaign to improve its effectiveness. Businesses should use data and analytics to track the performance of the campaign and adjust as needed.

Step-by-Step Instructions for Launching Automated Email Campaigns with AI

1. **Set campaign goals and objectives:** Clearly define the goals of the email campaign, such as increasing sales, generating leads, or improving customer engagement.
2. **Segment the email list:** Use customer data and behavior to segment the email list. This allows for targeted and relevant communication with different groups within the targeted audience.
3. **Design the email campaign flow:** Plan the sequence of emails, including the triggers for sending them and the actions recipients should be encouraged to take. This creates a structured pathway for the campaign.
4. **Personalize content with AI:** Employ AI technology to tailor the content and timing of each email to the specific needs and behaviors of each segment. This personalization can significantly enhance engagement and conversion rates.
5. **Conduct a pilot test:** Before rolling out the campaign on a larger scale, test it with a small segment of the targeted audience to identify any issues and ensure effectiveness.
6. **Analyze and learn from the results:** After the campaign is launched, monitor its performance closely. Analyze the results to gain insights that can inform and improve future email campaigns.

Drip Marketing

Drip marketing is a form of email marketing that involves sending a series of targeted, personalized emails to subscribers over a period. Emails are designed to educate and inform subscribers about a particular product or service and encourage them to act. Drip marketing is an effective way to nurture leads and convert them into customers.

AI can help businesses create more effective drip marketing campaigns by using machine learning algorithms to analyze customer behavior and personalize the messages. AI can help businesses identify the most effective subject lines, images, and calls-to-action to use in their emails. AI can also help businesses determine the best time to send emails based on the recipient's behavior, such as when they are most likely to open an email or make a purchase.

To create a drip marketing campaign, businesses need to follow these steps:

- *Define the goal of the campaign:* The first step is to determine the goal of the campaign. Is it to promote a new product or service, nurture leads, or retain customers?
- *Identify the target audience:* The next step is to identify the target audience for the campaign. This could be based on demographics, interests, or behavior.

- *Develop a content strategy:* The next step is to develop a content strategy that will educate and inform subscribers about a particular product or service. The content should be personalized and relevant to the recipient's interests.
- *Use AI to personalize emails:* AI can be used to analyze customer behavior and personalize emails based on their interests and behavior. This includes personalized subject lines, images, and calls-to-action based on the recipient's behavior.
- *Set up the drip campaign:* The next step is to set up the drip campaign. This involves creating a series of emails that will be sent out over a period of time. The emails should be personalized and relevant to the recipient's interests.
- *Test and optimize:* The final step is to test and optimize the drip marketing campaign to improve its effectiveness. Businesses should use data and analytics to track the performance of the campaign and make adjustments as needed.

Using AI in Automated Email Campaigns and Drip Marketing

There are several ways that businesses can use AI to improve their automated email campaigns and drip marketing efforts. Here are some of the key ways AI can help:

- *Personalization:* AI can help businesses personalize their email campaigns by analyzing customer behavior and creating personalized messages. This includes personalized subject lines, images, and calls-to-action based on the recipient's behavior.
- *Timing:* AI can help businesses determine the best time to send emails based on the recipient's behavior, such as when they are most likely to open an email or make a purchase. This can increase the effectiveness of email campaigns and improve the chances of conversions.
- *Segmentation:* AI can help businesses segment their email list based on customer behavior and interests. This allows businesses to create targeted messages that are more likely to resonate with the recipient.
- *Optimization:* AI can help businesses optimize their email campaigns and drip marketing efforts by analyzing data and adjusting as needed. This can improve the effectiveness of campaigns and increase conversions.
- *Customer insights:* AI can provide valuable insights into customer behavior and preferences, allowing businesses to create more effective email campaigns and drip marketing efforts. This includes insights into customer engagement, purchase behavior, and preferences.

Tips for Using AI in Automated Email Campaigns and Drip Marketing

Here are some tips for using AI in automated email campaigns and drip marketing:

- Use AI to personalize messages based on customer behavior and interests.
- Use AI to determine the best time to send emails based on customer behavior.
- Segment the email list based on customer behavior and interests.
- Use AI to optimize email campaigns and drip marketing efforts.
- Use AI to gain insights into customer behavior and preferences.
- Test and optimize the email campaigns and drip marketing efforts regularly.

AI has revolutionized the way businesses approach email marketing. Automated email campaigns and drip marketing are two powerful tools that businesses can use to nurture leads, convert customers, and retain customers. By leveraging AI, businesses can create personalized messages, improve timing, segment their email lists, optimize their campaigns, and gain valuable insights into customer behavior and preferences. Businesses that embrace AI in their email marketing efforts are more likely to succeed in today's competitive digital landscape.

Using AI in Automated Email Campaigns and Drip Marketing: Step-by-Step Instructions

1. **Integration of AI with Email Marketing Platform:**

   - Connect the AI tool to the email marketing software.
   - Ensure proper data flow between the CRM and the AI tool for accurate analysis.

2. **Data Analysis for Personalization:**

   - Utilize AI to analyze customer interaction data to understand preferences and behaviors.
   - Allow AI to generate personalized subject lines, images, and calls-to-action for each recipient.

3. **Optimal Timing Prediction:**

   - Deploy AI algorithms to predict when recipients are most likely to engage with emails.
   - Schedule emails to be sent at times when each recipient is most active.

4. **Audience Segmentation:**

   - Use AI to dynamically segment the audience based on their behavior and interests.
   - Create tailored email campaigns for each segment to increase relevance and engagement.

5. **Campaign Optimization:**

   • Implement AI tools to continuously analyses campaign performance data.
   • Make data-driven adjustments to email content, design, and delivery strategies.

6. **Insights Gathering:**

   • Leverage AI to gain deeper insights into customer engagement and purchasing behaviors.
   • Apply these insights to refine the content and targeting of email campaigns.

7. **A/B Testing and Refinement:**

   • Conduct A/B testing on different elements of emails using AI recommendations.
   • Use the results to further refine and enhance campaign performance.

8. **Regular Updates and Maintenance:**

   • Keep AI models updated with the latest data for ongoing learning and improvement.
   • Regularly review AI insights and adapt strategies accordingly.

CHALLENGES AND LIMITATIONS OF USING AI FOR MARKETING AUTOMATION

Marketing automation is a process where technology is used to automate various marketing tasks, such as email marketing, social media marketing, lead generation, and lead nurturing. It involves the use of AI to streamline various marketing activities including lead generation, segmentation, personalized messaging, and predictive analytics. Despite its potential benefits, the implementation of AI in marketing automation comes with several challenges and limitations. This chapter discusses these hurdles in detail.

One of the key challenges is the quality and quantity of data required. AI systems need vast amounts of high-quality data to learn effectively and operate efficiently. However, marketing data can often be messy, inconsistent, and sometimes insufficient to train the algorithms accurately. Privacy concerns further complicate data usage, as consumers grow increasingly wary about how their information is handled. Strict regulations such as GDPR and CCPA dictate rigorous standards for data collection, storage, and usage, requiring companies to be transparent and compliant.

The complexity of AI technology itself poses another significant challenge. Implementing AI systems for marketing automation requires a deep understanding of AI, which many companies may lack. These systems are also expensive and require substantial infrastructure, posing a barrier particularly for smaller companies. Moreover, the maintenance and troubleshooting of AI systems can be problematic, impacting their accuracy and reliability.

Ethical considerations also come into play with AI in marketing. There's a risk of bias if AI systems are trained on non-representative datasets, which can lead to unfair outcomes in marketing strategies. Ethical and unbiased AI use is crucial to avoid perpetuating discrimination. Furthermore, AI systems, while powerful, lack emotional intelligence and creativity, which are vital in marketing to connect with customers on a more personal and creative level.

Finally, resistance to adopting AI technology can be a significant barrier. Employees might resist using AI systems due to fears of job replacement, and there may be a broader cultural hesitation towards AI technology. Despite these challenges, it's essential for companies to maintain human oversight to mitigate errors and ensure that AI systems align with marketing goals and ethics.

While AI has the potential to revolutionize marketing automation, there are several challenges and limitations that need to be considered. Data quality and quantity, privacy concerns, complexity of AI, cost of implementation, bias, and ethics, need for human oversight, lack of emotional intelligence and creativity, and resistance to change are all factors that can impact the effectiveness of AI for marketing automation. Companies need to be aware of these challenges and work to overcome them if they want to fully realize the benefits of AI for marketing automation. This may involve investing in high-quality data, ensuring compliance with regulations, hiring skilled AI professionals, addressing bias and ethical concerns, and providing adequate training and support to employees. With the right approach, AI can be a powerful tool for marketing automation, but it requires careful consideration and planning to ensure that it is used effectively and ethically.

Chapter 13 of the *AI Marketing Playbook* delved into the topic of marketing automation with AI. It explores how AI can be used to streamline marketing tasks, increase efficiency, and improve marketing outcomes. In this chapter, the authors discuss the different ways in which AI can be leveraged for marketing automation, successful marketing automation strategies that use AI, techniques for automating lead scoring and nurturing with AI, the role of AI in automated email campaigns and drip marketing, and the challenges and limitations of using AI for marketing automation.

Marketing automation refers to the use of software tools and technology to automate repetitive marketing tasks and processes. This can include tasks such as lead generation, lead nurturing, email marketing, social media management, and customer segmentation. The goal of marketing automation is to increase efficiency, save time, and improve marketing outcomes by delivering the right message to the right person at the right time. AI can be used to enhance marketing automation by enabling marketers to gain insights into customer behavior and preferences and automate tasks that were previously manual and time-consuming.

One of the most significant benefits of using AI for marketing automation is the ability to improve lead scoring and nurturing. Lead scoring refers to the process of assigning a score to a lead based on their level of engagement and likelihood to convert into a customer. Lead nurturing refers to the process of building relationships with leads over time by providing them with relevant and personalized content. AI can help automate these processes by analyzing data on customer behavior and preferences to identify which leads are most likely to convert and what content they are most interested in.

One example of a successful marketing automation strategy that uses AI is chatbots. Chatbots are computer programs that use NLP to simulate human conversation. They can be used to answer customer questions, provide product recommendations, and guide customers through the sales process. By leveraging AI, chatbots can analyze customer behavior and preferences to deliver personalized recommendations and responses, improving the customer experience and increasing the likelihood of conversion.

Another successful marketing automation strategy that uses AI is predictive analytics. Predictive analytics refers to the use of data, statistical algorithms, and machine learning techniques to identify the likelihood of future outcomes based on historical data. In marketing, predictive analytics can be used to identify which customers are most likely to convert, what products they are most interested in, and what messages will resonate with them. By using AI to automate predictive analytics, marketers can save time and resources while improving the accuracy of their targeting and messaging.

Techniques for automating lead scoring and nurturing with AI include using predictive lead scoring models, analyzing customer behavior and engagement metrics, and leveraging NLP to deliver personalized content. Predictive lead scoring models use historical data to identify which leads are most likely to convert based on their behavior and characteristics. Customer behavior and engagement metrics can be analyzed to determine which content and messaging is most effective at driving conversions. NLP can be used to analyze customer interactions and deliver personalized content and recommendations.

The role of AI in automated email campaigns and drip marketing is significant. AI can be used to analyze customer behavior and preferences to determine which messages and offers are most likely to resonate with them. Automated email campaigns and drip marketing can be set up to deliver personalized content based on customer behavior and preferences, such as abandoned cart reminders, product recommendations, and promotional offers. By automating these campaigns with AI, marketers can save time and resources while improving the relevance and effectiveness of their messaging.

There are several challenges and limitations of using AI for marketing automation. One of the most significant challenges is the need for high-quality data. AI relies on accurate and relevant data to deliver accurate insights and recommendations. If the data is incomplete or inaccurate, the insights and recommendations generated by AI will be less effective. Another challenge is the need for skilled personnel to develop and maintain AI models. AI requires expertise in data science, machine learning, and programming, and many marketing teams may not have the necessary expertise in-house. Additionally, there are ethical concerns around the use of AI for marketing automation, particularly around data privacy and the potential for bias in AI algorithms.

Despite these challenges, the use of AI for marketing automation has become increasingly common in recent years, as more and more businesses recognize the benefits of automating repetitive marketing tasks and leveraging data insights to improve marketing outcomes. As AI technology continues to evolve and improve, it is likely that people will see even more sophisticated and effective marketing automation strategies that use AI in the future.

CHAPTER 14

USING ARTIFICIAL INTELLIGENCE (AI) FOR SALES ENABLEMENT

C hapter 14 of the *AI Marketing Playbook* explores the use of AI for sales enablement. The chapter covers a wide range of topics related to sales, including how AI can be used for sales enablement, examples of successful sales enablement strategies that use AI, the role of AI in lead generation and qualification, sales forecasting with AI, and the impact of AI on sales productivity and efficiency. This discussion will examine these topics in detail.

First, the chapter explores how AI can be used for sales enablement. Sales enablement is a process of equipping sales teams with the right tools, resources, and information to engage with prospects effectively, nurture relationships, and close deals. AI technology can help sales teams improve their performance by providing insights into customer behavior, identifying the most promising leads, and automating routine tasks.

One way AI can be used for sales enablement is by analyzing data on customer behavior and preferences to identify patterns and trends. With this information, sales teams can tailor their approach to each prospect, making it more likely that they will close a deal. An AI-powered tool can analyze a customer's browsing and purchasing history to suggest products or services that they are likely to be interested in. This can help sales teams to make more relevant and personalized recommendations, which can improve the chances of a sale.

Another way AI can be used for sales enablement is by automating routine tasks, such as data entry and lead qualification. By automating these tasks, sales teams can save time and focus on more important activities, such as building relationships with prospects and closing deals. An AI-powered lead qualification tool can analyze a prospect's behavior and demographics to determine their likelihood of becoming a customer. This can help sales teams to prioritize their efforts and focus on the most promising leads.

Following are some examples of successful sales enablement strategies that use AI. One example is the use of chatbots to engage with prospects and provide them with information about products and services. Chatbots use natural language processing (NLP) and machine learning (ML) algorithms to understand the customer's query and provide relevant responses. This can help to provide a seamless customer experience and reduce the workload of sales teams.

The use of predictive analytics to identify the most promising leads. Predictive analytics involves analyzing historical data to predict future outcomes. In the context of sales, predictive analytics can be used to identify the leads that are most likely to become customers. This can help sales teams to prioritize their efforts and focus on the leads that are most likely to result in a sale.

The role of AI in lead generation and qualification is another important topic covered in Chapter 14. Lead generation involves identifying potential customers who may be interested in a product or service. Lead qualification involves determining whether a lead is likely to become a customer based on their behavior and demographics.

AI can be used to automate lead generation and qualification, making it faster and more efficient. AI-powered tools can analyze data on a prospect's behavior, such as their browsing history and social media activity, to determine their likelihood of becoming a customer. This can help sales teams to prioritize their efforts and focus on the most promising leads.

Sales forecasting with AI is another important topic covered in Chapter 14. *Sales forecasting* involves predicting future sales based on historical data and market trends. AI can be used to analyze data on customer behavior, market trends, and other factors to make more accurate sales forecasts. This can help sales teams to plan their activities and resources more effectively, leading to improved performance and profitability.

The impact of AI on sales productivity and efficiency is a key topic in Chapter 14. AI can help sales teams to automate routine tasks, such as data entry and lead qualification, freeing up time for more important activities such as building relationships with prospects and closing deals. AI can also provide sales teams with insights into customer behavior and preferences, enabling them to tailor their approach and make more relevant and personalized recommendations. This can lead to improved customer satisfaction and higher sales conversion rates.

Moreover, AI can help to reduce errors and improve the accuracy of sales data. By automating data entry and analysis, AI can reduce the risk of human error and provide more accurate and reliable data for sales teams to work with. This can improve the quality of decision-making and lead to better business outcomes.

Chapter 14 of the *AI Marketing Playbook* provides a comprehensive overview of how AI can be used for sales enablement. AI can help sales teams to improve their performance by providing insights into customer behavior, automating routine tasks, and making more accurate sales forecasts. Successful sales enablement strategies that use AI include chatbots for customer engagement, predictive analytics for lead qualification, and automation for lead generation. AI can have a significant impact on sales productivity and efficiency, leading to improved performance and profitability.

Step-by-Step Instructions for Implementing AI in Lead Generation and Qualification

1. **Define Lead Qualification Criteria:** Begin by clearly defining what makes a lead qualified for a specific business. Consider factors like demographic details, engagement activities, purchase history, and specific interests.

2. **Select an AI Tool:** Choose an AI platform or tool that aligns with lead qualification criteria and can integrate with existing CRM and sales systems. The tool should have capabilities in data analysis, pattern recognition, and predictive modeling.

3. **Integrate Data Sources:** Ensure the AI tool has access to comprehensive data sources, including CRM, Web site analytics, social media interactions, and any other customer interaction platforms. This integration is crucial for a holistic view of potential leads.

4. **Configure the AI System:** Set up the AI tool to process and analyze the integrated data. The system should be configured to apply predefined lead qualification criteria and score leads based on their potential to convert.

5. **Train the AI Model:** Utilize historical sales and lead data to train the AI model, helping it learn and improve its accuracy in identifying and qualifying leads.

6. **Monitor AI Performance:** Regularly assess the AI system's performance. Evaluate how well the AI-qualified leads align with actual sales outcomes and make necessary adjustments to improve accuracy.

7. **Refine and Iterate:** Continuously refine the AI model based on ongoing data and feedback. Adjust the lead qualification criteria and scoring system as needed to enhance lead targeting and conversion rates.

8. **Integrate Insights into Sales Strategy:** Ensure the insights generated by the AI system are effectively integrated into the sales team's strategies, enabling them to prioritize and act on the most qualified leads efficiently.

HOW AI CAN BE USED FOR SALES ENABLEMENT

AI has become an integral part of modern business operations, especially when it comes to sales enablement. With the rise of data analytics and ML technologies, businesses can now leverage AI to gain a competitive edge and drive better sales results.

This section will explore how AI can be used for sales enablement, including its benefits, challenges, and best practices.

Benefits of Using AI for Sales Enablement

Not only does this improve the customer experience, but it also helps sales teams close deals more efficiently.

Best Sales Prediction

AI can also help companies improve their sales forecasting capabilities. By analyzing historical sales data, customer behavior and market trends, AI algorithms can predict future sales trends with high accuracy. This allows companies to adapt their sales strategies accordingly and stay one step ahead of the competition.

Simplified Sales Process

AI can automate many time-consuming and repetitive tasks in the sales process, such as data entry and lead qualification. This allows sales teams to focus on high-value activities like generating leads and closing deals.

Challenges of Using AI to Help Sales

While the benefits of using AI to increase sales are significant, companies must also consider some challenges.

Data Quality

AI relies heavily on data to generate insights and predictions. Therefore, it is important for companies to have high-quality and accurate data to ensure that AI algorithms make informed decisions. When data is incomplete, outdated, or inaccurate, it can lead to inaccurate forecasts and poor sales performance.

Implementation

Implementing AI into an existing sales process can be challenging. Businesses need to ensure that AI technology is compatible with their existing systems and that their sales team is professionally trained to use it. Additionally, companies must be willing to invest in the hardware and software infrastructure required to support AI technology.

Privacy and Security

AI algorithms rely on large amounts of data to generate insights and predictions. This data may include sensitive customer information such as personal and financial information. It is therefore important that companies have robust data protection and security measures in place to protect this information from unauthorized access and theft.

Best Practices for Using AI to Empower Sales

To maximize the benefits of using AI in the sales process and minimize the challenges, companies should follow these best practices. Emphasizing collaboration between AI tools and human insight can lead to more nuanced customer interactions and improved sales tactics. Additionally, continuously monitoring and refining AI algorithms based on real-time feedback and sales outcomes can drive further enhancements in sales effectiveness and efficiency.

Set Clear Goals

Before implementing AI to enable sales, companies need to establish clear goals and objectives. This ensures that AI technology is used to solve specific problems and produce meaningful results.

Choose the Right AI Technology

There are many different AI technologies to enable sales, including predictive analytics, NLP, and chatbots. Organizations need to choose the technology that best fits their goals and mission.

Form Sales Teams

Sales teams need to be professionally trained in the effective use of AI technology. This includes understanding how technology works, how to interpret the information generated by the technology, and how to incorporate that information into a sales strategy.

Monitor and Evaluate Results

After implementing AI technology, it is important for companies to monitor and evaluate performance. This includes measuring the impact of the technology on key metrics like lead conversion rates and revenue and making any necessary adjustments.

Continuous Improvement of Data Quality

As mentioned previously, data quality is critical to the success of sales-focused AI. Therefore, companies should have processes in place to continuously improve the quality of their data, such as regular data cleansing and validation.

Privacy and Security Troubleshooting

Companies should deploy robust privacy and security measures to protect sensitive customer information. This includes implementing data encryption, access controls and other security measures to prevent unauthorized access and theft.

There are many ways companies can use AI to increase sales. The following are some examples.

Main Score

AI can help companies improve their lead scoring process by analyzing data about a prospect's behavior, preferences, and interactions with the company. By anticipating the likelihood of a lead becoming a sale, sales teams can focus their efforts on the most promising prospects.

Personalized Recommendations

AI can generate personalized recommendations and messages based on customer behavior, preferences, and history within the organization. This helps sales teams develop a more personalized approach to selling, which leads to more conversions and increased revenue.

Sales Forecast

AI can help companies predict future sales trends with high accuracy by analyzing historical sales data, customer behavior and market trends. This allows companies to adapt their sales strategies accordingly and stay one step ahead of the competition.

Chatbots

Chatbots are AI-powered tools that enable businesses to automate customer interactions, for example, answering frequently asked questions and making product recommendations. This frees sales teams to focus on higher-value activities like generating leads and closing deals.

AI has become a valuable sales tool that offers many advantages such as better lead scoring, personalized sales approaches, better sales forecasts, and optimized sales processes. While there are also challenges such as data quality and privacy and security concerns, companies can follow best practices to maximize the benefits of AI to enable sales. The use of AI technology can help companies stay ahead of the competition and achieve better sales results.

Successful Sales Enablement Strategies that Use AI

In recent years, artificial intelligence (AI) has revolutionized the way businesses approach sales enablement. AI-powered sales enablement strategies have become increasingly popular, thanks to their ability to provide personalized insights and recommendations for each customer, streamline the sales process, and improve overall sales performance. This chapter explores examples of successful sales enablement strategies that use AI, and how they are helping businesses drive revenue growth.

AI-Powered Content Creation

An important part of sales enablement is providing sales teams with relevant and engaging content to use in the sales process. AI-powered content creation tools can help streamline this process by automating the creation of personalized content based on customer data. These tools use ML algorithms to analyze customer data such as browsing history, purchase history, and social media interactions to identify patterns and preferences. This data is then used to create targeted.

Content that Resonates with Each Customer

HubSpot's content strategy tool uses AI to help companies create a content strategy that is aligned with their target audience. The tool analyzes customer data, identifies topics, and keywords that resonate with the target group. It also includes suggested themes and formats that might be effective based on past performance data.

AI-Based Lead Score

Evaluating potential customers is key to selling. Each prospect is assigned a score based on their interest, engagement, and fit with the profile of the company's target customers. This helps sales teams prioritize and focus on the leads most likely to convert.

AI-powered lead scoring tools use ML algorithms to analyze customer data and identify patterns and behaviors that indicate a high likelihood of conversion. This data may include Web site interactions, email opens and clicks, social media interactions and other relevant data points. The algorithms then use this data to rank each prospect based on their likelihood of converting.

Salesforce's Einstein Lead Scoring uses AI to analyze customer data and score each lead based on the likelihood of conversion. The tool considers various data points, including purchase history, email engagement, Web site interactions, and more. This helps sales teams focus their efforts on the leads most likely to convert and increase their chances of success.

Sales Forecasts Are Based on AI

Sales predictions are the key to enabling sales. It involves forecasting future earnings based on past performance data and other relevant factors. Accurate sales forecasts help companies plan sales strategies, allocate resources, and set revenue targets.

AI-powered sales forecasting tools use ML algorithms to analyze past performance data and identify patterns and trends that can be used to predict future sales revenue. These tools can also consider external factors such as market trends, economic indicators, and competitor performance to create more accurate forecasts.

InsideSales.com's Predictive Pipeline uses AI to provide sales teams with accurate sales forecasts. The tool analyzes past performance data, identifies patterns, and trends that can be used to predict future sales revenue. It also considers external factors such as market trends and economic indicators to create more accurate forecasts.

Sales Coaching Based on AI

Sales coaching is an important part of sales support. This includes providing sales teams with feedback, guidance, and training to help them improve their performance. AI-powered sales coaching tools can help streamline this process by providing personalized feedback and recommendations based on each salesperson's performance data.

Chorus.ai's Conversation Intelligence feature uses AI to analyze sales pitches and provide feedback and recommendations to sales teams. The tool analyzes each merchant's performance data, such as call duration, talk time and interaction rate, and provides personalized feedback and suggestions for improvement. This helps sales teams improve efficiency and increase sales.

Engagement in AI-Supported Sales

Sales engagement involves interacting with prospects across multiple channels like email, social media, and phone calls to build relationships and increase conversions. AI-powered selling tools can help streamline this process by providing each customer with personalized recommendations based on their behavior and preferences.

The SalesLoft Sales Engagement Platform uses AI to provide each customer with personalized recommendations. The tool analyzes customer data such as previous interactions, purchase history, and social media behavior to provide sales teams with personalized recommendations for each customer. This helps sales teams build stronger customer relationships and increase the likelihood of conversion.

AI-powered sales strategies have become increasingly popular in recent years due to their ability to provide personalized insights and recommendations for each customer, streamlining the sales process and improving overall sales performance. Examples of successful sales enablement strategies that leverage AI include AI-powered content creation, lead scoring, sales forecasting, sales coaching, and sales engagement. By leveraging AI, companies can improve their sales performance, drive revenue growth, and strengthen their customer relationships.

THE ROLE OF AI IN LEAD GENERATION AND QUALIFICATION

Lead generation and qualification is a crucial aspect of any business, as it helps in identifying potential customers and generating revenue. In recent years, the use of AI has significantly transformed the lead generation and qualification process, making it more efficient and effective. AI technology has enabled businesses to automate and streamline their lead generation and qualification process, thereby reducing manual intervention and errors. This chapter will discuss in detail the role of AI in lead generation and qualification.

What Are Lead Generation and Qualification?

Lead generation is the process of identifying potential customers for a company's products or services. It includes various marketing strategies like email marketing, content marketing, social media marketing, and so on. On the other hand, lead qualification is the process of determining whether a lead is a good fit for the business or not. It consists of analyzing a range of factors such as budget, planning, decision-making powers, and so on. of the lead.

The Role of AI in Lead Generation and Qualification

AI technology has transformed the lead generation and qualification process by providing businesses with advanced tools and techniques to automate and streamline the process. Following are some ways AI can help generate and qualify leads.

Identification of Potential Contacts: AI

Technology can analyze customer data and behavior to identify the prospects most likely to convert. AI can analyze data from various sources such as Web site traffic, social media, email marketing, and so on. Identify potential buyers. This helps businesses focus their marketing efforts on the right audience and increase their chances of conversion.

Personalization of Communication

AI technology can personalize communications with prospects by analyzing their behavior and preferences. AI can analyze data such as browsing history, search queries, and so on. to personalize communication with potential customers. This helps businesses build stronger relationships with potential customers and increase their chances of conversion.

Main Score: AI

AI technology can analyze a range of factors such as overall budget, schedule, decision-making powers, and so on, to evaluate potential customers based on their conversion potential. This helps businesses prioritize leads and focus their efforts on leads that are most likely to convert.

Automated Lead Nurturing

AI technology can automate the lead nurturing process by sending personalized messages to potential leads at the right time. AI can analyze data like email open rates, click-through rates, and more. AI can send messages that are more likely to convert prospects into customers.

Chatbots

AI-powered chatbots can help businesses connect with potential customers in real-time. Chatbots can answer frequently asked questions, provide personalized recommendations, and even book appointments. This helps businesses provide better customer service and increase conversion chances.

Predictive Analytics

AI-powered predictive analytics can analyze customer data and behavior to predict the likelihood of conversion. This helps businesses focus their efforts on the leads most likely to convert, increasing their chances of success.

Qualification of the Prospect

AI-powered lead qualification tools can analyze a range of factors such as budget, schedule, decision-making powers, and so on, of a prospect to determine if a prospect is a good fit for the company or not. This helps companies focus their efforts on leads that are most likely to convert and avoid wasting time and resources on leads that are unlikely to convert.

Advantages of Using AI to Generate and Qualify Leads

Efficiency

AI-powered lead generation and qualification tools can significantly reduce the time and effort required to identify and qualify leads. This helps companies focus on other important aspects of their business and increase their overall efficiency.

Accuracy

AI-powered lead generation and qualification tools can analyze customer data and behavior more accurately than humans. This helps companies make more informed decisions and avoid mistakes that can lead to missed opportunities.

Personalization

AI-powered lead generation and qualification tools can personalize communication with potential leads and provide them with a better customer experience. This helps businesses build stronger relationships with potential customers and increase their chances of conversion.

Economy

AI-powered lead generation and qualification tools can help businesses reduce marketing costs by focusing on leads most likely to convert. This helps companies optimize their marketing spend and get a better return on investment (ROI).

Scalability

AI-powered lead generation and qualification tools can handle large numbers of leads, making it easier for companies to grow their business. This helps businesses expand their customer base and increase sales.

AI technology has radically changed the lead generation and qualification process, making it more efficient, accurate and cost-effective. AI-powered tools can help businesses identify leads, personalize communications, capture leads, automate lead nurturing, use chatbots for engagement, perform predictive analytics, and qualify prospects. These benefits help businesses optimize their marketing spend, achieve a better ROI, and grow their customer base. As AI technology evolves, expect further innovations in lead generation and qualification, making it an even more important aspect of any successful business strategy.

Step-by-Step Instructions: Implementing AI for Lead Generation and Qualification

1. **Define Lead Generation and Qualification Goals:** Start by clearly defining what the overall goals are with AI in the lead generation and qualification process. Set specific, measurable objectives like increasing lead volume, improving lead quality, or reducing the time and cost per lead.

2. **Select the Appropriate AI Technology:** Choose AI tools that are suited for lead generation and qualification tasks. These could include ML algorithms for predictive analytics, NLP for chatbots, or data mining tools for identifying patterns in customer behavior.

3. **Integrate AI with Existing Data Sources:** Ensure that the AI system can access and process data from various sources, such as a CRM system, Web site analytics, social media platforms, and email campaigns. This integration is crucial for the AI to have a comprehensive view of potential leads.

4. **Develop AI-Driven Lead Scoring Models:** Use AI to create lead scoring models that automatically evaluate leads based on their likelihood to convert. These models should consider a range of factors such as demographic details, online behavior, engagement levels, and past interactions with the specified brand.

5. **Implement AI-Powered Chatbots for Initial Engagement:** Deploy AI-driven chatbots on the specified Web site and social media channels to engage with visitors, answer their queries, and collect lead information. Chatbots can qualify leads by asking predefined questions and analyzing responses.

6. **Automate Lead Nurturing with AI:** Set up AI systems to automate the lead nurturing process. This can include sending personalized emails, content recommendations, and targeted offers based on the lead's behavior and interaction history.

7. **Monitor AI Systems and Analyze Performance:** Regularly review the performance of AI tools to ensure they are effectively identifying and qualifying leads. Analyze metrics such as lead conversion rates, engagement levels, and ROI to gauge the success of AI implementations.

8. **Refine and Optimize AI Processes:** Based on performance data and feedback, continuously refine AI models and processes. Update lead scoring criteria, adjust chatbot interactions, and tweak automated nurturing campaigns to improve lead generation and qualification outcomes.

SALES FORECASTING WITH AI

Sales forecasting is an essential element of business planning that provides insights into future sales trends, demand patterns, and customer behavior. Sales forecasting with AI is a powerful tool that leverages ML algorithms to analyze historical sales data, market trends, and customer behavior to generate accurate sales forecasts. Chapter 14 of the *AI Marketing Playbook* explores in detail how AI can be used for sales forecasting and the benefits it can bring to businesses.

Sales forecasting with AI involves the use of algorithms that can analyze large volumes of data to predict future sales trends. These algorithms use statistical and mathematical models to identify patterns, trends, and anomalies in sales data. These patterns are then used to predict future sales trends, considering market dynamics, customer behavior, and other external factors.

The first step in sales forecasting with AI is to gather and organize relevant data. This includes historical sales data, customer data, and market data. Historical sales data can be used to identify patterns and trends in sales, while customer data can provide insights into customer behavior, preferences, and purchase history. Market data, including economic indicators, industry trends, and competitor data, can also be used to inform sales forecasts.

Once the relevant data is gathered, AI algorithms are used to analyze the data and generate sales forecasts. These algorithms can be trained on historical data to learn from past sales trends and identify patterns and anomalies in the data. They can also be used to analyze market data and customer data to identify trends and factors that may impact sales.

One of the key benefits of sales forecasting with AI is its ability to generate accurate sales forecasts. AI algorithms can analyze large volumes of data and identify patterns and trends that may not be visible to human analysts. This can result in more accurate sales forecasts that consider a wide range of factors, including market dynamics, customer behavior, and external factors such as economic indicators and industry trends.

Another benefit of sales forecasting with AI is its ability to generate forecasts quickly and efficiently. AI algorithms can analyze large volumes of data in a fraction of the time it would take human analysts to do so. This can help businesses to make more informed decisions more quickly and respond more effectively to changes in the market.

Sales forecasting with AI can also help businesses to identify opportunities for growth and optimization. By analyzing sales data and identifying patterns and trends, businesses can identify areas where they can increase sales and optimize their operations. They may identify products or services that are selling well and invest in marketing campaigns to promote these products or services further.

There are several different types of AI algorithms that can be used for sales forecasting. These include regression analysis, time-series analysis, and ML algorithms such as neural networks and decision trees. Each of these algorithms has its strengths and weaknesses, and the choice of algorithm will depend on the specific requirements of the business.

Regression analysis is a statistical technique that can be used to identify relationships between variables. It can be used to predict future sales based on historical sales data and other variables such as marketing spend, pricing, and customer demographics. Time-series analysis, on the other hand, is a statistical technique that is used to analyze time-series data, such as sales data over time. This technique can be used to identify trends and patterns in sales data and to generate forecasts based on these patterns.

ML algorithms such as neural networks and decision trees are more complex than regression analysis and time-series analysis. These algorithms can analyze large volumes of data and identify complex patterns and relationships between variables. They can also be used to generate forecasts based on these patterns and relationships. However, they require more data and more computational resources than regression analysis and time-series analysis.

Sales forecasting with AI is a powerful tool that can help businesses to generate more accurate sales forecasts, identify opportunities for growth and optimization, and respond more effectively to changes in the market. By analyzing historical sales data, customer data, and market data, AI algorithms can identify patterns and trends that may not be visible to human analysts. This can help businesses to make more informed decisions and respond more quickly to changes in the market. Additionally, by using ML algorithms, businesses can continuously improve their sales forecasting models as more data becomes available.

Overall, sales forecasting with AI is a crucial tool for businesses that want to stay ahead of the competition and make more informed decisions about their sales and marketing strategies. By leveraging AI algorithms, businesses can generate more accurate sales forecasts, identify opportunities for growth and optimization, and respond more quickly to changes in the market. As AI technology continues to evolve, expect to see even more advanced sales forecasting techniques that will help businesses to stay ahead of the curve and achieve their goals.

Step-by-Step Instructions: Developing and Implementing AI-Based Sales Forecasting Models

1. **Identify Business Goals:** Clearly define what the overall goals with the sales forecasting model. This could include increasing revenue, improving inventory management, or optimizing marketing spend.

2. **Gather and Prepare Data:** Collect historical sales data, along with other relevant data such as market trends, customer demographics, and economic indicators. Clean and preprocess the data to ensure it is accurate and suitable for analysis.

3. **Select the Right AI Model:** Choose an AI model that fits forecasting needs. Options may include time series analysis, regression models, or ML algorithms like neural networks or decision trees.

4. **Train the Model:** Use historical data to train the AI model. This process involves adjusting the model parameters so it can accurately identify patterns and make predictions based on the data provided.

5. **Validate the Model:** Test the model with a separate set of data to validate its accuracy. Adjust the model as necessary to improve its predictive capabilities.

6. **Implement the Model:** Once validated, integrate the AI model into business processes. Ensure it can access real-time data and update forecasts accordingly.

7. **Monitor and Refine:** Regularly monitor the model's performance and make adjustments based on new data and changing market conditions. This will help maintain the accuracy of forecasts over time.

8. **Use Insights to Inform Decisions:** Utilize the insights gained from the AI model to make informed strategic decisions in areas like inventory management, pricing strategies, and marketing campaigns.

The Impact of AI on Sales Productivity and Efficiency

The emergence of AI) has had a tremendous impact on the world of sales. With the increasing number of businesses implementing AI technology in their sales process, it is evident that AI has become an essential part of modern sales strategies. AI has made it possible to automate many of the tedious and repetitive tasks involved in sales, enabling sales teams to focus on the more important and complex tasks that require human intervention. This chapter will explore the impact of AI on sales productivity and efficiency.

AI-Powered Sales Analytics

One of the significant advantages of AI in sales is its ability to analyze substantial amounts of data quickly and accurately. AI-powered sales analytics provide sales teams with insights into customer behavior, buying patterns, and preferences, which can help them make informed decisions. By analyzing customer data, AI can help sales teams understand the needs of their customers and develop personalized strategies to meet those needs.

AI-powered sales analytics can also help sales teams identify potential opportunities and risks, allowing them to make more informed decisions about how to allocate their resources. AI-powered predictive analytics can help sales teams identify leads that are most likely to convert into customers, allowing them to focus their efforts on those leads and improve their chances of success.

AI-Powered Sales Analytics: Step-by-Step Instructions

1. **Data Collection:**

   - Compile sales data, customer interactions, and feedback across all platforms.
   - Ensure data quality by validating, cleaning, and standardizing the collected data.

2. **AI Model Training:**

   - Use the prepared dataset to train AI models on patterns of customer behavior and purchasing history.
   - Test the AI models to ensure accuracy in predictive analysis.

3. **Insight Generation:**

   - Deploy AI analytics tools to sift through data and generate insights on customer preferences and buying patterns.
   - Create visualizations and reports to make the insights accessible and understandable for the sales team.

4. **Strategy Development:**

   - Use AI-generated insights to tailor sales strategies for different customer segments.
   - Develop personalized marketing campaigns based on predictive analysis.

5. **Opportunity and Risk Identification**

   - Utilize AI to identify potential sales opportunities and risks in the pipeline.
   - Adjust resource allocation to capitalize on opportunities and mitigate risks.

Automated Lead Generation

Another critical area where AI has had a significant impact on sales is lead generation. With AI-powered lead generation tools, sales teams can automate many of the tasks involved in the lead generation process. AI-powered tools can identify potential leads by analyzing customer data and behavior, enabling sales teams to focus their efforts on leads that are most likely to convert into customers.

AI-powered lead generation tools can also help sales teams personalize their approach to each lead by providing insights into the lead's preferences, needs, and interests. This can help sales teams develop a more effective and personalized approach, improving their chances of success.

Automated Lead Generation: Step-by-Step Instructions

1. **Lead Data Aggregation:**

   - Integrate AI lead generation tools with a CRM to collect potential lead information.
   - Analyze customer data and behaviors across various touchpoints.

2. **Lead Scoring:**

   - Implement AI algorithms to score leads based on their likelihood to convert.
   - Prioritize leads that show a higher propensity for conversion.

3. **Personalization:**

   - Use AI to uncover insights into each lead's preferences, needs, and interests.
   - Customize communication and sales approaches to align with these insights.

4. **Engagement:**

   - Automate initial lead engagement with personalized emails and messages.
   - Set up notifications for sales teams to take over when a lead shows high engagement.

Automated Sales Forecasting

Sales forecasting is another area where AI has had a significant impact. AI-powered sales forecasting tools can analyze historical sales data, customer behavior, and market trends to provide accurate and reliable sales forecasts. This can help sales teams develop better sales strategies and allocate resources more effectively.

AI-powered sales forecasting tools can also help sales teams identify potential risks and opportunities, allowing them to adjust their strategies and make informed decisions about how to allocate their resources.

Automated Sales Forecasting: Step-by-Step Instructions

1. **Historical Data Analysis:**

   - Input historical sales data into a AI forecasting tool.
   - Allow the AI to identify trends and patterns from past performance.

2. **Market Trend Integration:**

   - Feed market trend data into the system to enhance forecasting accuracy.
   - Adjust for seasonal fluctuations and market shifts.

3. **Forecast Generation:**

   - Run the AI tool to generate sales forecasts for different timeframes.
   - Review and validate forecasts against known variables and market conditions.

4. **Actionable Insights:**

   - Translate forecasts into actionable insights for resource allocation.
   - Make strategic decisions based on forecasted sales volumes and customer demand.

AI-Powered Customer Service

Customer service is another area where AI has had a significant impact. AI-powered chatbots and virtual assistants can help businesses provide 24/7 customer support, answering customer questions and resolving issues in real-time. This can help businesses improve their customer satisfaction rates and reduce their customer service costs.

AI-powered customer service tools can also help businesses personalize their approach to each customer by providing insights into their preferences and needs. This can help businesses develop more effective and personalized customer service strategies, improving their chances of success.

Automated Sales Processes

AI has had a significant impact on sales processes. With AI-powered sales automation tools, sales teams can automate many of the tasks involved in the sales process, such as lead qualification, follow-up, and scheduling. This can help sales teams save time and focus their efforts on more important tasks, such as closing deals.

AI-powered sales automation tools can also help businesses improve their sales processes by identifying areas that need improvement and suggesting ways to optimize them. This can help businesses improve their sales efficiency and effectiveness, leading to increased sales and revenue.

The impact of AI on sales productivity and efficiency cannot be overstated. AI-powered sales analytics, lead generation, sales forecasting, customer service, and sales automation tools have all helped businesses improve their sales processes, resulting in increased sales and revenue. As AI technology continues to evolve, it is likely that people will see even more significant impacts on the world of sales, making it an exciting time for businesses.

Step-by-Step Instructions: Enhancing Sales Productivity with AI

1. **Evaluate Sales Processes:** Start by identifying the sales tasks that are repetitive, time-consuming, and prone to human error. These might include data entry, lead qualification, follow-up scheduling, or report generation.

2. **Select Suitable AI Tools:** Choose AI tools that can automate the identified tasks effectively. Look for solutions with features like CRM integration, predictive analytics, NLP, and automation capabilities tailored to sales processes.

3. **Integrate AI Tools with Existing Systems:** Ensure the selected AI tools integrate seamlessly with existing sales and CRM systems. This integration allows for automated data flow and analysis, providing real-time insights and recommendations to sales teams.

4. **Train the Sales Team:** Conduct training sessions for the sales team to familiarize them with the new AI tools. Focus on how these tools can streamline their workflow, automate mundane tasks, and free up their time for more strategic activities.

5. **Set Up Automation Workflows:** Configure the AI tools to automate specific tasks like lead scoring, prioritization, email follow-ups, and meeting scheduling. Set up triggers and actions within the AI system to perform these tasks based on predefined criteria.

6. **Monitor and Optimize:** Continually monitor the performance of AI tools and their impact on sales productivity. Gather feedback from the sales team to identify areas for improvement and optimize the AI systems accordingly.

7. **Analyze AI-Driven Insights:** Utilize the AI tools' analytics and reporting features to gain insights into sales trends, customer behavior, and team performance. Use these insights to make data-driven decisions and adjust sales strategies for better outcomes.

8. **Encourage Continuous Learning:** Promote a culture of continuous learning and adaptation within the sales team. Encourage them to leverage AI-driven insights and automation to refine sales tactics and improve engagement with leads and customers.

In Chapter 14 of the *AI Marketing Playbook*, the use of AI for sales enablement was thoroughly discussed. The chapter began by explaining how AI can be used for sales enablement, with a focus on automating repetitive tasks, improving sales forecasting accuracy, and enhancing sales productivity and efficiency.

One of the primary ways AI can be used for sales enablement is through lead generation and qualification. AI algorithms can be used to sift through vast amounts of customer data, identifying potential leads and filtering them based on various criteria such as demographics, behavior patterns, and engagement levels. This process can be done more efficiently and accurately than a human, freeing up time for sales reps to focus on high-value prospects.

Several examples of successful sales enablement strategies that use AI were also provided in the chapter. One such example is the use of chatbots to engage with customers in real-time, providing personalized recommendations, and answering queries promptly. The use of predictive analytics to identify the most promising leads, allowing sales reps to focus their efforts on the customers who are most likely to convert.

In addition to lead generation and qualification, AI can also be used for sales forecasting. AI algorithms can analyze historical sales data and market trends to provide accurate predictions of future sales volumes. This information can help sales teams make informed decisions about resource allocation and sales strategies, enabling them to optimize their performance and achieve better results.

The impact of AI on sales productivity and efficiency was also discussed in detail in the chapter. By automating repetitive tasks and providing real-time insights, AI can help sales reps work more efficiently and focus on high-value activities. AI-powered tools can analyze customer behavior patterns, identifying buying signals and providing prompts for reps to act. This process can help reps engage with customers more effectively, leading to higher conversion rates and increased revenue.

The chapter also discussed some of the potential challenges and limitations of using AI for sales enablement. Some companies may struggle to integrate AI tools into their existing sales processes or may lack the resources or expertise to effectively leverage AI technology. Additionally, there are concerns around data privacy and security, as well as potential ethical concerns around the use of AI in sales and marketing.

Overall, the chapter highlighted the significant potential benefits of using AI for sales enablement, including improved lead generation, sales forecasting accuracy, and sales productivity and efficiency. While there are certainly challenges and limitations to consider, the use of AI in sales enablement is a growing trend that is likely to continue shaping the future of sales and marketing in the years to come.

ETHICAL CONSIDERATIONS AND THE FUTURE OF ARTIFICIAL INTELLIGENCE (AI) IN MARKETING

Chapter 15 of the *AI Marketing Playbook* delves into the ethical considerations and the future of AI in marketing. Artificial intelligence (AI) has revolutionized the way businesses market their products and services. However, as with any technology, there are ethical implications to consider. This chapter explores the ethical considerations when using AI in marketing, potential concerns, the importance of transparency and privacy, the future of AI in marketing, and the role of human expertise and creativity. The following summarizes some of what is discussed in this chapter.

Ethical Considerations When Using AI in Marketing

AI in marketing presents ethical considerations, especially when it comes to personal data usage. Marketers are collecting vast amounts of personal data from customers, which can be used to create personalized marketing campaigns. However, the use of personal data raises concerns about privacy, security, and transparency. Marketers must ensure that they obtain consent from customers before collecting and using their data, as well as complying with data protection laws.

Another ethical consideration is the use of biased data. AI algorithms are only as good as the data that is fed into them. If the data used to train the algorithm is biased, then the results will be biased as well. This can lead to unfair discrimination against certain groups of people, such as minorities or women. It is important to ensure that the data used is diverse and representative of the population.

Potential Ethical Concerns with AI in Marketing

There are various potential ethical concerns with AI in marketing, including:

- *Invasion of privacy:* Marketers using AI may collect vast amounts of personal data without obtaining proper consent or informing customers about the use of their data. This can be seen as an invasion of privacy.
- *Discrimination:* As mentioned earlier, AI algorithms can be biased if the data used to train them is biased. This can lead to unfair discrimination against certain groups of people.
- *Manipulation:* Marketers can use AI to manipulate customers into buying products or services that they may not need or want.
- *Transparency:* Customers may not always be aware that they are interacting with AI, which can lead to a lack of transparency.

The Importance of Transparency and Privacy When Using AI in Marketing

Transparency and privacy are critical when using AI in marketing. Customers have the right to know when they are interacting with AI and what data is being collected from them. Marketers must be transparent about how they use customer data and ensure that they comply with data protection laws. This includes obtaining proper consent before collecting and using customer data.

THE FUTURE OF AI IN MARKETING: EMERGING TECHNOLOGIES AND TRENDS

The future of AI in marketing looks promising. Emerging technologies such as chatbots, voice assistants, and virtual reality (VR) and augmented reality (AR) are changing the way customers interact with brands. These technologies allow for more personalized and engaging experiences, which can lead to increased customer satisfaction and loyalty. AI-powered chatbots can provide 24/7 customer service and support, which can improve customer experiences and reduce costs for businesses.

The Role of Human Expertise and Creativity in AI-Powered Marketing

While AI is changing the way businesses market their products and services, human expertise and creativity remain essential. AI algorithms are only as good as the data that is fed into them, and human experts are needed to ensure that the data is diverse and representative of the population. Additionally, humans are needed to analyze the results generated by AI algorithms and make decisions based on that analysis. Creativity is also important when using AI in marketing. AI algorithms can provide personalized recommendations, but it takes human creativity to design engaging campaigns and experiences that resonate with customers.

AI has revolutionized the way businesses market their products and services. However, there are ethical considerations to consider, including invasion of privacy, discrimination, manipulation, and transparency. Marketers must be transparent about how they use customer data and ensure that they comply with data protection laws. Looking toward the future, emerging technologies such as chatbots, voice assistants, and virtual and AR will continue to shape the way customers interact with brands. However, human expertise and creativity will remain essential in ensuring that AI-powered marketing is both effective and ethical. By considering the ethical implications of AI in marketing and prioritizing transparency and privacy, businesses can build trust with their customers and create meaningful experiences that benefit both the customer and the business.

ETHICAL CONSIDERATIONS WHEN USING AI IN MARKETING

The rapid development of artificial intelligence (AI) has brought unprecedented opportunities to the field of marketing. AI enables companies to process vast amounts of customer data quickly, accurately, and efficiently, leading to better customer segmentation, personalized product recommendations, and improved customer engagement. However, AI-powered marketing also raises ethical concerns. This section explores the ethical considerations that companies must consider when using AI in marketing.

- *Transparency:* One of the most significant ethical concerns regarding AI in marketing is transparency. Consumers have a right to know when they are interacting with an AI-powered system. It is not ethical to use AI to deceive or mislead customers into thinking they are interacting with a human being. Companies must be transparent about their use of AI and provide clear information about when customers are interacting with AI.
- *Privacy:* Another ethical consideration is privacy. AI requires vast amounts of data to learn and make predictions. Companies must be transparent about what data they collect, how they use it, and who has access to it. They must also ensure that they are collecting data in compliance with data protection regulations such as GDPR (General Data Protection Regulation) and CCPA (California Consumer Privacy Act). Customers should have the right to control their data and decide how it is used. Companies must respect these rights and ensure that customer data is kept secure.
- *Bias AI:* This can be biased, reflecting the biases of its creators and the data it is trained on. This can lead to discrimination and unfair treatment of certain groups of customers. Companies must ensure that their AI systems are designed to be fair and unbiased. This requires a diverse team of creators and data sets that are representative of the entire customer population. Companies must also regularly monitor their AI systems for bias and take steps to correct any issues that arise.

- *Customer autonomy:* AI can be used to influence customer behavior, by using personalized product recommendations or targeted advertising. While this can be a powerful marketing tool, companies must respect the autonomy of their customers. They should not use AI to manipulate customers or make decisions on their behalf without their consent. Customers must be given the freedom to make their own choices and decisions.
- *Safety:* AI-powered marketing must also prioritize safety. Companies must ensure that their AI systems are secure and cannot be hacked or manipulated. They must also ensure that their AI systems do not pose any physical or emotional harm to customers. AI-powered chatbots must be designed to handle sensitive information appropriately and avoid causing emotional distress to customers.
- *Accountability:* Companies must take responsibility for the actions of their AI systems. They must be accountable for any harm caused by their AI systems and take steps to rectify any issues. Companies must also be transparent about how their AI systems work and how decisions are made. Customers should be able to understand how their data is being used, and companies must be able to explain any decisions made by their AI systems.

While AI has tremendous potential to revolutionize marketing, it also raises significant ethical concerns. Companies must be transparent about their use of AI, respect customer privacy and autonomy, ensure that their AI systems are unbiased and secure, and take responsibility for the actions of their AI systems. By prioritizing these ethical considerations, companies can harness the power of AI to improve customer engagement while also promoting trust and respect with their customers.

POTENTIAL ETHICAL CONCERNS WITH AI IN MARKETING

AI is revolutionizing the way businesses operate, particularly in the field of marketing. AI can automate many tasks that were once done by humans, such as analyzing customer data, creating personalized content, and predicting customer behavior. While AI has the potential to improve marketing effectiveness and efficiency, it also raises ethical concerns.

Ethical concerns with AI in marketing arise from the potential for the technology to be used in ways that could harm customers or violate their privacy. This chapter will explore several examples of ethical concerns with AI in marketing and discuss their history.

Targeted Advertising

One of the most common uses of AI in marketing is targeted advertising. AI algorithms analyze customer data to create personalized advertisements that are more likely to resonate with individual customers. While targeted advertising can be effective, it also raises ethical concerns.

In 2018, Facebook was caught up in a scandal involving Cambridge Analytica, a data analytics firm that used data obtained from Facebook to influence the 2016 US presidential election. The firm used AI algorithms to analyze Facebook users' data, including their likes and dislikes, to create personalized political ads. The scandal sparked a conversation about the ethics of targeted advertising and the need for greater transparency in how companies use customer data.

Another example of targeted advertising raising ethical concerns is the use of AI to create discriminatory advertisements. In 2016, ProPublica published an investigation revealing that Facebook's advertising platform could be used to create discriminatory ads that excluded certain groups, such as African Americans and Latinos, from seeing job listings. The investigation highlighted the need for greater regulation of AI in advertising to ensure that it does not perpetuate discrimination.

Personalization

AI can also be used to create personalized content, such as product recommendations and email marketing campaigns. While personalization can improve customer engagement and conversion rates, it also raises ethical concerns.

One potential ethical concern with personalization is the use of AI to manipulate customers' emotions. In 2014, Facebook conducted an experiment in which it manipulated the content of users' news feeds to see how it would affect their emotions. The experiment sparked outrage and raised concerns about the ethics of using AI to manipulate human behavior.

Another potential ethical concern with personalization is the use of AI to create deepfakes, which are highly realistic images or videos that are manipulated to misrepresent someone or something. Deepfakes can be used to create false advertising, spread misinformation, and manipulate public opinion.

Privacy

AI in marketing also raises concerns about privacy. AI algorithms analyze vast amounts of customer data to create personalized advertisements and content. While this can be beneficial for businesses and customers alike, it also raises concerns about data privacy.

In 2019, Amazon's Ring doorbell came under scrutiny for its data privacy practices. The doorbell uses AI to analyze video footage and identify potential threats, such as burglars and trespassers. However, the doorbell also collects vast amounts of data on its users, including their comings and goings, which raised concerns about how the data could be used and who would have access to it.

Another example of privacy concerns with AI in marketing is the use of AI chatbots to collect customer data. Chatbots are becoming increasingly popular in customer service, as they can automate many tasks and provide 24/7 support. However, some chatbots are programmed to collect customer data without their consent, which raises concerns about data privacy.

Bias

AI in marketing raises concerns about bias. AI algorithms are only as unbiased as the data they are trained on, and if the data is biased, the algorithm will be too. This can lead to discriminatory marketing practices that perpetuate stereotypes and marginalize certain groups.

In 2018, Amazon came under fire for its AI-powered recruiting tool, which was found to be biased against women. The tool was trained on resumes submitted to Amazon over a ten-year period, which were predominantly from men. As a result, the tool started to favor male candidates and penalize resumes that included terms such as "women's," "female," and "she." The incident highlighted the need for greater diversity in AI training data and for humans to monitor and correct bias in AI algorithms.

AI in marketing has the potential to improve marketing effectiveness and efficiency, but it also raises several ethical concerns. Targeted advertising, personalization, privacy, and bias are just a few examples of the ethical challenges that arise when AI is used in marketing. As the use of AI in marketing continues to grow, it is essential for businesses to be transparent about their data practices, ensure that their algorithms are unbiased, and prioritize the privacy and well-being of their customers.

Artificial Intelligence (AI) has revolutionized the way companies conduct their marketing campaigns. By utilizing AI, companies can analyze customer data and behavior to create more targeted and effective advertising strategies. However, AI has also raised potential ethical concerns in marketing. This chapter will provide examples and detail the history of these ethical concerns in AI marketing.

The following list describes some examples of potential ethical concerns with AI in marketing:

- *Privacy:* One of the most significant ethical concerns surrounding AI in marketing is privacy. The use of AI in marketing allows companies to collect and analyze substantial amounts of data about customers, including personal information such as age, gender, location, and search history. This data can be used to create targeted advertising campaigns that are tailored to individual customers' interests and preferences. However, this collection of data raises concerns about privacy and security. Customers may feel that their personal information is being exploited and used for marketing purposes without their consent.

- *Bias and discrimination:* AI is only as unbiased as the data that it is fed. However, the data that AI is fed is not always objective, and it can contain inherent biases. AI may be fed data that is skewed toward a particular demographic or region. This can result in discriminatory marketing campaigns that exclude certain groups or individuals. Bias in AI can also perpetuate and reinforce stereotypes, leading to further discrimination.
- *Misleading advertising:* AI-powered advertising can be more targeted and effective than traditional advertising methods, but it can also be misleading. Companies can use AI to create highly customized and personalized advertisements that may exaggerate the benefits of their products or services. This can lead to customers being misled about the quality or effectiveness of a product, which can harm the brand's reputation and erode customer trust.
- *Manipulation and addiction:* AI-powered marketing can also be used to manipulate customers and promote addiction. Companies can use AI to analyze customer behavior and create highly effective advertising campaigns that exploit customers' vulnerabilities. Social media platforms can use AI to identify users who are more likely to engage with certain types of content and bombard them with ads or notifications. This can lead to addiction and other negative outcomes, such as reduced productivity or increased anxiety.
- *Lack of transparency:* The use of AI in marketing can also raise concerns about transparency. Customers may not be aware that their data is being collected and used for marketing purposes. Furthermore, the algorithms used by AI may be complex and difficult to understand, making it difficult for customers to know how their data is being used. This lack of transparency can erode trust and undermine customer relationships with brands.
- *Privacy breaches:* AI-powered marketing campaigns can also lead to privacy breaches. Companies may store substantial amounts of customer data, and if this data is not adequately protected, it can be vulnerable to hacking or other forms of cyber-attacks. A privacy breach can result in the loss of sensitive customer information, such as credit card details or social security numbers, which can cause significant harm to customers and damage a company's reputation.
- *Automation and job loss:* The use of AI in marketing can also lead to automation and job loss. AI can automate many of the tasks that were previously performed by humans, such as data analysis and ad targeting. This can lead to job losses in the marketing industry, which can have a significant impact on the workforce.

AI has the potential to revolutionize marketing and provide significant benefits to companies and customers. However, it is essential to be aware of the potential ethical concerns surrounding AI in marketing. Privacy concerns, bias and discrimination, misleading advertising, manipulation and addiction, lack of transparency, privacy breaches, automation and job loss are all issues that need to be addressed. Companies must take steps to ensure that they are using AI in an ethical and responsible way, and that they are protecting the privacy and security of their customers' data.

THE IMPORTANCE OF TRANSPARENCY AND PRIVACY WHEN USING AI IN MARKETING

AI has transformed the marketing industry by enabling businesses to analyze large volumes of data and make informed decisions. As AI becomes more prevalent in marketing, it is essential to prioritize transparency and privacy to build trust and maintain consumer confidence. This section will explain the importance of transparency and privacy when using AI in marketing and explore the benefits of transparency and privacy for both businesses and consumers.

Transparency refers to the openness and clarity of information provided to consumers about how their data is being collected, used, and stored. Privacy, however, is the protection of personal information from unauthorized access or disclosure. Both transparency and privacy are essential for building consumer trust, which is crucial in today's digital age. When businesses are transparent about how they use consumer data, they create a sense of trust and transparency that fosters brand loyalty and customer engagement.

One of the main benefits of transparency in AI marketing is that it builds trust and establishes brand credibility. Consumers are becoming increasingly concerned about their data privacy, and businesses that are transparent about their data collection practices can help alleviate those concerns. When consumers are confident that their data is being collected and used appropriately, they are more likely to engage with a brand and make a purchase. Conversely, when consumers do not trust a business, they are less likely to engage with that brand and may even switch to a competitor.

Another advantage of transparency is that it can help businesses identify potential ethical concerns and mitigate them before they become a problem. AI algorithms that rely on biased data can perpetuate discriminatory practices, and businesses that are transparent about their data collection and analysis can identify these biases and correct them before they cause harm. Similarly, businesses that are transparent about their use of AI can help consumers understand how AI is being used to personalize their experiences and make informed decisions about their data privacy.

Privacy is also critical in AI marketing because it protects consumers from unauthorized access to their personal information. When businesses collect and store data about their customers, they have a responsibility to protect that data from cybercriminals and other malicious actors. This is particularly important in the marketing industry, where data breaches can result in the theft of sensitive information such as credit card numbers and social security numbers. Businesses that prioritize privacy can build consumer trust by demonstrating their commitment to protecting personal information.

In addition to protecting consumer data, privacy can also help businesses comply with legal and regulatory requirements. In many countries, including the United States and the European Union, there are strict regulations governing the collection and use of personal data. Businesses that fail to comply with these regulations can face hefty fines and damage to their reputation. By prioritizing privacy, businesses can demonstrate their commitment to complying with these regulations and avoiding legal and regulatory penalties.

Overall, transparency and privacy are essential in AI marketing to build trust, establish credibility, and protect consumer data. To achieve these goals, businesses can take several steps, including:

- *Being transparent about data collection practices:* This includes informing consumers about what data is being collected, how it is being used, and who it is being shared with.
- *Providing consumers with control over their data:* This includes giving consumers the option to opt-out of data collection and allowing them to review and delete their data.
- *Prioritizing data security:* This includes implementing strong security measures to protect consumer data from cybercriminals and other malicious actors.
- *Complying with legal and regulatory requirements:* This includes understanding and complying with local and international data privacy laws and regulations.

Transparency and privacy are critical in AI marketing to build trust and protect consumer data. By prioritizing transparency and privacy, businesses can build brand credibility, comply with legal and regulatory requirements, and mitigate potential ethical concerns. Businesses that prioritize transparency and privacy in their AI marketing efforts will be better positioned to succeed in the digital age.

THE FUTURE OF AI IN MARKETING: EMERGING TECHNOLOGIES AND TRENDS

Artificial Intelligence (AI) is no longer a distant concept, but an emerging reality that is fast reshaping the world. In recent years, AI has found widespread application across various industries, including marketing. AI has revolutionized the way marketers engage with customers, by providing new and innovative ways to gather insights and make informed decisions. Looking toward the future, the role of AI in marketing is only set to grow, with innovative technologies and trends emerging that will further enhance its capabilities. However, as AI continues to advance, it is important that ethical models and standards are put in place to ensure that it is used responsibly and for the greater good.

Emerging Technologies and Trends

Natural Language Processing (NLP)

Natural language processing (NLP) is a subset of AI that focuses on understanding human language. In marketing, NLP can be used to analyze customer feedback, social media posts, and other forms of unstructured data to gain insights into customer behavior and preferences. NLP can also be used to develop chatbots that can engage with customers in a more personalized and human-like manner.

Predictive Analytics

Predictive analytics uses data mining, machine learning (ML), and other AI techniques to analyze data and make predictions about future events. In marketing, predictive analytics can be used to forecast customer behavior, predict which products or services will be popular, and identify high-value customers. This allows marketers to make data-driven decisions and optimize their marketing strategies.

Computer Vision

Computer vision is the ability of machines to interpret and understand visual data from the world around them. In marketing, computer vision can be used to analyze images and videos to gain insights into consumer behavior. Computer vision can be used to analyze social media posts and identify products or brands that are being featured in user-generated content.

Augmented Reality (AR) and Virtual Reality (VR)

AR and VR are technologies that overlay digital information onto the physical world or create a completely immersive digital environment. In marketing, AR and VR can be used to provide customers with interactive product experiences. Customers can use AR to see how furniture would look in their home before making a purchase or use VR to experience a virtual tour of a hotel before booking a room.

Personalization

Personalization is the process of tailoring marketing messages and experiences to individual customers. AI can be used to gather data on individual customers and create personalized content that resonates with them. This can include personalized product recommendations, customized email marketing campaigns, and personalized Web site experiences.

Ethical Models and Standards

Transparency

Transparency is key when it comes to AI in marketing. Companies should be open and honest about how they are using AI, what data they are collecting, and how that data is being used. This includes providing clear and concise explanations of how AI algorithms work and how they make decisions.

Privacy

Privacy is a major concern when it comes to AI in marketing. Companies must ensure that they are collecting customer data ethically and that they are protecting that data from misuse or unauthorized access. This includes complying with data protection laws and regulations, such as GDPR and CCPA, and being transparent about what data is being collected and how it will be used.

Bias

Bias is a major issue in AI, and it can have grave consequences for marketing. AI algorithms can be biased if they are trained on biased data or if they are designed in a way that reflects the biases of their creators. To avoid bias in AI marketing, companies should ensure that their algorithms are tested for bias and that they are using diverse and representative data sets.

Accountability

Accountability is crucial when it comes to AI in marketing. Companies must take responsibility for the decisions made by their AI algorithms and ensure that they are using AI in an ethical and responsible manner. This includes ensuring that AI algorithms are not making decisions that are discriminatory, harmful, or unethical, and that they are being constantly monitored and reviewed.

Human Oversight

Human oversight is necessary to ensure that AI algorithms are being used ethically and responsibly. While AI can automate many tasks and processes, there should always be a human in the loop to ensure that the decisions made by the AI are ethical, transparent, and fair. Human oversight can also help to identify and address any issues or biases that may arise.

AI is set to revolutionize marketing, with modern technologies and trends emerging that will further enhance its capabilities. As AI continues to advance, it is important that ethical models and standards are put in place to ensure that it is used responsibly and for the greater good. Companies must be transparent, protect privacy, avoid bias, take accountability, and have human oversight to ensure that their use of AI in marketing is ethical and responsible. By doing so, they can harness the power of AI to create more personalized and engaging experiences for their customers while maintaining their trust and loyalty.

THE ROLE OF HUMAN EXPERTISE AND CREATIVITY IN AI-POWERED MARKETING

Artificial intelligence (AI) has been transforming the marketing industry for some time now, providing businesses with advanced tools to help them make data-driven decisions, optimize marketing campaigns, and achieve better results. However, AI-powered marketing is not just about using technology to automate tasks and analyze data. It also involves human expertise and creativity to make the most of the technology and deliver effective marketing strategies that engage and convert customers. This chapter will explore the role of human expertise and creativity in AI-powered marketing.

The Importance of Human Expertise in AI-Powered Marketing

While AI can analyze vast amounts of data and detect patterns that humans may not be able to identify, it is not a substitute for human expertise. AI-powered marketing requires the input of skilled professionals who can interpret data, develop insights, and make strategic decisions that align with the goals of the business.

One area where human expertise is particularly critical is in selecting the right AI technology for the task at hand. With so many AI tools and platforms available, it can be challenging to determine which one will best meet the needs of the business. Marketing professionals with knowledge of AI can evaluate different solutions and determine which ones are the most suitable for their specific requirements.

Another area where human expertise is crucial is in developing and refining the algorithms that power AI models. AI models are only as good as the data they are trained on, and marketing professionals with domain expertise can identify the most relevant data sources and help ensure that the models are accurate and effective.

Human expertise is essential in interpreting the results generated by AI. While AI can generate insights and recommendations, it still requires humans to make sense of these results and use them to inform marketing decisions. Skilled marketing professionals can translate AI-generated insights into actionable strategies that drive business growth.

The Role of Creativity in AI-Powered Marketing

AI-powered marketing is often associated with data analysis and automation, but creativity is also critical to success. While AI can help identify patterns and generate insights, it cannot create compelling content or design engaging campaigns on its own. Creative marketing professionals are still necessary to develop effective messaging and design campaigns that resonate with customers.

One area where creativity is particularly important is in content marketing. AI can identify the topics and keywords that are most likely to attract attention, but it is up to human content creators to develop content that is informative, engaging, and relevant to the target audience. Skilled content creators can use AI-generated insights to inform their content strategy and develop content that resonates with customers.

Similarly, creativity is also critical in designing effective campaigns that engage customers and drive conversions. While AI can help optimize campaigns and identify the most effective channels and messaging, it is up to human marketers to develop campaigns that are visually appealing, emotionally resonant, and aligned with the brand's values.

Creativity is also necessary in evaluating the results of AI-powered marketing campaigns. While AI can provide detailed analytics and insights, it is up to human marketers to interpret these results and make decisions that will drive future success. Skilled marketers can use their creativity and expertise to develop new strategies, tweak campaigns, and adjust messaging based on the insights provided by AI.

AI-powered marketing is transforming the way businesses approach marketing, providing advanced tools and capabilities to help them make data-driven decisions, optimize campaigns, and achieve better results. However, the success of AI-powered marketing depends on human expertise and creativity. Marketing professionals with knowledge of AI can help select the right technology, refine algorithms, and interpret results. Skilled content creators and designers can use AI-generated insights to develop compelling content and campaigns that engage customers and drive conversions. The most successful AI-powered marketing strategies will combine the best of human expertise and creativity with the power of AI technology.

AI has been transforming the marketing industry for some time now, providing businesses with advanced tools to help them make data-driven decisions, optimize marketing campaigns, and achieve better results. However, AI-powered marketing is not just about using technology to automate tasks and analyze data. It also involves human expertise and creativity to make the most of the technology and deliver effective marketing strategies that engage and convert customers. This chapter will explore the role of human expertise and creativity in AI-powered marketing.

The Importance of Human Expertise in AI-Powered Marketing

While AI can analyze vast amounts of data and detect patterns that humans may not be able to identify, it is not a substitute for human expertise. AI-powered marketing requires the input of skilled professionals who can interpret data, develop insights, and make strategic decisions that align with the business's goals.

One area where human expertise is particularly critical is in selecting the right AI technology for the task at hand. With so many AI tools and platforms available, it can be challenging to determine which one will best meet the business's needs. Marketing professionals with knowledge of AI can evaluate different solutions and determine which ones are the most suitable for their specific requirements.

Another area where human expertise is crucial is in developing and refining the algorithms that power AI models. AI models are only as good as the data they are trained on, and marketing professionals with domain expertise can identify the most relevant data sources and help ensure that the models are accurate and effective.

Human expertise is essential in interpreting the results generated by AI. While AI can generate insights and recommendations, it still requires humans to make sense of these results and use them to inform marketing decisions. Skilled marketing professionals can translate AI-generated insights into actionable strategies that drive business growth.

Step-by-Step Instructions: Navigating the Future of AI in Marketing

1. **Stay Informed About AI Trends:** Regularly research and monitor the latest developments in AI technology, particularly those relevant to marketing, such as chatbots, voice assistants, and augmented reality. Attending industry conferences, participating in webinars, and subscribing to relevant publications.

2. **Evaluate Current Technology Stack**: Assess existing marketing technology and identify areas where AI can add value. Consider how integrating new AI technologies could enhance customer experiences and improve marketing efficiency.

3. **Identify Ethical Considerations:** Understand the ethical implications of deploying AI in marketing. Consider issues like data privacy, transparency, and the potential for bias. Develop guidelines and policies to address these ethical concerns.

4. **Develop a Strategic Plan:** Create a roadmap for integrating AI into the marketing strategy. This should include specific goals, the AI technologies that will be adopted, timelines, and budget considerations.

5. **Build or Enhance Skills:** Ensure the team has the necessary skills to work with AI technologies. This might involve hiring new talent with AI expertise or providing training for existing staff.

6. **Experiment with AI Solutions:** Start small by implementing pilot projects or trials with AI technologies like chatbots or voice assistants. Analyze the outcomes and iterate based on the results.

7. **Focus on Customer Experience:** Design AI implementations with a strong focus on enhancing the customer experience. Ensure that AI tools are user-friendly, add value to customers, and align with their preferences and expectations.

8. **Ensure Data Integrity and Security:** Invest in robust data management and security practices. Ensure that customer data used by AI systems is accurate, collected ethically, and protected from unauthorized access or breaches.

9. **Monitor and Evaluate AI Performance:** Continuously track the performance of AI initiatives against defined KPIs and adjust, as necessary. Regularly review the ethical impact of AI tools and address any issues that arise.

10. **Adapt and Innovate Continuously:** As AI technology evolves, be prepared to adapt strategies, and explore innovative ways to leverage AI in marketing. Stay agile and open to evolving the approach based on technological advancements and market dynamics.

Chapter 15 of *AI Marketing Playbook* covered various topics related to the ethical considerations and future of AI in marketing. The following is a summary of the key points discussed:

Ethical Considerations in AI Marketing

The chapter highlighted the importance of ethical considerations in the use of AI in marketing. It discussed the need for transparency and accountability in AI decision-making processes, especially in situations where these processes have significant impacts on human lives. The chapter also stressed the need for ethical and legal frameworks to govern AI usage in marketing.

Potential Ethical Concerns with AI in Marketing

The chapter provided examples of potential ethical concerns with AI in marketing. These concerns included issues around privacy, bias, and discrimination in data collection, analysis, and usage. The chapter also discussed the potential for AI algorithms to amplify existing inequalities and biases in marketing and advertising.

Transparency and Privacy in AI Marketing

The chapter emphasized the importance of transparency and privacy when using AI in marketing. It discussed the need for businesses to inform their customers about the use of AI technologies in marketing and to ensure that customer data is collected and used in ways that are transparent and compliant with relevant data protection regulations.

Future of AI in Marketing

The chapter also discussed the future of AI in marketing, highlighting emerging technologies and trends that are likely to shape the industry in the coming years. These included the growing use of chatbots, voice assistants, and virtual and augmented reality in marketing, as well as the potential for AI to enable hyperpersonalization of marketing messages and to improve customer engagement and retention.

Role of Human Expertise and Creativity in AI-Powered Marketing

The chapter emphasized the critical role of human expertise and creativity in AI-powered marketing. It discussed how AI technologies can help marketing professionals make data-driven decisions and optimize marketing campaigns but noted that human creativity and expertise are still needed to develop effective messaging and design engaging campaigns that resonate with customers.

Chapter 15 of the *AI Marketing Playbook* covered various topics related to the use of artificial intelligence in marketing. These include personalized marketing, customer segmentation, predictive analytics, chatbots, and voice assistants. This chapter also provides insights into how AI can improve customer engagement and loyalty.

The chapter began by highlighting the importance of personalized marketing in today's competitive business landscape. Personalized marketing involves tailoring marketing messages and experiences to individual customers based on their unique preferences and behavior. The chapter explains how AI can help marketers achieve this by analyzing customer data and providing insights into their preferences, interests, and buying habits.

Next, the chapter discussed the role of customer segmentation in effective marketing. Customer segmentation involves dividing a company's customer base into distinct groups based on common characteristics such as demographics, behavior, or preferences. The chapter explains how AI can improve customer segmentation by analyzing large amounts of customer data and identifying patterns and trends.

The chapter then delved into the use of predictive analytics in marketing. Predictive analytics involves using ML algorithms to analyze past data and predict future outcomes. The chapter provides examples of how predictive analytics can be used to identify potential customers, forecast demand, and optimize pricing strategies.

The next section of the chapter focused on chatbots and their role in customer service. Chatbots are AI-powered virtual assistants that can interact with customers via text or voice. The chapter explains how chatbots can improve customer engagement by providing fast and personalized responses to common inquiries.

The chapter discussed the use of voice assistants in marketing. Voice assistants are AI-powered devices such as Amazon Alexa or Google Assistant that can interact with customers via voice commands. The chapter provides examples of how voice assistants can be used to improve customer engagement and loyalty, such as providing personalized recommendations and creating a seamless shopping experience.

Throughout the chapter, the author emphasizes the importance of using AI in marketing to improve customer engagement and loyalty. The author also highlights the potential challenges of using AI, such as privacy concerns and the need for transparency in how customer data is collected and used.

Overall, Chapter 15 of the *AI Marketing Playbook* provides a comprehensive overview of how AI can be used to improve marketing strategies and customer engagement. It emphasizes the importance of personalized marketing, customer segmentation, predictive analytics, chatbots, and voice assistants in achieving these goals. The chapter provides real-world examples of how companies have successfully implemented AI in marketing and offers insights into the potential challenges and opportunities of using AI in this context.

AI marketing offers businesses the ability to understand their customers on a deeper level and create personalized experiences at a scale. By using ML algorithms, businesses can analyze customer behavior, personalize content, automate marketing processes, and improve sales productivity. While AI has been around in marketing for some time now, its potential for growth and impact on the industry is still being realized. As technology evolves, there are exciting new trends emerging, such as voice-activated interfaces, natural language processing, and computer vision.

However, it's important to keep in mind that AI in marketing also poses potential ethical concerns such as privacy, transparency, and bias. The responsibility falls on businesses to ensure they are using AI in an ethical manner that is fair to their customers. Additionally, human expertise and creativity in marketing cannot be replaced entirely by AI. Instead, AI should be used as a tool to augment human capabilities and drive innovation.

Overall, the *AI Marketing Playbook* provides a comprehensive guide for businesses to leverage the power of AI in their marketing strategies. By understanding the basics of AI and ML, preparing data for AI, and implementing AI-powered solutions, businesses can stay competitive and provide better experiences for their customers. The future of AI in marketing is exciting, and with the right approach, businesses can stay ahead of the curve and drive growth.

INDEX

A

A/B testing, 2, 66–7, 146
accessibility features, 181
accountability, 105
accuracy, 104
act, feedback loop, 59
ad
   copy creation, 10
   optimization, 124
advanced data security measures, 39
advertisement, 115
AI marketing
   advantages, 13
   benefits, 1–4
   elevating traditional marketing
     techniques with, 2
   evolution, 8–9
   harnessing the power, 5
   history
     big data, 6–7
     dawn of, 6
     personalization and automation, 7–8
   impact
     enhancing personalization and
       customer experience with AI, 9
     marketing's future, expanding role
       of, 10
     predictive analytics and forecasting,
       10
     revolutionizing marketing analytics
       and optimization through AI, 9
   innovative optimization and efficiency,
     5–6

   personalization and targeting, 5
AI-powered
   advertising campaigns, 5
   algorithms, 73, 185
   analyses, 10
   backlink analysis, 177
   chatbots, 116–17, 126
   consumer behavior assessments, 61
   consumer segmentation, 52
   content creation, 12, 20, 228–9
   customer service, 239
     future, 93–4
     virtual assistants, 91
     voice-enabled interfaces, 91–3
   lead nurturing tools, 213
   lead scoring models, 213
   personalization, 181
   picture identification, 53–4
   predictive analytics, 125
   predictive analytics tools, 131
   sales analytics, 236–7
   SEO strategies, 173
   systems, 19
   technologies, 19
   tools, 6
Airbnb, 50, 117, 146, 184–5
Alexa, 8
Amazon, 5–6, 52, 54, 70, 72, 132–3, 150,
   158, 192–3, 211
Amazon Alexa, 11, 91
Amazon SageMaker, 43
Amazon Web Services (AWS), 45–6
analyze feedback, 59

anomaly detection, 22
AnswerThePublic, 170
artificial intelligence (AI)
    algorithms types, 235
    analytics platforms, 3
    -based lead score, 229
    chatbots, 9
    clustering and segmentation in customer
      analysis, 57–8
    customer segmentation, 52–3
    customers understanding
      Amazon, 54
      Netflix, 54
      Starbucks, 54–5
    ethics and transparency, 173
    feedback loops in customer analysis,
      58–61
    image enhancement, 181
    image recognition, 53–4
    in marketing, ethical considerations,
      243–6
    into marketing playbook, 209
    marketing strategies, 27, 36, 38
    optimization, 5
    personalization, 73
    predictive analytics, 48–50, 127–44
    sentiment analysis, 50–1
    techniques for creating customer
      personas using AI, 55–7
audience
    segmentation, 132
    sentiment analysis, 119–20
augmented reality (AR), 102, 252
Autoencoders in deep learning, 41
automated A/B testing, 181
automated content generation, 12
automated emails, 151–2
    campaigns, 207, 214–18
automated keyword research, 168
automated lead generation, 237–8
automated sales
    forecasting, 238–9
    processes, 239–41
automated segmentation, 66
automated subtitling and transcription, 181
autonomous vehicles, 22
autoregressive integrated moving average
  (ARIMA), 138–9

B

backlink monitoring, 172
banking and finance, 82
behavioral analysis, 158
behavior-based triggers, 66
bias
    and discrimination, 74
    ethical considerations, 248–50
    and fairness, 104
big data, 6–7
BI platforms, 43
BlueBot, 83
boost efficiency, 14
brand ambassadors, 121–2
brand reputation monitoring, 120
Brandwatch, 118
BrightEdge, 166, 193
budget-friendly innovation, 1
BuzzStream, 171
BuzzSumo, 172

C

call-to-action (CTA) buttons, 161
campaign analysis, 172
Canva's design tool, 193
Capital One, 82
Carnegie Learning, 17
characteristics of products, 36
chatbots, 3, 7, 207, 228
    AI for social media marketing, 113–15
    AI-powered customer service
      future, 93–4
      virtual assistants, 91
      voice-enabled interfaces, 91–3
    banking and finance, 82
    benefits of using, 80–1
    and conversational marketing, 124
    for customer support, 211
    designing conversational interfaces for
      conversational interface design, 85
      practices for designing conversational
        interfaces for, 85–8
    e-commerce and retail, 81–2
    health, 83–4
    marketing automation, 209
    practices for training, 88–90
    social media marketing, 116–17
    travel and hospitality, 83

classification algorithms, 21
cleaning data, data hygiene and quality, 32
client
    engagement, 12
    feedback, 36–7
cloud-based platforms, 30
cloud-based storage solutions, 37
clustering, 22
    and segmentation in customer analysis,
      57–8
Coca-Cola, 53, 117
cognitive behavioral therapy (CBT)
    techniques, 83
collaborative filtering, 22, 64, 67, 143
collect feedback, 59
common data enhancement techniques, 103
common data preprocessing techniques,
    39–42, 45
competitive analysis, 184
competitive edge, 59
competitor analysis, 174
compliance checks, 182
comprehensive data backup and recovery
    plan, 39
compression and resizing, 181
computer vision
    in marketing, applications, 101–2
    technologies and trends, 252
consent, 104
consumer
    behavior and preferences, 58
    data and track customer interactions, 43
    loyalty, 72
    responses to advertising, 100
content
    analysis for engagement, 181
    -based filtering, 22, 64, 67, 143
    creation, 112–13, 158, 168
    for customer, 229
    distribution, content marketing, 190–1
    email marketing with AI, 148
    optimization, 66, 165, 169, 179–80,
      184–5
    personalization, 132–3
    tagging and classification, 180
content management system (CMS), 106
content marketing
    analysis, 191–2
    creation, 188–9
    different audience segments with AI,
      198–201

distribution, 190–1
effectiveness, 201–5
ideation and creation, AI role, 194–8
optimization, 189–90
personalization, 190
strategies that use AI, 192–4
continual learning, 106
conventional marketing methods, 13
conversational interface, 86–7
conversion rate optimization (CRO), 162
conversion rates, 63
convolutional neural networks (CNNs), 22,
    103
correct errors, 35
correlation analysis, 40
cost, AI for social media marketing, 115–16
cost-benefit analysis, 76
creative content generation, 2
credit card fraud, 22
cross-departmental collaboration, 4
cross-sell and up-sell opportunities, 130
cross-validation, 136
customer
    analysis, 61
    behavior, 10, 38
    behaviors and preferences, 10
    churn prediction analytics, 129
    emotions and sentiments, 51
    engagement, 3, 63
    experiences, personalization, 130
    feedback loops, 59
    loyalty and growth, 54
    personas creation using AI, 55–7
    record, 35
    retention, 59, 76
    satisfaction, 9
    segmentation, 22, 26, 43, 52–3
    service departments, 9
    service interactions, 48
    transactions, 36–7
customer behavior, 54, 132, 140
    prediction models, 60
    and preferences, 224
customer lifetime value (CLV), 76
customer relationship management (CRM),
    43, 56
    software, 45
    systems, 26, 35
customer relationship management (CRM)
    systems, 65, 213
customer satisfaction, 117

and business performance, 60
and feedback, 76
feedback loop, 59
levels, 60
and loyalty, 80
customization, 19
custom ML models, 56
custom thumbnail creation, 181

D

data
analysis and modeling, 26
audit, data hygiene and quality, 32
augmentation, 104
cleaning, 26, 39, 41
dictionary or schema, 38
expansion, 103
governance, 31, 33
governance policies, 37
hygiene and quality, 29–33
increase, 103
integration, 31, 40–2
management for AI marketing, 45
mining, 8–9
normalization, 41
preparation, for artificial intelligence
common data preprocessing
techniques, 39–42
data hygiene and quality, 29–33
data preprocessing methods, 30
machine learning algorithms,
structure data for, 33–6
optimizing data collection and
storage for AI applications, 30
revolutionizing AI marketing with
tools and platforms, 30
strategies for collecting and storing
data, 36–9
structuring data for ML algorithms,
29–30
tools and platforms, 42–6
pre-processing in ML, 41–2
reduction, 41–2
security, 31, 74
data hygiene and quality, 33
silos, 31
standardization processes, 38
storage performance, 39
transformation, 40–2
validation, 31–2

volume, 31
warehouses, 30
data collection, 26
and labeling, 24
and preparation, 135
data management platforms (DMPs),
36–337
data quality
AI for social media marketing, 115
and integrity, 38
data science, 16
in AI marketing, 25–7
decision-making task, 22
decision trees, 22, 48, 135
algorithms, 21
Deep Q-Networks (DQN), 23
deep reinforcement learning, 21
delivering personal touch, 1
design, 10
focused marketing efforts, 58
Digital Equipment Corporation, 160
dimensionality reduction, 40–1
distance-based algorithms, 36
distributed file systems, 30
drip campaign, 216
drip marketing, 215–18
drones, 22
dynamic content, email marketing with AI,
152–3
dynamic content personalization, 211

E

e-commerce
platforms, 5
product listings, 100
and retail, 81–2
retailer, 96
sites, 12
Web sites, 9
effectiveness, 146–7, 160–4
efficiency, 2
email
campaigns and drip marketing, 208
crafting, 172
layouts on email performance, 161
marketing with AI, 211
A/B testing, 146
automated emails, 151–2
benefits of AI in, 154
content, 148

conversion rate optimization (CRO), 162
dynamic content, 152–3
effectiveness, 146–7, 160–4
history, 160
natural language processing (NLP), 154–5
optimization, 145
personalization, 145–7, 149–50
personalizing email content with AI, 157–60
predictive analytics, 146, 148–51, 155
product recommendations, 147
segmentation, 145, 148
step-by-step instructions, 148
subject lines, 147
testing, 145
spam classification, 22
emotion detection, 99–101
engagement, 75
enhanced automation, 154
Eno, 82
ensemble learning, 104
errors
correction, 40
and inaccuracies in customer interactions, 81
ethical considerations
with AI in marketing, 243–6
and best practices, 10
bias, 248–50
ethical models and standards
bias, 253
human oversight, 253
privacy, 253
transparency, 252–3
human expertise and creativity in AI-powered marketing, 244–5, 253–9
in AI-powered marketing, 254
creativity role, 254–5
future, 257
importance, 255–7
potential ethical concerns with, 257
role, 257–9
transparency and privacy in AI marketing, 257
personalization, 247
privacy, 247–8
targeted advertising, 246–7
technologies and trends

augmented reality (AR) and virtual reality (VR), 252
computer vision, 252
natural language processing (NLP), 252
personalization, 252
predictive analytics, 252
transparency and privacy, 244, 250–1
when using AI, 104–6
ethical guidelines, 10
ethical models and standards
bias, 253
human oversight, 253
privacy, 253
transparency, 252–3
explain ability, 74
exploratory data analysis (EDA), 42
exponential smoothing (ES), 139
exponential transformations, 42

F

Facebook, 124
Facebook Messenger chatbot, 117
face recognition, 16, 98, 102
fairness, 74
fashion detection model, 103
feature extraction, 24, 41
feature scaling, 41
feature selection, 40–1
and engineering, 135
feedback, 86
loops in customer analysis, 58–61
financial services firm, 131
follow-up automation, 172
forecasting customer behavior, 7
fraud detection, 22
future trends in AI marketing
automated content creation, 12
from chatbots to advanced conversational AI, 11
image and video recognition, 12
predictive analytics, 11–12
scaling personalization with AI, 11
voice search optimization, 11

G

generalization ML, 24
Google Analytics, 170
Google Cloud, 45–6

Google Cloud AI Platform, 43
Google Cloud Natural Language, 50
Google Home, 11, 91
Google's Smart Bidding feature, 9
Grammarly, 146

H

handling data for AI marketing, 42
history, 13, 110
H&M, 211
Hootsuite Insights, 118, 161
HubSpot, 43, 133, 185, 211
human expertise and creativity in AI-
  powered marketing, 244–5, 253–9
    in AI-powered marketing, 254
    creativity role, 254–5
    future, 257
    importance, 255–7
    potential ethical concerns with, 257
    role, 257–9
    transparency and privacy in AI
      marketing, 257
human surveillance, 105
hybrid models, 64, 67
hyperparameters, 136

I

IBM's Watson Content Hub, 212
IBM Watson, 7, 50, 55, 166
IBM Watson Analytics, 194
IBM Watson Health, 17
IBM Watson Marketing Insights, 161
ideal customer profile (ICP), 212
image and video recognition with artificial
  intelligence, 22, 53–4, 124, 174
    application, 96
    computer vision in marketing,
      applications of, 101–2
    e-commerce retailer, 96
    ethical considerations when using AI,
      104–6
    optimization, 185
    SEO, 169
    strategies
      emotion detection, 99–101
      face recognition, 98
      object detection, 98
      visual search capabilities, 99

training image recognition models,
    techniques for
      convolutional neural networks
        (CNNs), 103
      data increase, 103
      learning together, 104
      learning transfer, 103
    video content, 96
Inception v3 model, 103
incomplete or inconsistent data, 31
influencer marketing, 115, 126
insights and improvements, 181
insurance fraud, 22
integrating AI into marketing strategies, 3–4
integrating feedback loops, 59
interpretability, 136
iterative learning, 172

J

Jarvis, 172
JPMorgan Bank, 17

K

key buying signals, 212–13
key performance indicators (KPI), 76, 147,
    177
keyword clustering, 185
keyword research, 166, 184
K-means, 22
k-nearest neighbors, 41

L

label encoding, 42
language translation, 22
lead generation, 224
    and qualification, 225, 230–4
lead scoring, marketing automation, 209
learning together, 104
learning transfer, 103
lightning-fast processing, 2
linear regression, 135
link building, 165, 168, 171
Local SEO, 169
logistic regression, 135
Lumen5, 194

M

machine learning (ML), 134, 140

algorithms for supervised learning, 20–1
algorithms for unsupervised learning, 21
applications, 22–3
basics, 16
book's format, 19
chatbots and consumer support, 20
customization, 19
data examination, 19
data science in AI marketing, 25–7
definition, 16–18
making content, 19–20
step-by-step instructions, 18
training data for ML, 23–5
types, 15
machine learning algorithms, 136
machine learning (ML) algorithms, 1
marketing automation
    AI into marketing playbook, 209
    automated email campaigns, 214–18
    challenges and limitations, 218–21
    definition, 219–20
    drip marketing, 215–18
    email campaigns and drip marketing, 208
    strategies, 207
    techniques for automating lead scoring and nurturing with AI
        AI-powered lead nurturing tools, 213
        AI-powered lead scoring models, 213
        customer relationship management (CRM) system, 213
        ideal customer profile (ICP), 212
        key buying signals, 212–13
    use AI, 208–9, 211–12
marketing automation platforms, 43
marketing campaigns, 14, 41
    optimization predictive analytics, 130
marketing industry, 12
    improvements, feedback loop, 59
    influence of AI on, 13
    predictive analytics in, 139
    upcoming trends, 13–14
MarketMuse, 193
Marketo, 43
Marriott International, 83
mean absolute error (MAE), 123
Microsoft Azure, 45–6
Microsoft Azure Machine Learning, 43
Min-Max scaling, 41
missing data handling, 39
ML platforms, 43

model
    performance and reliability, 136
    selection and training, 135
multimedia integration, 189

N

narrow AI, 16
natural language chatbots, 85
natural language generation (NLG) technology, 193
natural language processing (NLP), 2, 19–20, 22, 55, 82, 154–5, 158, 174, 184–6, 208
    predictive analytics, 142–3
    technologies and trends, 252
NetBase Quid, 161
Netflix, 5, 7, 10, 54, 63, 66, 71, 73, 77, 125, 133, 150, 158–9, 212
neural networks, 36, 48, 135
    and decision trees, 235
Nielsen, 100
NLP algorithms, 10
normalization, 40

O

object detection, 98
object recognition for personalized experiences, 102
one-hot encoding, 42
ongoing monitoring and maintenance, 31
online
    advertising industry, 5
    grocery store, 77
    retailer, 130
on-premises databases, 38
optimization
    email marketing with AI, 145
    of marketing, 26
overall profitability, 3

P

Pardot, 43
performance tracking, 181
personalization, 2, 86, 145–7, 149–50, 168
    AI personalization, 72
        automate individualized experiences with, 72
        examples of, 72–3
        at scale, 71

AI-powered email, 158–60
benefits, 157–8
communication plans, 53
of content, 132–3
content creation, 43
content marketing, 190, 192
content recommendations, 207
customer engagement strategies, 50
email campaigns, 65–6
email content with AI, 157–60
ethical considerations, 247
ethical considerations when using AI,
   73–5
leveraging AI for personalized content
   recommendations, 67–8
marketing automation, 208–9
personalized pricing, 68–9
personalized website experience, 69–70
predictive analytics for, 64–5
pricing, 68
product recommendations, 64
recommendation systems, 3
ROI measurement, 75–7
social media marketing, 116
strategies, 70–1
and targeting, 26
technologies and trends, 252
physiological responses, 100
pinpoint accuracy, 1
policy gradient, 21
Power BI, 43
predicting customer abandonment, 132
prediction accuracy, 24
predictive analytics, 2–3, 12, 43, 48–50, 93,
  146, 148–51, 155, 158, 169, 194
   with artificial intelligence (AI), 127–44
   definition, 220
   in marketing, 139
   marketing automation, 209
   methods of time series analysis and
      autoregressive integrated moving
         average (ARIMA), 139
      exponential smoothing (ES), 139
      machine learning (ML), 140
      regression analysis (RS), 140
   natural language processing, 142–3
   predictive modeling with machine
     learning algorithms, 134–7
   recommendation systems, 143–4
   sales enablement, AI for, 224
   and social media marketing, 121–3

strategies
   audience segmentation, 132
   personalization of content, 132–3
   predicting customer abandonment,
      132
   predictive scoring of leads, 133–4
technologies and trends, 252
time series analysis
   history of, 137–8
   in marketing, 138–9
   and predictive analytics, 137
   types, 129–31
predictive content creation, 212
predictive keyword analysis, 175
predictive lead scoring, 10, 133, 207
predictive modeling with machine learning
  algorithms, 134–7
predictive scoring of leads, 133–4
pregnancy prediction model, 5
preprocessing steps, validation of, 42
Principal Component Analysis (PCA), 22,
  40–1
privacy, 73–4, 104
   concerns, AI for social media marketing,
     115
   ethical considerations, 247–8
proactive decision-making, 50
product recommendations, 10, 147
purchase records, 36

Q

Q-learning, 21, 23
QlikView, 43

R

random forests, 48, 135
Rank Brain, 185
real-time analysis, 154
real-time insights, 3
recommendation systems, 22, 143–4
   predictive analytics, 143–4
recurrent neural networks (RNNs), 22
regression, 22
   algorithms, 21
   analysis, 235
regression analysis (RS), 140
regularization, 135
regular monitoring and maintenance, data
  hygiene and quality, 33

reinforcement learning, 15, 17, 21–2
remove duplicates, 39
resource constraints, 31
return on investment (ROI), 3, 201
  of personalization, 63, 75–7
robot's navigation, 22
root mean squared error (RMSE), 123
R-squared to measure performance, 123

S

sales coaching, 230
sales enablement, AI for
  AI-based lead score, 229
  AI-powered content creation, 228–9
  benefits, 226–7
  content for customer, 229
  customer behavior and preferences, 224
  lead generation and qualification, 224–5,
    230–4
  practices for, 227–8
  predictive analytics, 224
  sales coaching, 230
  sales engagement, 230
  sales forecasting with AI
    AI algorithms types, 235
    AI-powered customer service, 239
    automated lead generation, 237–8
    automated sales forecasting, 238–9
    automated sales processes, 239–41
    benefits, 234
    developing and implementing, 235–6
    neural networks and decision trees,
      235
    regression analysis, 235
    Sales productivity and efficiency,
      236–7
  sales forecasts, 229
sales engagement, 230
Salesforce, 43
Salesforce Einstein, 56, 161
sales forecasting with AI, 130, 228–9
  AI algorithms types, 235
  AI-powered customer service, 239
  automated lead generation, 237–8
  automated sales forecasting, 238–9
  automated sales processes, 239–41
  benefits, 234
  developing and implementing, 235–6
  neural networks and decision trees, 235
  regression analysis, 235

Sales productivity and efficiency, 236–7
sampling, 40
SAS developed software solutions, 7
scalable data storage solution, 38
scaling, 40
scikit-learn in Python, 23
search engine optimization (SEO), 193
  AI and search engines, 175
  AI for, 165–6
  AI-powered keyword research, 170
  AI-powered link building, 171–3
  applications of AI for, 169–70
  benefits of AI for, 168
  challenges of AI for, 168–9
  content creation, 178–9
  content optimization, 170, 179–80
  future, 167
  image optimization using AI, 173, 180–3
  keyword research, 176–7
  NLP, 183–6
  optimizing content for search engines
    with AI, 166–7
  predictive analytics using AI, 171
  strategies that use AI, 166
  techniques for keyword research with
    AI, 166, 173–5
  video optimization, 180–2
  voice search, 182–3
  voice search optimization using AI, 170
search engine results pages (SERPs), 167–8
segmentation, email marketing with AI, 145,
  148
self-driving automobiles, 22
semisupervised learning, 15
sentiment analysis, 22, 50–1, 142
  social media marketing, 117–20
Sentiment Analyzer, 50
Sephora, 71, 117, 124, 152, 159
Siri, 8
social listening, 110–12
social media
  activity, 48, 67
  data, 139
  dynamics and customer behaviors, 123
  engagement, 11
  interactions, 36–8
  listening tools, 45
  monitoring platform, 100
  platforms, 35, 50
social media marketing, 193
  AI for

advertisement, 115
challenges, 115
chatbots, 113–15
content creation, 112–13
cost, 115–16
data quality, 115
influencer marketing, 115
privacy concerns, 115
social listening, 110–12
history of AI, 110
impact of AI, 124–6
and predictive analytics, 121–3
predictive analytics and social media
marketing, 121–3
strategies
chatbots, 116–17
personalization, 116
sentiment analysis, 117–20
split ratio, 36
Spotify, 71, 73, 146, 158
Sales productivity and efficiency, 236–7
standardization and normalization, data
hygiene and quality, 32
Starbucks, 54–5, 71
step-by-step instructions, 148
subject lines, 147
subpar data quality, 37
subscriber behavior, 156
supervised learning, 15, 17, 22, 134
algorithms for, 20–1
support vector machines (SVM), 21, 41
survey results, 36–7

T

Tableau, 43
tailor marketing messages, 14
Talkwalker, 118
targeted advertising, ethical considerations,
246–7
techniques for automating lead scoring and
nurturing with AI
AI-powered lead nurturing tools, 213
AI-powered lead scoring models, 213
customer relationship management
(CRM) system, 213
ideal customer profile (ICP), 212
key buying signals, 212–13
technologies and trends

augmented reality (AR) and virtual
reality (VR), 252
computer vision, 252
natural language processing (NLP), 252
personalization, 252
predictive analytics, 252
Tesla's Autopilot technology, 17
testing, email marketing with AI, 145
text mining, 142
third-party data providers, 35, 37
time series analysis
history of, 137–8
in marketing, 138–9
and predictive analytics, 137
autoregressive integrated moving
average (ARIMA), 139
exponential smoothing (ES), 139
machine learning (ML), 140
regression analysis (RS), 140
T-Mobile, 133
T-Mobile's Next Best Action program, 132
topic modeling, 142, 185
tracking consumer responses, 100
training data, 23–5
training image recognition models,
techniques for
convolutional neural networks (CNNs),
103
data increase, 103
learning together, 104
learning transfer, 103
transactional data, 38
transaction records, 48
transfer learning, 104
TransferWise, 82
transformer models, 22
transparency, 104
and accountability, 73
and privacy, ethical considerations, 244,
250–1
travel and hospitality, chatbots and AI-based
customer service, 83

U

unsupervised learning, 15, 17, 22
algorithms for, 21
user behavior
analysis, 166
patterns, 36

V

VGGNet, 103
video
    content, 96
    surveillance, 96
virtual assistants, 91, 93–4
virtual reality (VR), 252
    and augmented reality (AR), 12
visual search capabilities, 99
voice
    -activated assistants, 8
    -activated interfaces, 93–4
    -enabled interfaces, 91–3
    search, 8, 167, 186
    search optimization, 169, 174–5, 185

W

Web analysis, 36–7
web analytics platforms, 45
Webmaster guidelines, 173
Web site analytics, 48, 65
well-structured data breach, 37

Y

Yoast SEO, 166
Your.MD, 83

Z

Zoho, 43

www.ingramcontent.com/pod-product-compliance
Lightning Source LLC
La Vergne TN
LVHW022303060326
832902LV00020B/3241